MAS

$30.00

I0576553

1st UK

ON
AND OFF
THE ROCKS

ON AND OFF THE ROCKS

Selected Essays 1968–1985
by Jim Perrin

London · Victor Gollancz Ltd · 1986

First published in Great Britain 1986
by Victor Gollancz Ltd,
14 Henrietta Street, London
WC2E 8QJ

© Jim Perrin 1986

*British Library Cataloguing in
Publication Data*
Perrin, Jim
   On and off the rocks: selected essays
   1968–1985.
   1. Mountaineering—History—20th
   century
   I. Title
   796.5′22′0924   GV199.89

   ISBN 0-575-03810-1

Designed by John Grain
Photoset in Great Britain by
Rowland Phototypesetting Ltd,
Bury St Edmunds, Suffolk
and printed and bound by
Billings & Son Ltd, Worcester

"Childlike, I danced in a dream;
Blessings emblazoned that day;
Everything glowed with a gleam;
   Yet we were looking away!"

By the same author:

MENLOVE
The Life of John Menlove Edwards

*Frontispiece: New Morning, Mowing
Word, Pembroke (photo: Malcolm
Griffith)*

CONTENTS

Foreword by Sir Jack Longland   8
Introduction and acknowledgements   10

Part One: The Gilded Calamity

Where the Need Exists: a Reverie   13
"A Small, Gothic Cathedral of a Mountain"   17
On Mountain Designs, and the Designs of Men   22
A Sacrificial Mountain?   26
Vast Landscapes   30
Mind has Mountains   36
Idyllic Hills   40
Landscape with Figures   45
Ireland, Radnor   49
Black Earth, Black Light   55
Up Here, Down There   59

Part Two: On the Rocks

In Praise of Jamming   65
Right Unconquerable—a Gritstone Paean   68
Whatever Happened to the Wet Days?   70
The Great Wall of Craig y Forwyn   73
"Denn bleiben ist nirgends"   75
Street Illegal   78
Taxation no Tyranny   81
The Gate of Horn   85
The Land That Time Forgot   88
Fictive Heroes   97

Part Three: The Human Factor

Chaplin as Mountaineer: H. W. Tilman   105
The Craftsman: Pat Littlejohn   112
Role-model: Jill Lawrence   119
Two sketches: John Redhead, Robin Hodgkin   121
Prankster, Maniac, Hero, Saint and Fool:
Al Harris   124
The Ice Climbers: A Literary Discourse   128
John Hoyland: the Missing Dates   135
Chris Bonington at Fifty: Sketches from
the Life   144

Part Four: The Nature of the Beast

A Note on Commitment   156
Trains, Cafes, Conversations   158
Ogwen Historical   161
Country Matters   170
Partners   175
Venues   178
A Valediction   184
For Arnold Pines   186

LIST OF PHOTOGRAPHS

New Morning, Mowing Word, Pembroke 2

Afon Glaslyn 12

Statue of Hedd Wyn, Trawsfynydd 14

Tryfan and Llyn Ogwen 15

The West Face of Tryfan and Afon Ogwen 18

Tryfan from the East 19

North Peak of Tryfan from the summit 21

"Rosie, being a fell-runner, and my dog, being a dog, loped rapidly off into the distance . . ." 23

Footpath maintenance work in Snowdonia 23

Pen y Gadair and Cyfrwy 24

Llyn y Gadair 25

The Llanberis Track and railway from above Clogwyn Du'r Arddu 27

The Wayfarer Plaque at the Nant Rhydwilym 31

Moel Sych from the East 32

Tony Shaw on the Berwyn ridge above Llyn Lluncaws 33

Corndon Hill from Pole Bank, Long Mynd 39

John Greenland on the first ascent of Heart of Darkness, Mowing Word 41

Dièdre Sud, Mowing Word. Jan Rawlinson climbing 42

Cwm Pennant and Bwlch Dros Bern from the summit of Moel Hebog 43

Ruined cottage, North Wales 47

Ireland: "A few feet of cracked chimney breast maintained some pretence of uprightness" 50

William Perrin on Llanbedr Hill 51

Modern farming and forestry—Mid-Wales 52

Snowdon from Moel Siabod 55

"The shadow at my feet had spilled over with shocking suddenness and streamed out to the horizon" 57

"I . . . rested finally among some boulders suffused with the last of the western light" 58

Berwyn lower slopes—bare tree, conifers and phosphate 62

Berwyns—"the primality of all high places" 63

Elegug Tower, first ascent, 1970. Peter Biven and Jim Perrin 64

Suicide Wall, Cratcliffe Tor 66

Roger Alton on New Morning, Mowing Word 67

Neb Direct, Ed Wood climbing 68

Mandy Glanville on Right Unconquerable 69

"A race against failing strength and breath" 70

Vember—the Drainpipe Crack 71

Charlie Fowler launches out on the Great Wall of Craig y Forwyn 73

Andy Pollitt traversing the Great Wall 74

Brant, Clogwyn y Grochan, Ann Hardwick leading 76

Brian Wyvill and Sam Whimster on The Strait Gate 77

The Cyfrwy Arete 78

Hardd, Carreg Hyll Drem   82

Left Wall, Dinas Cromlech. The author with Barry Ingle   83

Gate of Horn; the first ascent   87

". . . the group dynamics of mixed adolescent parties"   90

". . . they proceeded to climb the Idwal Slabs in a single rope"   91

". . . she held herself in such a manner that a susceptible man might have fallen in love with her there and then"   92

Tennis Shoe   94

"Helyg has more clutter of redolence than . . . anywhere else in Wales"   95

Megalith, Newton Head, Pembroke. Keith Robertson climbing   99

Meshach, 1963. The author cheating   101

Silly Arete. Matt Fisher seconding   103

Stennis Head; Ben Wintringham "resting"   104

H. W. Tilman   106

H. W. Tilman with the bicycle he rode across Africa. (Taken outside Bod Owen, May 1977)   109

Pat Littlejohn   113

Deep Space, Mother Carey's Kitchen. The author and Roger Alton climbing the classic Littlejohn route   115

Jill Lawrence on Tower Face, Stanage   119

Jill Lawrence on the Left Unconquerable   120

John Redhead   121

John Redhead on Cock Block, Clogwyn y Grochan   122

Al Harris   124

Harris bouldering on Fach Wen   125

"Oh, fuck, no, he's done it!" The Atomic Finger Flake   127

John Hoyland in 1934, a month before he died on Mont Blanc   135

The third ascent of Pigott's Climb, Clogwyn Du'r Arddu, 1928. Ted Hicks leading   139

John Hoyland and John Jenkins on top of Glyder Fach, July 1934   143

Chris Bonington   145

"A willingness to embrace new ideas"   153

Pex Hill balletics—choreography by Martin Boysen   160

Paul Williams on the Holly Tree Wall   163

Rusty Baillie on Suicide Wall Original Route   167

The Milestone Buttress   169

Stag-hunting in Devon—a country "sport"   171

Pincushion and Silly Arete, Tremadog   175

"That inveterate, lead-hogging god" Martin Boysen   177

A seasick Joe Brown   179

Gogarth Bay   181

Joe Brown attempts to hold the cliff in place—Cilan Head   183

Yr Elen and Carnedd Llywelyn from Cwm Llafar   189

Castell y Gwynt, Glyder Fawr   191

Foreword by Sir Jack Longland

THIS SELECTION OF essays written by the best of our young writers on mountain themes will, I believe, attract not only climbers and country-lovers, but also other discerning readers who have no special interest in rocks and hills and what goes on amongst them. Blake wrote that "Great things are done when men and mountains meet", but it is rare for accounts of these meetings to be worth even cursory literary comment. It is all too easy, on the other hand, for them to be pompous or inflated or both, but this is a trap into which Perrin never falls. He pinpoints wonder, humility and, just occasionally, cocky pleasure in unexpected success, but he never strays far from his main theme of what we can learn from mountains and from the humans who respond to them in such a diverting variety of ways.

It is no business of the writer of its Foreword to summarize all of Jim Perrin's fascinating book, but among many pieces I particularly like and admire, perhaps my favourite is "Up Here, Down There"—a tale of chancey conditions which pulls out from a few snatched mountain hours every last ounce of wonder and self-resource, and at the end triumph, and the solace of remembrance of things past: this is the essence of Jim Perrin at his best—vivid recording, rigorous honesty, deeply felt empathy: all that and in this instance the company of a faithful and possibly slightly bewildered dog!

To make technical descriptions catch the inexpert reader's attention is not easy, either in climbing or in most other sports, but the pieces in Part Two of this book, "On the Rocks", succeed in doing just that. Witness "Right Unconquerable—a Gritstone Paean": the climb is a short but revolutionary first ascent by the almost legendary Joe Brown (who appears as a climbing companion in an essay from Part Four, "Venues"). Perrin's account of it admirably conveys the excitement to be found on our dour Derbyshire millstone-grit edges. Or there is "Whatever Happened to the Wet Days", which sets against the superbly gymnastic feats of today's young aces on sunlit overhangs or sports-hall climbing walls the older discipline of routes strugglingly fought out with chilling rain running up your sleeve and overflowing your boots, and the unique feeling of achievement when you crawl out at the top. Climbing has many mansions, and the most glittering are not necessarily the best.

His examination of "The Human Factor" exemplifies Perrin's skill —the biographer as miniaturist, as in his perceptive, affectionate and admiring portrait of a man who will remain endlessly elusive—H. W. Tilman. Among the modern stars, I am sure the portraits of Pat Littlejohn and Jill Lawrence will hold the reader who is never likely to become a rock-climber. "The Ice Climbers" is delightful in exhibiting a first-class writer/climber appraising and saluting his peers, Bill Murray and Tom Patey, in both these categories. And then there is, light-heartedly, our *preux chevalier*, Chris Bonington, casually and domestically sketched in, with a deep understanding of the problems with which his chosen career has confronted him. He comes out likeable, honourable, candid and dedicated.

I have tried to give some impression of this book's insight, strict honesty of observation and judgement; of its communication to others of that vision of "The Ramparts of Paradise"—and they are ramparts to be climbed, not gates to be passed easily through—to which, through mists and disillusionments and failures and losses, the author has kept steadily faithful. It is a good book, and a worthy successor of his justly-praised biography, *Menlove*.

BAKEWELL 1986   JACK LONGLAND

Introduction: The Ramparts of Paradise

IN ROBERT ROBERTS'S haunting autobiographical account of a Salford slum childhood, *A Ragged Schooling*, there occurs the following passage:

> One sunny Wednesday afternoon [Mother] took me to Peel Park. We sat on a high esplanade and looked far over the countless chimneys of northern Manchester to the horizon. On the skyline, green and aloof, the Pennines rose like the ramparts of paradise. "There!" she said, pointing. "Mountains!" I stared, lost for words.

When I first read this simple anecdote, unconnected with anything else in the book, it brought an instant shock of recognition, jolting me back into my own childhood. To be born in any of the great northern industrial cities is to be within sight of hills from the earliest years. I was brought up in areas of Manchester where conditions had changed little, apart from the damages of war, in the forty years since the time about which Robert Roberts wrote. I remember standing as a child in this or that of the city's scuffed green spaces—Seymour or St George's Park, or more salubriously Platt Fields, which allow the horizon to rear up beyond the hemming streets—and seeing the hills there, blueygreen, far away, mysteriously desirable, like the realization of a hymn or a dream.

So it was inevitable that I should find my way to them. The larger parks of Heaton and Lyme, at the edge of the city (in what is now modishly termed by town planners or countryside and population managers the urban fringe), led out there. Lyme Park in particular swelled up on the Derbyshire border into the ridge running from Black Hill to Sponds Hill. When I first panted up on to it, at the age of twelve, it was by the track through the wood, where the clean brown loam lay bare beneath the trees, patched with vivid green moss and patterned by the brilliant orange of fallen beech leaves.

After the wood's boundary wall, the path broached the steep moor to Bowstonegate. To arrive there was to encounter a vision which stopped my breath. Beyond were rocks, hills, valleys leading off amongst them, glimpses of a plain spreading westward and still more hills on its farther side.

I kept on throughout that day and the next, scrambled on the rocks of Windgather, straggled across Shining Tor in a bright wind, climbed Shuttlingslow, searched among the trees of Back Forest for the secretive green cleft of Lud's Church, and followed the River Dane out west with the Welsh hills of my father's family in the faintest distance. It is a journey which, in a sense, has never ended.

I cannot imagine a passion which could have been more fulfilling than the one I conceived then for the hills—their rocks, ridges, histories, moods, people. It is one which has lasted unabated to the present and will surely continue lifelong. It has been, as passions always are, an educative force and the impressions I have gained from it, of joy, frustration, ambition, anger, friendship, beauty, love (and chiefly, I hope, the latter) are what I have reflected upon and tried to write about. Some of these pieces I may have outgrown; there are tricks of style which I no longer own and conclusions with which I may no longer agree. But like Tennyson's Ulysses, "I am a part of all that I have met", and I cannot thus honestly discard them.

The experiences which mountains and the many activities which take place upon them have bestowed have been enormously worthwhile. In the larger scale of things the ones recorded here might not register, but it is the intimate, honest and personal response which concerns me, available at any level of activity, communicating not by the distancing effect of achievement but through the common factor of humanity. If I have succeeded here and there in making in my readers' minds the same sort of vital connection which Robert Roberts's story made in mine, then I have done my job as a writer, and perhaps enticed those readers to join me on what may not always have been "the ramparts of paradise", but have certainly been a liberation and inspiration in my life.

On a more mundane note, these pieces are a personal choice from amongst a much larger body of journalism produced over a long period of years. Many of them have a strong autobiographical element, and I hold to Gramsci's argument that everyone has the rights and individual richness of perception to produce such work. In some cases, the articles were cut about to suit the purposes of magazine or newspaper publication. Where it seemed necessary, passages have thus been reinstated. This introduction is a fitting place to record my thanks to all the editors who have given encouragment over the years: Nigel Rogers, who wheedled out of me the first piece I ever wrote, in gratitude to whom it is included here; Chris Brasher and Walt Unsworth—their willingness to publish only qualified by embargoes on the political or libellous; Ken Wilson, with whom I have gleefully disagreed on most things for more years than I care to remember; his two gifted successors, Bernard Newman, and the late Tim Lewis, of charitable heart and savage intellect; Geoff Milburn, indefatigably enthusiastic; and Geoff Birtles, who has given me the writer's best possible discipline—my own head (within the noose of a regular deadline). To Sir Jack Longland, who contributes the foreword, I owe a great personal debt of thanks, as I do also to the photographers, whose pictures are credited in the text which they grace.

Finally, this book is dedicated to my father, Stanley Perrin, who was born and died in Robert Roberts's Salford. His comments to me —"What d'you want to be always reading them books for?" "You stay away from those rocks!"—though never unkindly meant, are ones I have consistently disregarded for most of my life. Perhaps, "there on the sad height", he would now understand why.

1: THE GILDED CALAMITY

The landscape of Wales has a powerful appeal to incurable romantics (or natural depressives?) such as myself. Perhaps it is the attraction of the marginal—the rough hills and crags, the ravaged industries, the legend-teeming sunset seas on which imagination sets the mortally wounded king's barge floating out to Avalon. And a culture which still rages, to keep its light from dying.

There is a solace about the indefinable and the evanescent, just as there is a sadness in too perfect a beauty. An extract from an essay by Camus for me captures exactly the essence and the mood of these almost-too-lovely hills of Wales, and gives this section of the book its title:

> *In such spots one can understand that if the Greeks knew despair they always did so through beauty and its stifling quality. In that gilded calamity, tragedy reaches its highest point.*

The tragedy is not just one of a frequently embittered national consciousness. It is also to do with a country whose spiritual image is polished until at times the brass shows through the gilding, and the material texture of which by contrast—the landscape which is its most lovely and perfect asset—becomes more battered and irremediably tarnished as each year passes by.

The dozen essays gathered here are all set in the Welsh hills or borders. Since I first knew this country, 25 years ago, it has enthralled me, and I have never tired in the attempt to convey what it means, and has meant, to me. The first piece is autobiographical, and tells of how the spell was first cast.

Where the Need Exists: A Reverie
1983; High 1985

> ". . . the speed, the swiftness, walking into clarity,
> Like last year's bryony are gone."
>
> Ivor Gurney,
> "On High Hills"

IT RAINED ALL night in that gusty, lashing manner of the Welsh uplands, and when I rose in the morning the valley was flooded from side to side. Looking down over this scene, it brought to me with extraordinary vividness a kind of dream of former things. I give it here, not as something outgrown, but as a few stones in the arch of

Opposite: Afon Glaslyn (photo: Malcolm Griffith)

13

Statue of Hedd Wyn, Trawsfynydd

experience. Perhaps if they were removed and examined too closely, the whole edifice would crumble. We have to take on faith our interpretations of the past . . .

On a rainy April morning over twenty years ago, a young boy was walking along the road between Pont y Pant and Dolwyddelan in North Wales. Mist wraiths skirled amongst dwarf oak woodland on the hillsides above, and the rain marched in gleaming columns down the valley, beating an incessant counterpoint of downpour and drip. A steady trickle ran from the boy's hat-brim on to his oilskin cape, to which his rucksack gave a curiously tilted and purposeful parasol shape as he plodded up the road, veering to the crown here and there to avoid stippled puddles or encroaching pools. Down to his left winterblack trees formed cutwater vees on the spreading plain of flood, and little island pastures were newly green where they rose from the grey watersheen. The boy's boots had taken on the texture of wet cardboard, and the baggy flannel trousers he wore were dark and sodden from thigh downwards. For all that, there was an obduracy and resolution in his step as he paced forwards. Hearing the sound of an engine, and tyres plashing along the road behind him, he eased up from his hunched stride, leant left-handed against a wall, half-turned and stuck out his thumb. The grey Morris van drew up beside him, he thrust himself in, and they set off, worn gearbox clicking and whining through the ratios, along the streaming road. A mile or so farther on the van turned down a steep, rough track and pulled up in front of a large house. Driver and boy emerged, and the latter was ushered through a white door into the kitchen beyond.

Before I take you into that kitchen, I will tell you something about this boy. He has just turned thirteen, and for all the usual reasons of adolescence and some which are uniquely his own, he is painfully self-conscious. He lives in Manchester, in the very middle of that grimy, smog-ridden city, in a flat above a city-centre office-block of which his father is the caretaker. The streets in which he grew up were bulldozed away three or four years beforehand, their groundplan quite gone, their place taken by harsh crescents of concrete flats, where once there were damp rosettes and the smell of soot, dirt and the closeness of crumbling brick. He attends a grammar school in a middle-class area of his home-town and, caught between snobbery and allegiance, hates something about this weekday, workaday scenario which he cannot quite define, though he hates it with excruciating, bitter hostility. On the day of which I write, he probably has a week or so of his Easter holiday left, perhaps a pound in his pocket, and in his rucksack a couple of packets of porridge, a paraffin bottle, blanket, pan, and primus stove. He will sleep where he can—barn or shed, bus shelter or forestry plantation—and intends making for Ffestiniog or Bala on this night, to climb Arenig Fawr on the following day.

Tryfan and Llyn Ogwen

In the kitchen, the driver sat the boy down while his wife threaded and fussed through the room's clutter of furniture with the practised dexterity and hipswerve of a Welsh fly-half taking on the Irish pack. The kettle boiled, tea was made and handed round, the boy's flannels steamed and turned pale by the fire, and the talk began. You should understand that there was a need in this boy for a landscape carved from rock and spirit and the natural responses of men—more than a need, a passion for such. There was a craving in his soul for beauty and poetry and permanence to set against the transience and squalor of his own beginnings, the harshly mechanistic uncomprehendingness of school and home society. This was a willing listener, and the talk had begun.

Preliminaries differ the world over. An Indian will ask you if you are married and how many children you have. Englishmen ask for the Test Match score. This Welsh couple, old, childless and kindly, asked where I was from, what my religion was, and then told me—their proudest boast—of the preachers who had lived in the house. And the conversation went on from there: the castle above; the pulpit rock of Rhys Goch in Cwm Cynfal; the slate-ranked generations in the chapel yard from this single house; the *fable* of a society in whose composition doctor and vicar, quarryman, cowman, shepherd, drunkard and fool were distinguished by richness of language, imagination, and humanity alone.

There is a vivid picture in my mind of the wife standing at her door and waving; small, bulking a little at bosom and hip, her wrinkled face shrewd and gladdening as the man and boy set off back to the delivery round. And I have vivid flashes of the places, the talk, the people of that day from time to time, for it was one of continual magic. I will describe one incident, to serve for the rest.

Some time about lunch, they stopped in the straggling grey downhill, upland village of Trawsfynydd. The boy's new friend stood bareheaded in the still-falling rain by the statue of Hedd Wyn to tell him the story—poet and farmer's boy from Cwm Prysor, killed in France in the Great War, news of his death arriving on the morning he was awarded the bardic chair at the 1917 National Eisteddfod, which thereafter was known, from its black-draped chair, as "Eisteddfod Gadair Du". The thrill of feeling which shot through the boy in response to this story, its charge of raw sentiment, remains with him still, its pulses still travelling along the arteries of belief, its presence more archetypal than actual now in his mind.

But to return to that day in the rain—the man and boy standing by the statue, and the boy asking for some lines of Hedd Wyn's—to which request the man obliged by repeating the following quatrain:

> Dim ond lleuad borffor
> Ar ffin y mynydd llwm,
> A swn hen Afon Prysor
> Yn canu yn y cwm.

(Nothing but the purple moon on the end of the leaden mountain, and the sound of the old River Prysor singing in the valley.)

It was a "nothing but" which carried with it a desired magical everything. It set the grey universe humming as, drawn up to his full five-and-a-half feet of height, hair plastered thinly to his scalp under the glistening copper statue, he breathed and whispered it out to the clean wind of a wet Welsh street. Little more need be said. If you have listened attentively, you will know what the day brought. But I will add a coda, lest you think impressionable youth incapable of discernment. Very recently, I met the old man again, sat by his fire through the space of an afternoon as the light faded and night fell. He was retired, his wife was ten years dead, and daily he sat by his fire reliving the days. He had aged and shrunk, but still seemed sweet at the core though his skin was shrivelled and seamed. The voice I remembered was a little tremulous now across the deep basses, but its images were fresh and clear. He talked of frost-crystals hanging from wires in the winter I was born, "like notes of music written on a page", and voiced his thankfulness for having lived his life in such a place: "I look up at Moel Siabod; it is different every day, a different light every time I look, and they try to tell me there is not a God!"

The mechanics of our speech might bring us contradiction now, but his knowledge and his vision were an education to me once, when the need was there to be fulfilled. They imparted to me a sense of place, a richly-informed love of a particular landscape, were a catalyst, a creative agent. What blooms in the imagination lives on in the perceiving eye, glows out through words and memories that others may share its colours and fragrance, is passed on, translated, and perhaps eventually dies.

If you can write profiles of people, then why not of mountains? Instead of recounting the high points of a career, speak of the routes to a summit. Anthropomorphize, if you will, on feature and form, describe the unique presence and texture. And what are history and association but the human dimensions of the subject? And talking of subjects, is there a worthier one than Tryfan?

"A Small, Gothic Cathedral of a Mountain"
High 1982

THERE IS THE remarkable fact of its summit, at 3,010 feet, being a mere half-mile from the road. Not that the near point is anything like the best from which to view the mountain. Better to approach from the traditional angle, along the Nant y Benglog from Capel Curig. Then at any season, in any caprice of weather, it is capable of surprising you. The eastern aspect of the mountain is one of the great sights amongst our British hills. It is supremely elegant; dove-grey, or like shot silk in sunlight after rain, it glistens or glows as the mood takes it, and underpins such ephemera of light with a formidably balanced architectonic splendour—a small, Gothic cathedral of a mountain which seizes upon our imagination so as almost to exaggerate the effect of its own shapeliness.

It doesn't, of course, take everyone so. George Borrow, for instance, passed this way in 1854, but was too busily engaged in showing off his Welsh to do anything more than dismiss it brusquely as "the second hill on the left". And the motor-coaches which chug by on the A5 summerlong, a-tilt and agog with blue-rinsed, craning ladies, perhaps find more of interest in the two "figures" perched on top, than in the perfect buttresses from which they spring.

But for all that, Tryfan has never lacked admirers. Thomas Pennant, looking down on the mountain from the plateau of the Glyders in 1781, described it thus: "In the midst of the vale far below rises the singular mountain Trevaen, assuming on this side a pyramidal form, naked and very rugged." Pennant's accompanying artist, Moses Griffiths, etched

*The West Face of Tryfan and
Afon Ogwen*

a splendid counterpoint to the words. At the close of the eighteenth century, the Reverend William Bingley climbed to the summit: "We could scarcely take a dozen steps together in any place without at the same time using our hands." Bingley goes on to note, of the two summit figures, that "a female of an adjoining parish was celebrated as having often made this daring leap".

So much for those who consider daring in the mountains as a latter-day commodity—I know many present-day walkers and climbers who would blench at the thought of jumping from Adam to Eve, or vice versa. (Which stone obelisk is Adam, and which Eve, is one of the great topics of ribald discussion; geology and biology are not mutually helpful here.) It should be said, though, that this "daring leap" by which you gain the freedom of Tryfan, for all the airiness of its position, is little more than a long step. But perhaps we should climb our mountain first?

There are popular ways up mountains, and there are good ways up mountains, and they are not necessarily, nor even all that frequently, one and the same. The popular way up Tryfan is to leave the road somewhere near Gwern y Gof Uchaf, follow a path beneath the striking inclined slab of Little Tryfan, which has given a traditional rock-climbing introduction to generations of beginners, cross some marshy ground, and then, by means of a vegetatious, steep and gravelly little gully, gain the lower end of the Heather Terrace, a prominent feature which traverses beneath the cliffs of the mountain's East Face. At its end you reach the summit by means of the South Ridge, which offers little of interest to the scrambler, but does lay claim to fame as one of the few easiest ways up a British hill which still necessitates the use of hands. At this point, no doubt a clamour will go up from multitudes of clever readers who, by dint of a judicious elbow here and knee there, have taken up the gauntlet and reached the

Tryfan from the East (photo: John Cleare)

summit without having laid hand upon the parent body. Good luck to them; they illustrate, rather than dispute the point.

To my way of thinking the Heather Terrace is quite the most tedious line of ascent on the mountain. It is bad enough when used just as a means of reaching the climbs on the East Face. Without their attraction as objective, it becomes insufferably dreary. Its outlook is restricted to the boggy hollow of Cwm Tryfan, as anonymous a place as Wales has to offer, and the Terrace itself is no more than a wide shelf of scarred and decomposing rubble. Its attractions are minimal. The best way of ascending the mountain, beyond any doubt, is by the shortest line on the map, conveniently delineated by the North Ridge. Sixty years ago, the Abraham brothers included this as one of the "Easy courses" for rock-climbers in their British Mountain Climbs. It is not in any sense a rock-climb, but it is one of the most invigorating of mountain scrambles.

We start where the tenth milestone from Bangor once stood, beneath the clean buttress of rock to which it gave a name. The path climbs round to the left of the Milestone Buttress, quite steeply, beneath the sombre left-hand facet known as the Back of the Milestone, which, even in these days of climbing's population explosion, has still not gained the popularity it deserves—climbers, as any walker will tell you, are the most conservative creatures.

After a few minutes' walk you reach a broad, heathery shoulder characterized by a network of paths and a large cairn, as well as the usual proliferation of smaller ones. Cairn-building seems to have been a popular pastime in Snowdonia at least since Neolithic times. I, for one, find it less than gratifying that in this small matter we have progressed little since the Stone Age. Nowadays we build more of them, with less artistry, and to no good purpose. The sight of them rouses me to furious orgies of destruction.

From the shoulder, the Heather Terrace creeps off at the left-hand end; the North Ridge lies above and across to the right. The responsible advice would be to pick your way across to the left, and strike back by vague paths to reach the ridge somewhere near the Cannon, the prominent howitzer-shaped block visible on the crest of the ridge from all points west. The best advice, given dry conditions and some ability on rough ground, is to take as direct a course as possible, and throughout its length tease out all the little problems, the clean rock walls, firm holds, and blocky risings, all placed there as if by kindly Providence for your special delectation. You can suit it anywhere to your own standard, and it is all mottled, rough-textured, open and delightful. Or you can avoid it as you please, circuitously. Archer Thomson's is the definitive statement: "On its broad crest, wayward humours and lively impulses may be indulged with impunity."

Before a flat stretch of ground leading to the abrupt rise of the North Peak, you encounter the Notch, which has a fearsome reputation of sorts, being rather exposed, seemingly unavoidable, and distinctly polished. The Nor' Nor' Gully rises to the Notch from the east, giving a useful alternative scramble to those who have quickly tired of the Heather Terrace's resistible charms. After the Notch, you are left with a pleasing final scramble to the North Peak, and five minutes thence should see you to Adam and Eve.

Because of its proximity to the road, the summit of Tryfan gives an exceptional feeling of height. It is quite spectacularly elevated. There is no sense of remoteness or wide horizons. South and north, higher

peaks lie close at hand. But it is wonderfully aloof. It has another, to my mind inestimable, virtue. Unlike almost every other mountain summit in Britain, there is no summit cairn. The natural features preclude that and suffice.

North Peak of Tryfan from the summit

There are two viable descents. One leads back to the col between the North and Central Peaks, then skitters down scree-paths on the west side and so to the A5. It is fast, steep—and hard on the knees. The gentler way is to follow the South Ridge down to Bwlch Tryfan, turn right (if you are not heading on up the Bristly Ridge) and follow the Miners' Track past Llyn Bochlwyd, in its grand mountain cwm, whence a steep and uncomfortable descent for a few hundred feet from the toe of the Gribin Ridge ends at a marshy area separating us from the Cwm Idwal path. Over to the right is the mountain, the outline of the ridge we have climbed, its massive shape sculpted by forces powerful beyond our understanding. We place ourselves upon these rocks and hills, and for the brief years of bodily strength at our command, we make the effort to climb. We think and dream and sometimes die upon them, interpret them, for all their vast indifference, in the facile forms and varieties of our own minds. Momentarily, we shrill along them, and perhaps more lastingly, but not by much, we despoil them, or write about them. At the end of the day, as we descend from them, each into his darkening valley, their forms thicken and resolve into the perfect simplicity of night, until we know them no more. And these activities of ours amongst them are sometimes seen as conquests . . .

For the hill-walker the two most popular mountains in North Wales have long been Snowdon and Cader Idris. The heavy usage this implies has brought its own peculiar problems, which have not even yet been found susceptible to universally acceptable solutions. The following two essays discuss some of the issues involved, and catch me in two minds about the remedies which have been applied.

On Mountain Designs, and Designs of Men
High 1982

A WEEK OR SO ago I met my friend Rosie Naish in Tremadog and we drove down in the rain to Cader Idris. I have walked up Cader, or climbed on its cliffs in summer and winter, many times over the last twenty years. It is a favourite mountain of mine, and I do not recall ever having had a bad day on it, which is probably why we forced ourselves out into the pelting rain on this dismal morning to climb it once again.

Rosie, being a fell-runner, and my dog, being a dog, loped rapidly off into the distance, leaving me trailing slowly behind on the long slog up to Rhiw Gwredydd. I caught up with them eventually on the zig-zag path up to the bwlch. My dog, associating stops with food, was all quivering expectation, whilst Rosie was glowering at a large wire-netting cage, prominently positioned in a gully just above the path, which enclosed in perfect cuboid form several hundredweight of scree.

"What on earth's that?" she demanded, as I sagged down beside her.

"It's to stop erosion. They're all over the place these days," I replied, not giving it a second look.

She rounded on me: "Just look at it! How did it get there? It's like something out of a scrapyard," she ranted as, startled, I gave it my full attention.

"I suppose it is a bit out-of-keeping," I mumbled, in an attempt to pacify.

"Out-of-keeping! It's hideous—I'd sooner have the erosion," she stormed, then swung on her heel and streaked up to the bwlch, leaving my dog and me to pant along behind. With the rain still sweeping down and thoughts of the wire fences, the concrete steps to.the summit, and the stinking slum of a hut up there, I began to entertain doubts as to the day's success.

The ridge greeted us with a fierce wind, inhibiting further conversation and gusting at our backs as we skipped and strode along the boggy whaleback by an over-cairned and paint-marked path which was very

obviously patched, straitened, and maintained. Quite suddenly, a great rift appeared in the mist, blue sky gleamed above, and the wind, as if in benediction for the faith of our setting forth, scoured the mountain free of cloud. We huddled in the lee of the summit cairn, watched the resident flock of ravens, most joyful of aerial acrobats, and shared chocolate above a sparkling, sun-bathed landscape. I tried to put the case for prevention of erosion on mountain paths. The statistics slid glibly off my tongue: 220,000 people climbing Snowdon in the year to June 1980; the summit a mass of boulder-scree denuded of vegetation; high rainfall gouging out gullies where the paths climb the slopes, depositing sediment which kills off further vegetation; over £200,000 per annum spent on the National Park's five-year management scheme for Snowdon; a further contribution this year from the Welsh Development Agency; work for people on job-creation schemes; Government approval through the suave personage of Mr Nicholas Edwards . . .

Above left: "Rosie, being a fell-runner, and my dog, being a dog, loped rapidly off into the distance . . .

Above right: Footpath maintenance work in Snowdonia (photo: Steve Ashton)

Somehow, the more I said, the less conviction it carried. All the arguments and impressive analyses of the conservationists, all the worthy and honourable voluntary labour of army apprentices or field corps workers, all the science and reasoned argument was being gently drummed away by its own insistency. A couplet of William Blake's came into my head:

To cast off Bacon, Locke, and Newton from Albion's covering,
To take off his filthy garments and clothe him with imagination.

Could the scientists and conservators and practical men-of-work devise nothing more imaginative than rubble-filled cages of wire to stop the ruin of our hills? The question, of course, is transparently unfair, but it has a certain validity. It always strikes me as a curious anomaly that the Snowdon Summit Hotel should have been designed by Clough

Pen y Gadair and Cyfrwy (photo: Steve Ashton)

Williams-Ellis, whom many would consider a man of vision. As we sat there on the summit of Cader, looking out to the cloud-encircled peaks of Central Snowdonia, I wondered whether there was not a strong element of hubris in our modern preoccupation with that area of concern which hides from definition behind such arcane terms as resource management in conservation, ecospherical control studies, landscape utilization theory, and a hundred other ponderous conference-title themes and autisms of our scientocratic world.

I keep, in loose form, what used to be called a commonplace book, and one quotation therein on which my eye lights with frequent and unwavering distaste is that of a medical researcher, American inevitably, and quoted in the risible American periodical *Newsweek*: "We cannot duplicate God's work, but we can come very close." Well, fifteen years have elapsed since this was said, and no doubt they now think they can come even closer. I was reading this week a booklet produced by that notorious body, the Central Electricity Generating Board, on a hydro-electric project in Mid-Wales. Over four pages it carried "before and after" photographs of a weir, obviously a showpiece, at Felin Newydd. The "before" picture showed a rough, rocky stretch of water flowing into a tiny gorge under a very utilitarian bridge—just the sort of scene you come across throughout Wales, and which constitutes something of the particular charm of the place. The "after" picture was an abstract design of curves, walls and arches in gleaming white which would have graced any new shopping centre in Birmingham, Coventry or the like. The text underneath was educative; it taught us poor, benighted savages what a huge improvement was the latter over the former. It told us how poor, hard-run Nature often fell short of the highest standards, but with judicious or even extensive help from man, the JCB, and pre-cast, reinforced concrete, even the simplest scene could be rendered a beauty spot of momentous impact. The architect, whose aesthetic sense no doubt handsomely lines his pocket, explained how he had decided to "change what natural beauty was already there into something . . . rather more sophisticated."

Well—who am I to argue with the thousands, the day-trippers, car-drivers and coach-tour operators who each year choose to file in and admire the beauty and ingenuity of Rheidol, Stwlan, Traws-fynydd, Dinorwig? And that attitude being abroad, can we wonder that the maintainers and advisers, the constructors of footpaths, car parks, toilets and restaurants, consider their work to be an unqualified good? Perhaps they are the rightful descendants of Kent, Repton, or Capability Brown, with reinforced concrete instead of clear vistas, wire mesh and slit-pipe drainage in the place of water and planted trees. Perhaps on our mountains we are about to witness a new era of landscape gardening and improvement to equal any-thing at Blenheim or Stowe. If we prefer climbing brick walls to rock-faces, then why not the synthetic mountain? Perhaps the summit of Snowdon will soon be gracefully re-modelled in textured concrete* to prove finally that man can cap anything Nature can achieve.

Amidst musings like this we set off from the summit of Cader, skittered and crashed down the Foxes' Path, and brought up for a moment by the shore of Llyn y Gadair. Looking back up at the vastness of this thousand-foot, worn chute of scree, a glow of satisfaction crept in that it would never be susceptible to the control of wire-mesh conservationists—that it would moulder on thus through aeons. I remembered the times and seasons I had come down that way: the first time alone in mist and rain when I was fourteen, bound for the youth hostel at Pont ar Eden; or the occasion ten years ago when Martin Boysen and I had snatched one of the steep and difficult ice-gullies right of Cyfrwy as it dripped and thawed, and coming down the Foxes' Path in the sunset, points of rock speared through melt-holes in the snow, each rimmed with red-glinting ice so that the whole slope seemed strewn with fiery rosettes in the fading light. There was a small solace thus to be set against the meshed blocks and injunctions not to stray, in that mood and season will always mask men's efforts and reclaim their own.

We set off down from the llyn by sheep pastures and heathery descents, untrodden and unmarked. As we picked our way down by an exquisite stream avenued about with rowan, holly, alder and birch, a dipper worked fastidiously over green-mossed rocks and through a glitter of spray. A grey pall of cloud still lay heavily across the great peaks to the north. By the time we reached the car park, the rain had started again.

Llyn y Gadair

* A scheme along these lines has actually been put forward in a Countryside Commission report.

A Sacrificial Mountain?
High 1984

THERE IS A poem entitled "Snowdon" by Geoffrey Winthrop Young in which he exhorts us to "Look forward fifty tens, and fifty more" years and view the mountain again at that time:

> Other the boys, other their transient fame,
> Snowdon will look the same

The statement is, of course, rich with irony. Snowdon is not the same as it was in the early decades of the century, when the poem was written. Geoffrey Young could never have envisaged a time when in excess of half a million people every year (according to 1984 statistics) would walk on the mountain. Even though he himself was instrumental in the use of mountains as an educational medium, he surely never foresaw the endless parade of children escorted up and down the Miners' Track every day of the season. And equally surely, he never dreamt, in the days when the Pig Track or the track up to Lliwedd were no more than flattenings of the turf and a few nail-scratches here and there on the rocks, of the state to which the mountain would be reduced by two or three decades of such heavy use—livid, pale scars everywhere, widening and deepening by the year, rain-scoured, cracked by the droughts of summer, the turf stripped, the scree run piecemeal down denuded slopes.

I used, for the problem has been creeping up on us for some years, to wonder what could be done. I have even used this journal to voice doubts about some of the workmanship which has taken place in the name of footpath maintenance in Snowdonia—*gabions* (wire-mesh cages filled with rubble) obtrusively sited on the path up Cader Idris, for example, I found particularly irritating. When I took this point up with John Ellis Roberts, Head Warden of the Snowdonia National Park, his response was diplomatic on the question of the Cader Idris *gabions*, but he was not discouraged by my apparent hostility to the work being carried out: "Why," he suggested, "don't you come out for a day on Snowdon and let me show you the sort of things we've been doing there?"

"Any pretext for a day away from the desk," I thought, and arranged a date for the grand tour of inspection. In the interim, the controversy over footpaths on Snowdon bubbled up on to the front page of a North Wales local paper, where the story began: "Footpaths built on Snowdon by the National Park Authority are described as 'vandalism' by a Beddgelert climber who sees the paths 'reaching motorway proportions'." So my interest was keenly whetted as I climbed into the Park Warden's white Land Rover one sunny morning and drove round to Pen y Pass.

Our first stop was by Llyn Llydaw, where John was to explain to the

leaders of a group from the British Trust for Conservation Volunteers the work he would like them to undertake. He praised them for previous work done on the Pig Track, and then outlined the present task, with a slightly apologetic air about its seeming simplicity: "Far better that you do a good job on this than that we give you a harder task with which you're perhaps less well able to cope." The work, he explained to them, involved reconstructing the banks of a stream above the path, using *gabions*, which he asked them, with a wry grin in my direction, to conceal very carefully under large stones. The purpose of the work was to ensure that the stream, even in times of heavy rainfall, channelled directly into a large drainage pipe under the path.

His volunteers happy with their allotted role, we drove on up towards Glaslyn and stopped just beyond an outcrop of rock which John told me had recently been blasted. A team of full-time estate workers were reconstructing the path at this point, and for the first time I saw the contrast between the restored and unrestored sections of path. Behind us, the path was spruce, even-surfaced, with large slabs firmly delineating the outer edge and a neat drainage ditch on the uphill side. Ahead of us, all was rubble and ruin. There was a definite appeal in the tidiness of what had gone before compared to the dereliction in front. The workmanship of this permanent team is of impeccably high standard. Gritting my teeth, I was forced to admit that the restored path looks better than the ravaged section to come.

The Llanberis Track and railway from above Clogwyn Du'r Arddu (photo: Eric Whitehead)

We walked on to Glaslyn. On the way up I had remarked how wide and prominent the path to Lliwedd now was, but a surprise was in store at Glaslyn. I hadn't been this way up Snowdon in summer for several years, and looking up at the zig-zags, they seemed less prominent, less messy, less sprawling and eroded. A careful look revealed that the line of the path now is straightened and directed by lines of *gabions*.

Back in the car park at Pen y Pass, we set off up the Pig Track. It has been delicately re-ordered. In places little boundary lines of stones, like a Chinese rockery, define the path. I mocked them, and John vouchsafed the reply that his estate workers wouldn't have put in that touch. In the sections I remembered as having been boggy, drainage ditches carry away the water and the path cruises effortlessly on. To each side the bare, scarred areas to which the path had previously spread are now grassing over again. We hopped over a boulder-field. "Not much needs to be done about this," John remarked, "and anyway, it gives them a taste of the real thing," he added, with a smile.

A little farther on we came to the point which was obviously the focus for all the furore in the press. The army had recently blasted a small bluff of rock in order to make the line of the path easier and more attractive, and to discourage spreading diversions to the right. They had been very enthusiastic with their explosives and it still looked a mess—the rock heavily shattered and scattered all around. It was the one really intrusive feature I saw all day, and it was obviously a sore point, for it put John on the defensive straight away, explaining the need for some work at this point, justifying what had been done. Although nothing was said to this effect, I had the distinct impression that behind the official cover he was putting up, he too thought that in this instance things had gone rather far and that, although he would defend the action as a matter of policy, he would also be very careful not to let it happen again.

As John was taking me home he explained more to me about the Snowdon Management Scheme of which all this is a part: "One of the troubles," he told me, "is that the work was started too late. If we'd had paths with durable surfaces for people to walk on, and if we'd maintained them properly over the years, the mountain would not be in the savagely-scarred state we find it in today."

A day or two later I drove down to Penrhyndeudraeth to talk to the very capable new National Park Officer, Alan Jones. "Do you," I quizzed, "have an overall policy on the Snowdon footpaths?"

"Well, the policy related to Snowdon basically is that we accepted that there were no means of curtailing the use of Snowdon by the masses rather than by the more committed mountaineers and mountain-walkers, and therefore, being the highest mountain in England and Wales and thus the one which everyone wants to climb, it had to be 'sacrificed' for the masses and we had to try and cater for the problems which they caused."

"Any truth in the 'paths reaching motorway proportions' jibe?"

"No, I don't think there is. You see, Snowdon is used by the ordinary person who just wants to go wandering at leisure on the mountain, who's probably not particularly prepared for it—I know there's a mixture of users, but the ordinary tourists who come to North Wales use the mountain and they do so in their own way—summer clothes, shoes, whatever they happen to be wearing. If we accept, as we do in essence, that that is going to happen and that we should allow it to happen, since everyone has a legitimate desire to get to the top of the highest mountain in England and Wales, then I suppose the paths should be of a standard which allows them to do it with ease and safety (under summer conditions, of course) and with a minimum of disruption to the farming and nature conservancy going on around them."

I went away to ponder on that one. The maintained paths are not to the mountaineer's or committed hill-walker's taste, but yes, they do minimize the problems of erosion, and they are approved of by farmers and conservationists. It seems to me unarguable that the parts of Snowdon where the footpath work has taken place look in better condition now than they did before the work began. In principle, I most strongly disapprove of the army being asked to blast away bedrock. In practice, what has been done will certainly heal other scars very obvious to view. And in context, these blasting scars are very slight in comparison to the huge ones on Lliwedd or Bwlch Main where the footpaths have spread unchecked and undirected.

I don't want to approve, because my sentimental affection for the mountain demands that it be left untouched by human hand, but unless the hands are brought into play, the feet do the damage and what they do looks worse in the long run than good construction work on the paths, thoroughly and sympathetically integrated into the environment. So in the end I suppose that if I examine my objections, it comes down to a complaint that the ascent is being made easier for others. I might haze this over with apparent concern for the safety of those lured into high places by the ease of the ascent, but basically it comes down to that. And what sort of selfish and élitist plea am I allowing myself there? You can't say to people, "Stay away—this mountain's not for you unless you are of our creed." You can educate to a degree, you can provide the mountain with some protection against the ravages wrought upon it, but you cannot proscribe.

In the end, I came away feeling grateful rather than the contrary to John Ellis Roberts and his workers. And perhaps with a lingering hope that, given all this industry and care, "Snowdon will look the same" as it did in earlier days, before the half-million people a year took to its slopes. The Park Authority's solution is a pragmatic one to a difficult situation. As mountaineers, we should be very concerned not to dismiss it out of hand.

*Just as the importance of linear narrative has long been
underrated by literary fashion, so too can it be said that circular
walks are pleasant enough in their way, but there is a stronger
appeal in the idea of a journey between distant points—
especially when it lies across wild, high and trackless land.
No part of Wales better fits the description than the country
south and west of Bala, through which this itinerary struggles its
way.*

Vast Landscapes
1979, High 1985

WE ARE CAPABLE of the strangest actions, such as packing a rucksack
on a fine autumn morning, whistling the dog from her basket, and
setting out into the wilderness. On this October day, tired leaf-colour
revivified by a hint of the sere and the sun burning from a cloudless sky,
boiling the mist from each crucible valley, I was Ulysses, my back once
more to Ithaca, in quest of untravelled worlds:

> Full many a glorious morning have I seen
> Flatter the mountain tops with sovereign eye,
> Kissing with golden face the meadows green,
> Gilding pale streams with heavenly alchemy.

It was a good incantation to chant me up the muddy, narrow lane
which leads steeply out of the Dee Valley from opposite the chapel in
Glyndyfrydwy. You can use such a text as the basis for those intellectual gymnastics by which the walker's bane—an uphill path from the
outset—is turned into a staunchly rhythmical pleasure. My mantra had
induced the latter frame of mind by the time I reached the deserted
quarry east of Moel Fferna, first summit of the day. They always cause
me to linger, these stonecrop-and-wild-strawberry-covered wastes of
man's former enterprise in the Welsh hills. There are so many of them,
chipped into rounded flanks or burrowed under shaggy outcrops, the
vegetable life encroaching back on the mined rock's sterility, rabbits
scuttering across the mounds of slate to fracture their bittersweet calm
of brood and decay. The heather creeps in and mocks them, just as it
mocked my stupidity in attempting to walk on a compass bearing from
quarry to summit. If you find a path on the Berwyns which heads in
anything like your general direction, don't leave it lightly; there are
oceans of concealment amongst the heather to lead you out of your
depth. I made the summit in an ill temper, and the climate compounded it:

> Why didst thou promise such a beauteous day,
> And make me travel forth without my cloak,
> To let base clouds o'ertake me in my way . . . ?

Splashing along over Cerrig Coediog and Bwlch Croes y Wernen in a downpour, getting wetter and heavier-hearted by the minute and sunken into that withdrawn state of a man who endures his weather, I could only lament the glorious morning which had gone. A great bank of cloud, which had lain hidden behind the hill-massif to the west as I set out, now dominated the scene. Behind me and over to the north, hills beyond the Dee were sunlit. Here on top of the Berwyns, a harsh wind thrashed the rain into my face as I flailed along, possessed by infernal discontent.

Just before Nant Rhydwilym, however, by a green field incongruously intruded into the brown moor (why are they ploughing so high these days?), the rain stopped, and I steamed gently down to a sunlit lunch by the Wayfarer plaque.

My dog, a black labrador bitch who had frisked and busybodied across many more miles than her master by this time, sat and played Jack Sprat's wife with the apricots in a huge bag of dried fruit which I had brought along. A couple of walkers crossed the bwlch, talking between themselves of rain. To the west, the moorland ridge cleared of cloud, and heather glowed soft and warm as old tapestry. We set off at a fast pace and in very little time were resting again on top of Moel Sych, southernmost of the major Berwyn peaks.

I wonder if it's a mistake to embark on too long a walk, with too little time allotted. There are advantages, of course, but on sections like that from Nant Rhydwilym to Moel Sych, the urge is not to hurry but to dawdle, to sit and gaze. The valleys leading off east are beautiful in their blend of long perspective and intimate detail. Clee Hill, the Stiperstones and a fade of cloud beyond are the backcloth to scattered copses, brown slopes and solitary farms which lead the eye up into fine, sculpted cwms immediately below the ridge, along which latter the walking is smooth and easy. Sitting on top of Moel Sych, I was in a mood of buoyant optimism. The afternoon was young, the sun shone and the view spread wide. There was just one distraction, one flaw in this jovial mood. For by the cairn, studded tyre-tracks leading to them, I noticed three cans of petrol had been stacked, and they set me in a fury. You may think as you will of what I did; you may say it was irrational, irresponsible, untidy, stupid. But I took those three cans, loosened the tops, walked with them to the scarp edge and hurled them far out so that they landed amongst the screes trickling down to Llyn Lluncaws. And I was glad that I had done it and ranted passionate imprecations against those who had put them there. For what event they had been stored, I don't know. Perhaps it was hypocritical of me, for in the past I have ridden a motorcycle over Snowdonia hills. But in that place they seemed so incongruent, alien and intrusive that I was impelled to rid it of them.

Emptied, they must still rust there amongst the screes. Maybe those who had cached them by the cairn sensed what had been done and used

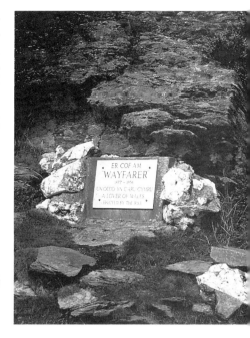

The Wayfarer Plaque at the Nant Rhydwilym

Moel Sych from the East (photo: Chris Jackson)

their own invective to direct the elements against me, for within ten minutes of leaving Moel Sych a west wind rose, bringing rain. The path towards Milltir Gerrig petered out amongst innumerable miry and heathery knolls; you could barely see a hundred yards. From Moel Sych to Milltir Gerrig is three miles; on the map, the gently falling contours arouse the expectation of ease. Don't be deceived. If I was feeling any guilt, the punishment was quickly to hand and long-drawn-out. By the time I reached Milltir Gerrig I was tired, dispirited, wet through, and time had passed. Car drivers on the Llangynog road glanced pityingly as I squelched past. Just west of the high point on the pass, I took a sodden track down to the right, and after a few hundred yards ducked into a copse of pine trees by a stream, where I took out my primus and brewed some tea.

The making of tea over a primus, particularly when you are cold and wet, is one of the great rituals in outdoor life. The stove itself is such a delightful machine. Mine is truly half-pint size and lives in a blue tin box secured by a band cut from an old inner tube. I love to see its gleaming brass tank and strutting legs, delight in the art of priming it so that, just at the exact moment, it growls into action. They call the noise it makes a purr, but it's not—it's a self-satisfied and distinctly loud little growl, like the noise made by gritting your teeth and breathing past the base of your tongue pressed on the roof of your mouth. And the elixir you can make upon it! The handful of tea thrown in the bubbling water, the jumping symmetries of amber jewels as you tap the side of the billy to settle the leaves, the rush of silence as you release the pressure valve.

Tony Shaw on the Berwyn ridge above Llyn Lluncaws

Hazlitt, they say, died of drinking strong, green tea; Samuel Johnson wrote in its defence; to me, squatting on my rucksack in a dripping copse, it was rebirth. With two pints of it infusing warmth throughout my body, I could look with equanimity on the bag of dried fruit's disintegration within my rucksack. I set off towards Hafod Hir in something like high spirits. My plan was to find the fork in the path over Hafod Hir to Melangell, and then to walk on compass bearings to Cyrniau Nod. It was a bad plan—no trace of a path exists over Hafod Hir—so after a time I abandoned it, and began the long flounder towards Cyrniau Nod. Imagine the scene—within yards of leaving the path you look back to find it has disappeared from view; the faint signs of previous passage ahead soon do likewise, and you are left to surf through waves of thigh-deep heather on to the first shallow whaleback. Beyond this, a wide, flat basin of heather, with ominous but rather lovely patches here and there of vivid green, stretches out to the foot of a great roll of hillside, dark against the western light, dark with heather, trackless—and this you must climb. It is ingrained in my memory as the archetype of suffering under a louring heaven. Its name, as I panted it over and over whilst scrabbling up that awful flank, sounded like the shuddering breaths of an exhausted man. Even the vegetation seems to have given up in the struggle to colonize its top, where patches of bare peat and gravel are punctuated by rotting wooden boundary posts.

All the valleys south and west were sombre with evening as I dropped down from the ridge and plunged through another boggy valley to a shooting cabin by a shaley gully in the east flank of Cefn

Gwyntog. There were dry wooden benches, a few spent cartridges on the floor and rain dinning on the tin roof. I should have taken it as my lodging for the night.

Instead, with an hour of daylight left, I scrambled up the shaley gully, crossed Cefn Gwyntog to the Afon yn y Groes, skirted a wood on its west bank and followed a wet path down to the Hirnant road. The last dozen miles from Moel Sych had been a version of Purgatory, but now there was the temporary release of coming down upon a road as the twilight closed into night. There was something about the atmosphere of the place which brought a poem of Lionel Johnson's into my mind:

> In Merioneth, over the sad moor
> Drives the rain, the cold wind blows:
> Past the ruinous church door,
> The poor procession without music goes.

It was quite dark by now, the wind blowing, and rain fell incessantly. A full moon shone through a gap in the clouds on a ruinous house. I looked for an entry but the windows were all securely fastened with boards and nails. My dog whimpered to heel, and I was half-relieved that we could not get in. We crept instead into a wood by the junction of the Afon Cwm Lloi and the Nant Nadroedd Fawr, probing far enough in to be out of sight of those boarded eyeless windows:

> Lonely she wandered out her hour, and died.
> Now the mournful curlew cries
> Over her, laid down beside
> Death's lonely people: lightly down she lies.

In the wood I put down my sack on the damp brown of the pine needles and fed my very wet dog, who was by now quite mystified as to what was going on and longing, I have no doubt, for her basket by the kitchen fire. I made a brew of tea and, too tired to eat, wriggled into sleeping bag and bivouac sack and tried to sleep. To no avail. My dog nosed her way to the depths of the bivouac sack and articulated her nightlong protest through shivers, kicks and groans. The rain dripped through the trees. Occasional vituperative sallies of wind spat drops across my face. I was wet, cold and aching. At the first glimmers of dawn I got up, still dressed in wet clothes, allowed myself the luxury of dry socks and lit the stove. Is there any more welcome sound than a primus growling into life on a cold morning?

I shall tell you about my rations. Apart from the tea and dried fruit (most of which latter had been brushed out of the rucksack at Milltir Gerrig, though bits still adhered to clothes and sleeping bag), I had brought a loaf, a pound of bacon and a bottle of brown sauce, and for a full hour on this raw morning my dog and I sated ourselves on bacon butties in a bout of ecstatic gluttony. Then we wiped or licked the grease from our mouths, packed things away, and by seven o'clock were following the forestry track along the south bank of the Afon Nadroedd Fawr.

The mist and I both draw a veil over the subsequent passage across to Ty Nant. To say it was wet and laborious would be the merest shorthand in describing the terrain. As for the prospect ahead, Landor's lines had come true:

> Soon shall Oblivion's deepening veil
> Hide all the peopled hills you see.

Where the Arans should have stood magnificently in view, there was just a deep pall of grey. But the main point was my manner of progress. By now every joint was grating and crackling in an extraordinary manner. The body's slow decay; it is odd how you can find a little wry humour in even the most exigent of truths. A path of sorts, downhill, brought some relief, and I hobbled along the road from Ty Nant like an eighty-year-old, thinking it quite a good bad joke.

Now I was in no fit state to seek out the courtesy path which starts from Pont y Pandy, to gain the Arans ridge from the north. I thought to take a chance on the route to the ridge by way of Llyn Lliwbran and turned off up Cwm Croes. Just before the point where I intended branching on to the grassy shoulder, a Land Rover came puttering down the track. I saluted the driver, and spoke accusingly to him in heavily North-Walian accented Welsh:

"Terrible weather—it's been raining on me all the way from Glyn-dyfrydwy." He'd taken in my crabbed motion along the road and the dejected dog at my heel, looked at me with an expression somewhere between questioning and suspicion. "Would you mind if I went up to have a look at Llyn Lliwbran?"

"*Arglwydd*, no, help yourself," the reply came in English. "You won't see much of it today."

He guffawed with laughter and drove slowly away, leaving me to strike up to the lake. I sat down by it—crow-coloured is what its name means in Welsh—and made a brew of tea on the pebbly strand whilst gazing at the cliff of Gist Ddu above, with its magnificent arete lines. I remembered doing one of them in the company of someone with a very bad stammer. I had led a long and hard pitch, with the difficult section right at the bottom and out of sight from my belay. There had been gruntings and a pull on the rope, I'd assumed he wanted slack, but when I paid some out the clear and agonized cry floated up: "Bastard!" I took in the rope quickly and no harm came of it, though whether he believed my protestations of good intent I don't know. The very triviality of the memory seemed to make it the more comic when set against the scale and presence of the cliff. On that fine day long-gone, in the right company and with the appropriate safeguards, it was climbable. But today, alone here with my dog and the streaming rock above me, I could no more have climbed it than I could have flown. Yet at the time it seemed a triumph, a victory?

The clouds were lifting. We scrambled round the side of the cliff, a little less stiffly now, and quickly gained the long ridge. It is one of those ascents which keeps promising completion, only to rear up again after the attained object. Eventually you arrive at the tiny pool of Llyn Pen Aran, and a little beyond it and only a little higher is the large cairn at the top of Aran Benllyn. Undulating over the minor rise of Erw y Ddafad Ddu—acre of the black sheep—the ridge then keeps at the 2,700ft level for over a mile to the Ordnance Survey pillar on top of Aran Fawddwy. It is rocky and rough, with an impressive, craggy slope on the east side. Once or twice, sunlight broke through the cloud cover and made the wet rocks glisten and their yellow lichens gleam. I was stumbling along, though, by now, and almost too thoroughly fatigued to enjoy it. We barely stopped on top of Aran Fawddwy, just trudged grimly on to the point where there is a startling transition from bouldery ground to easy grass, and you turn past the small monument and down the spur called Drws Bach to circle round the head of Hengwm and follow a slanting path which traverses the final steep hillside into Cwm Cywarch. The last three miles of road were rest after long labour. I was heading, if not for my own hearth at least for that of the Red Lion in Dinas Mawddwy. All the vast landscapes of the last two days were behind me, I was back in the intimate world of lanes, hedgerows and trees. There is surely a liberation amongst these hills—in their loneliness, across their untrodden miles. The wide skies and your own small figure journeying beneath them add an attraction moving towards the mystical, a freeing of soul in despite of the body's pain. And I still had the last stanza from Lionel Johnson's poem as a mantra to see me home:

> In Merioneth, the wind lives and wails.
> On from hill to lonely hill:
> Down the loud, triumphant gales,
> A spirit cries Be strong! and cries Be still!

The interplay between landscapes and the people who have lived there is more than just physical or historical—it inhabits an imaginative dimension as well, and can sometimes produce the most amusing results.

Mind Has Mountains
High 1985

THE SUN HAD all but disappeared behind a bank of cloud creeping round the foot of Corndon Hill when I first saw the figures. At their backs the twilight was gathering, enhancing the sinister effect of their gait—the tall one staggering forwards, with the short, squat creature gliding alongside, leaning against him. As they zig-zagged across the snow towards me I debated whether to lie down amongst the heather and let them pass, but thought better of such cowardice, strained my eyes to see what manner of company I was about to encounter, and carried on.

What cocktails the mind can shake up from its disparate resources! Here I was, stalking across the Long Mynd on a snowy February evening, my civilized veneer cracking by the second as there welled up inside me a primitive, superstitious dread: Edric and the Wild Hunt; Mary Webb's Stephen Southernwood looking on from back there by the Devil's Chair; Housman's landscapes of gallowtrees, wars, lost youth and expectant death . . .

There are some places which, before you ever visit them and whilst they are still *tabula rasa* to the physical eye, are written upon in the most vivid terms by the imagination. A journey of the mind's allurement precedes every worthwhile journey undertaken by mere force of breath and limb.

Let me sketch out one such. Its starting point is the September of 1962; a school classroom (from whence, at idle moments, glimpses of the Derbyshire hills), at the front of which a balding, slight, fierce, acerbic master, gowned and intense, is labouring with every trick and wile at his command to convey to those under his tutelage, if not a love then at least an understanding of Milton—not an easy task when faced with a group of fifteen or sixteen-year-old boys. But the performance he puts on is magisterial. This desiccated, stuffy school librarian sings out the blank verse in an extraordinary manner—there are no giggles, we are too afraid of his savage temper for that—but little by little, by the subtlest variations of emphasis and pace, he begins to impart to us the music and the magic of the poetry—it is the first book of *Paradise Lost*. I still remember with a shiver of pure sensual pleasure the dying fall of his voice in such lines as, "Thick as Autumnal Leaves that strow the brooks/In Vallombrosa."

By the time he comes to the stern, brief passage,

> Let none admire
> That riches grow in Hell; that soil may best
> Deserve the precious bane

I doubt if there is a boy in the room, even towards the end of a long double-period, who is not thoroughly entranced. Then, quite suddenly, his manner softer and abstracted now, he relaxes into one of the digressions which have brought the poem alive for us: "Whenever I read these lines, they put me in mind of a hill in Shropshire called the Stiperstones. On one side of it there are mines, and there's even a rocky outcrop on top called the Devil's Chair . . . I rather think I'm not alone in the identification, either, because the Shropshire writer Mary Webb called one of her novels *Precious Bane* . . . Woodall, be quiet!"

His cane crashed on the desk to end the reverie. The bell rang, books were put away, the lesson, and with it afternoon school, was over.

I still feel grateful to him for that moment of imaginative release, but we must press on to the next stage of the journey, which takes me—probably on the same evening—walking down the grim, black Victorian thoroughfare which is Manchester's John Dalton Street. There used to be, where it ran into Deansgate, a secondhand bookshop run by a shabby-suited, wheezing man in a stained, green cardigan:

"Mary Webb—yes, we've surely got something by her. *Precious Bane* you want? Look in the shilling-and-unders . . ."

I did as I was bidden, ran my fingers along the packed shelves in the back of the shop, and after searching diligently through, then questing back again, came up with one small volume in an odd, furry-feeling grey binding—*The Golden Arrow*.

"Haven't we got *Precious Bane*? There are usually quite a few of them in there. I tell you what—I'll throw something else in with this one. You can have them both for the same price."

He turned to the poetry section, picked out a very slim and battered edition, handed it to me, took my money—sixpence—and nodded me out of the shop.

Now at this point you might be expecting me to confess a lifelong affection for Mary Webb and Housman's *Shropshire Lad*—which was the book thrown in to make up the bargain lot. In fact, I've never had much of a liking for either of them, though it almost sounds like treachery to the schoolmaster and the bookseller to say so. There are a few poems of Housman's—"On Wenlock Edge the wood's in trouble" and "Into my heart an air that kills" amongst them—which belong with the unforgettable stock of knowledge you gain in those most intellectually acquisitive years of adolescence and are never thereafter, despite the most strenuous efforts, able to lose. And I find one novel of Mary Webb's, and a few other scattered passages from here and there amongst her writings, haunting and memorable. The conscious apparatus of both writers—Housman's soldier-lads and gallows-fodder, Mary Webb's awkward naivety of plot and character —I've always found slightly repellent. Yet despite that, the landscape in which both of them worked imaginatively is vividly alive to me. I can hear the sound of the wind-tossed trees on Wenlock Edge, see in my mind's eye the "flat, white stones that lay about . . . like tombstones with no name, no date, no word of hope, fit for the nameless dateless dead, beasts and men, who had gone into the silence of annihilation" on the Stiperstones.

For twenty-odd years I shunned these places. They seemed to me doom-laden, bleak and primitive—to be avoided if you wished to keep

Corndon Hill from Pole Bank, Long Mynd

your peace of mind. Then, one snowy February afternoon, I found myself with a few hours to spare in Church Stretton—beneath the Long Mynd, with Wenlock Edge stretching out eastwards and the Stiperstones over the hill to the west.

In the greater scheme of mountaineering things there's not much of a claim you can make for a ten-mile circuit around a smoothly-contoured hill which just fails to make 1,700 feet. But that is to discount the power of the mind:

> . . . mind has mountains; cliffs of fall
> Frightful, sheer, no-man-fathomed.

I paced around that hill in a frenzy of terrified expectation. It turned out to be less mild and gentle than it seemed on the map—the snow had blotted out road and track and reinstated the hill to its proper wildness, whilst wind and sun had buffeted and burnished the surface so that for long stretches you broke through a thin, hard crust into eighteen inches of soft snow, then suddenly by contrast skated across fields of white, pure ice. And all the while a thin, cutting wind ushered you along with the reminder that it would be in your face on the journey back. On top, all the outliers in this shoal of hills were clearly in view. I saw the Stiperstones for the first time, its shattered quartzite tors distinct against the western light.

But it was in the valley beyond that the fear started to grow upon me. There was one particular dilapidated farmhouse, the lane past it banked high with snow, where a face leant hard and unsmiling against a window to watch me pass by. I recalled Stephen Edwards, Menlove's brother, telling me of the occasion when a group of cretins gathered round him mowing and gibbering while he fished a river in this area one day, then they drew back and began to stone him from a nearby bridge.

A little farther on, searching for the right track from a farmyard, an arm slid over a stable door, released the bolt, and let out a pack of snarling dogs about my heels, which I fended off with a stick whilst holding my own dog up out of their reach.

By the time I turned back to regain the crest of the Long Mynd, my nerves were ragged. Even the rabbits which hopped in front of us up Pole Bank seemed invested with supernatural powers. And then, as we'd breasted the ridge and the light was failing fast, there was this staggering visitation to be faced.

Which is where we rightly descend into bathos. A couple of hundred yards more, and the spectral pair resolved themselves into—a man pushing a heavily-laden bicycle—an odd enough character to chance across on a twilight snowfield, but nothing more untoward than that. We hailed each other as the gap closed between us.

"You'll need your studded tyres on if you're riding that thing down the other side."

"Aye, well, I shall slide down on my bum if necessary."

A Midlands accent and a cheerful face beneath the peaked cycling cap, his steel-capped shoes scratching on the ice.

"Going to the Youth Hostel?"

"Aye."

"Well, you'll be there in time for tea."

"Oh, I've got it with me if I get stuck."

Conspiratorial grins to each other, a few more inconsequential remarks, and we parted company. I scarcely stopped giggling all the way back down the hill. Quite an ordinary, friendly sort of chap really, Edric, of the Wild Hunt . . .

To be asked to choose, for the delectation of the reader, your favourite places in Britain, and then to write an essay upon them, is a wonderful indulgence, and one which every good editor should allow his contributors. For me, the attraction is chiefly associative, and increases in power as the years pass.

Idyllic Hills
High 1984

ONE AUGUST DAY in 1969 Anne Davies and I abseiled down to a ramp in the bay just west of Mowing Word in South Pembrokeshire. In a little corner at the back of the ramp, ten or fifteen feet above high tide level, we found a large primus stove, some enamel saucepans, and a pile of ragged clothing. The white cliffs glared around, the sea lapped in gently towards us, we shrugged our shoulders and went off to climb.

Opposite: John Greenland on the first ascent of Heart of Darkness, Mowing Word

That night the wind rose and next day waves were running hard against the cliffs. When we came back a few days later the shabby encampment had gone without trace.

Why this should stick in my mind I do not know, but it does, surfacing now and then to prick me with the intimation that someone else considered the place special and gave to it a mystery. I have been back dozens of times since, threaded my rope through the clinking iron rings, themselves mysterious in origin, and skipped down the brief wall to climb, sunbathe, or explore; and always a pucker at the brow as I pass the former camp, an undefined hovering presence about the place.

All places that we like best have an atmosphere which blends familiarity with mystery, and our fondness for them is a synthesis of the two. If you like, they are two directions of thought, the one backwards into memory, pondering, re-assessing, mockingly or gratefully dwelling upon the moments of experience and time which made us what we are; the other curious, eager, probing, desirous of more and closer knowledge. How were the holds in that faint groove, with its ripple of orange lichen, over to the right of where we had climbed? What flowers grew on the other path to the hill's summit, which we never took?

The two places I like best are these: the stretch of coast between Barafundle and Broad Haven in South Pembrokeshire; and Cwm Pennant, with its surrounding hills, to the west of Snowdon. Both, for me, are rich in memory and desire. Let me take the seaward venue first.

Not much over a mile of coastline; two small bays, Barafundle and the nameless cove with the ramp mentioned in the first paragraph; limestone sea-cliffs, flat-topped, rising to 150 feet in the twin promontories of Stackpole Head and Mowing Word. Thus the outline —what of the texture? The subtle colourings and exquisite sea-carvings on these cliffs, their tide-level intricacies, the smooth, green, thrift-and-bugloss-starred turf of their tops, the path which rises through the oakwood from Barafundle to Stackpole Head, the wave-sound heard distantly through cliff-top chasms, the great, green rolling waves out of winter seas which pile, gather, hurl their spume high over the cliffs and recoil in swirling white chaos beneath, are all a part of that.

And so was the day we walked over from Stackpole Quay in the late afternoon, hid our rucksacks in a wood carpeted with rose-of-Sharon beyond the dunes at Barafundle, climbed in evening sunlight on Mowing Word, barnacled rock crunching above sluicing, indolent water, holds sharp and rough to the fingertip, the sure cling of friction, and granular dusty lichens glowing out warmly to the west. Afterwards we made camp in a little hollow among the dunes, far back and unseen from any path, built a small fire to cook over from the wood lying round

Dièdre Sud, Mowing Word. Jan Rawlinson climbing

about, and in the velvet air and darkness walked hand-in-hand and naked across an empty, washed beach into the cool shock of the water; play and laughter, foam sparkling with moonlight, all the uncluttered perfection of an elemental place, the salt taste on her lips, the warming flesh, waves and dreams and darkness.

There were other days encompassed by the place when the tender joy of this sensuality gave way to a brute ecstasy of steep rock, an awareness of strength, the perfect moment of the well-timed move whose memory lives on long after the body's capacity for it has gone. Or days when the enquiring mind drove around that arete, across that wall, through the cave with the incoming tide chasing past. These are all now assimilated into experience of place, the same flash of synaes-thetic charge can bring them all back. And tease at the half-forgotten urge to climb there and there, to swing again along that line of holds on a grey morning with the sea-fret beading your hair. That which I remember *is* and lives on into an eternal, singing present.

But not just from my experience. Throughout the four years I lived in Cwm Pennant, the sense grew on me that here was a landscape where every field-corner was thick with ghosts, where generations of men had played some cosmic chess-game, arranged and re-arranged stones into the temporary shapes of two or three hundred years, borrowed from here to build there, let frost and wind collapse and the grass wipe clean, and though the summit ridges could preside, curved and swooping, effortlessly elegant, each stone piece their own be-quest, they too were subject to the rules of the game, timed by the pulse of the sun.

Let me tell you something of the variety of the place: streams and woods, close turf with orchids and scabious, church and chapel, ridge and dome of hill, rough scree and a drift of bluebells like woodsmoke across a green shade, all intermingled, all shaken up together in this

Cwm Pennant and Bwlch Dros Bern from the summit of Moel Hebog

valley-vessel with its cliffed spur of Craig Isallt stopping up the end. These are abstractions and generalities. If you want the specific of rock, there is climbing in Pennant, on Craig Isallt—one of the great bouldering areas, or on the grassy, broken cliff of Craig Cwm Trwsgl at its head.

I remember a misty September day ten years ago on this cliff, rain falling as I abseiled down to clean the diamond-shaped slab now climbed by The Exterminating Angel. Daylong as the columns of rain swept by and imaginable shapes of mist streamed and whirled around, there was a murmur of voices in the cwm, echoing from the deserted quarry, clustering round the hut circles of an older time, swelling out and dying away, sometimes from the col up to my left, other times retreating past the tiny lake. As the mist thickened down towards night I coiled my dripping ropes and set off to the valley. All the way to the lip of the high cwm I was followed—by something which kept pace perfectly, prickled the hair on my scalp, slipped beyond sight as I turned to see, and was gone as inexplicably as it had come.

There have been pleasanter experiences for me in Pennant. Watching the peregrines, for example, and seeing the tiercel attract the falcon from her nest, she flying under him and upside down to catch the pigeon he dropped to her, then breaking away and back to the inaccessible ledge as he sported about her. Or the foxes, supposed to be so alert, yet one passed me amongst the summit rocks of Moel Hebog one morning, coat glistening rich chestnut in the just-risen sun, my dog and I sitting quite still and he not ten feet away so that his acrid stink had my bitch quivering with excitement. Other evenings in the summer we watched cubs playing outside their earth in a bank by Brithdir, delicately marked, robustly quarrelsome. And again, lest you think me oversentimental, one which ran through my flock of geese in clear mid-morning, tearing off a wing here, a shrieking head there as I watched helplessly from the hillside above.

Not that foxes were the only killers. There were summer nights on the river when the foxglove bloomed and Owen John Cwt-y-Bugail and I patrolled our favourite pools, where I held the lamp and carried the heavy battery as he poised, *trifar* in hand, fiercely intent above the water, eyes sharp and cold as any soldier hewing limbs at Pilleth or Mortimer's Cross five hundred years before; then the shaft's plunge into dark water, thrash and gleam of the stricken fish. Once the bailiff came along. That night we had two girls with us and no chance of escape. Two of us hid behind a bush, fish and lamp amongst the roots of a tree. Owen John and the other girl were on the grass, giggling, her knickers by her ankles and he on top of her by the time the bailiff flashed his lamp: "Oh, sorry mate. Have one for me while you're at it." And away he went.

The people are as much a part of the spirit of the place as the river or the hills. The old Welsh faces, the lingering conversations, the companionable crises of the farmer's year, the frenetic sweat and itch of stacking hay in a barn, pandemonious sadism at the sheep-dipping, the shepherding—that time in the late snow, the sheep tired with long labour and no option but to bare your arm to the elbow and push the breech lamb up and round before pulling it out, the lamb and your arm both marbled bloody and yellow against the white ground; hares boxing with young lambs, the season-to-season gradation of colour in so simple a thing as grass, and season to season likewise the swing of the sun north and south behind the flawless ridge each night at its setting. Then the man-made oddities in a landscape—not just the obvious ones—the water-wheel in Cwm Ciprwth, the isolated clumps of trees on Moel Lefn planted as shelter for the sheep, or the tower amongst the beeches above the ruins of Bryncir Hall—but also the stranger exiles—the prehistoric town on Braich y Gornel, the Welsh names and the oddness of their translations; market valley, Englishman's pass, pass of the two biers; the unaccountable cairns of Garnedd-goch; all of them fragments from the text of a lost story, beyond our power of imagination to recreate.

The very last night I spent in Pennant there was a girl with me, beautiful and long-golden-haired, whom I'd first seen walking through the flowery riverside meadow above Pont Cyfyng like the re-enactment of a myth. We sat by the ruined shell of a tower above Bryncir Hall, badgers playing on the hillside beneath, their black and silver coats bouncing in the joy, the grunt and tumble of their game, mindless, heedless, as we made our way down through the trees where the moonlight was translating all to longing, into the soft rustle, unfold, and intertwine of the valley and the stream and the falling night.

Next morning I was gone, and have not been back, except sometimes to climb by muddy tracks through the thick forest above Pont Cae'r Gors, past Ogof Owain Glyndwr, up to the firm and wrinkled rocks around the summit of Moel yr Ogof, to look from there into this enchanted place, out through Bwlch Dros Bern at its head to the glimmer of sand and wave along the west coast of Anglesey, and all along the Lleyn in front, its bays and little, jutty hills narrowing down and threaded by the old Saints' Road to Ynys Enlli, the mountains of Snowdonia grandly at my back, and a clamour of lost worlds reaching up through the swirl of time.

Cwm Pennant has figured in more than one piece I have written. It is a haunted valley for me—populous with phantoms. T. H. Parry-Williams, who was born just over the pass at the head of the valley, in Rhyd Ddu, caught the feeling memorably in a line from his poem "Hon":

"Mae lleisiau a drychiolaethau ar hyd y lle."
(There are voices and apparitions throughout the place.)

What follows is a ghost story of sorts, recounts a second meeting with the Cwm Trwsgl doppelgänger, and is entirely true.

Landscape with Figures
1975, Bangor University Journal 1981

I LEANT AGAINST an ash tree and looked down on the bridge. On Dartmoor it would have been called a clapper bridge, but this was the head of a Welsh valley. It was nothing more than two slabs of rock, narrow in relation to their length, spanning a point where the stream was channelled between high banks. The natural contours of the slabs were accentuated, hollowed out, though whether by the passage of feet or water I could not tell. It was mid-September. I had been watching a sewin in a pool by a copse of alder downstream. And following it, too, following its quickness, the silvery perfection of its form, until eventually it had arrowed its way out of the still pool and under the broken surface of the faster water, to be lost from sight.

So I left the stream to climb up and stand by the ash tree. The keys were hanging in heavy clusters. Some of them were littered about on the grass, and the leaves retained only a memory of green in their shrivelled browns. Above the skyline ridge, the clouds were grey. I was not looking directly at the farmhouse but, looking at it or not, just then I saw a figure come out of the door. I turned my head, puzzled, not quite sure of what I had seen. Nothing moved. Why should anyone have been in that place? It sufficiently aroused me from my lethargy to make me cross the bridge.

As I neared the house, a rabbit rose on its haunches, peered at me, and darted over the cropped turf to a hole in a bank grown with blackthorn. I stepped inside the door. There was a thick, sour smell, a mixture of elder, fungus and rotting plaster. The plan of the house was discernible. A few slimy remnants of wood poked out from holes halfway up the walls. In one corner a fragment of roof remained, supported on a beam jammed by chance against the leaning chimney stack. I went outside again, shrugged my shoulders, and set off briskly up the valley.

The path slanted steeply back across the hillside from the valley head, climbing round a spur to reach the old quarry tramway. I consciously enjoyed the pain of walking uphill, the heaviness of it, the mechanical labour of lungs and legs. There was a grim satisfaction in its dissociation from the processes of mind. And when it sent my head reeling with fatigue, I could turn on my heels, gaze down, and re-assert a mental ascendancy. I reached the tramway, its slightly sunken course plashy with water. The valley stretched seawards below me. A little patch of sunlight caught the outline of a castle on a rocky knoll by the coast. At the foot of the incline I stopped to piss against a broken column of slate. The wire it must once have supported now rusted in the sedge. I climbed the steps to one side of the incline. In places they had collapsed. For a few uphill paces, you could get into a rhythm, and then a disjunction, a faltering, as you picked your way from one remnant to another. Beyond the incline, a track contoured round a cwm, quite high and separate from the main valley, to slate workings at its head. Beyond that, the bwlch, a miry path down to the next village. In the bottom of the cwm, under a smooth-crowned and heathery cliff, a small lake had gathered behind the debris of a moraine. Rising trout pocked its surface; the wind rippled over it. Above the lake, stone hut circles and ruined sheepfolds existed in a strange synchronicity. I moved on along the track to the foot of the next incline. Some way up this, a terrace ran off on both sides. Rightwards, below a slope of shaly scree, a quarry hole had been cut down for eighty or ninety feet into the side of a natural outcrop. Its dripping back wall was streaked with brown, and studded here and there with dull mosses or brilliant green ferns. To the left, a tongue of firm-packed waste led out across the hillside. A line of roofless, low buildings had been built along it; in front of them, the stonecrop-carpeted belvedere of slate, looking down into the main valley.

I sat on a slab in the window of one of the buildings, my back to one wall, my feet against the other, trying to recreate the lives of the men

Ruined cottage, North Wales (photo: Ken Wilson)

who had lodged in these barracks. The creatures of my imaginings had not so much reality as a flicker of movement glimpsed by an averted eye. The spirit of their existence was dead to my conscious mind. The few surviving sons of the men who had built these walls would now themselves be old men. The thought did not depress me. The isolation of the place, the greyness of the sky, the feel of these cold and starless dog days, all had a numbing effect. I was no more than a figure in a landscape, wherein the failure of my will to imagine did not signify. I thrust my hands in my pockets, walked to the edge of the terrace, and looked up through gaps of former roof-trees to the bwlch.

To the north-west, the sky was darker. I thought to make the bwlch, and set off up the incline at a rapid pace, stumbling from time to time in my haste. At its top the incline met a second, shorter terrace. A few yards along to the right a parallel incline slanted down. The terrace ended against a little wall of rock, just before which I took a gravelly path which rose through a broad rocky gully to reach the col. A gate in the drystone wall marked the top. I leant against the wall, breathing hard. Another range of hills rose beyond. To both sides, valleys led off. A wind blew from the north-west; rain started to fall. Looking down the valley in that direction, ghostly shapes of luminous grey rain drifted towards me. The raindrops slashed down more vehemently. I turned up my collar and ran back down the gully.

It was at this point that a terror seized me. From the security of self-consciousness it is easy to suppose how silly you would look, how vain and futile, if you were being watched. But I was beyond that and near panic, running and skidding down the path. I jumped down on to the terrace, fell, picked myself up, ran to the incline and hurled on downwards regardless of my feet slithering on the wet slate. At the bottom was a steep slope of scree. I launched down it, rocks sliding beneath and around me. A large one bounded slowly past me, turned on end, almost stopping, then spun off down. It shot out into space. A moment's silence. I stopped, scree still trickling around me. A crash as the rock hit bottom. The edge of the hole was only feet away. A squall of hail hissed across the slope. I traversed the edge, my body arched rigid, and scrambled up on to the incline.

At the first terrace I halted, glanced about, shivered as I attempted to retain composure, and walked down, slowly. The feeling grew stronger, not just that I was being watched but that something was following me. The flesh on my back crawled; my scalp prickled with fear. I stopped to listen; nothing, beyond the suggestion of something silently behind me. I looked round. Nothing. I walked on and it followed me, keeping perfect time with me, gaining on me if I speeded up, holding back if I slowed down. Mist was rolling down from the cliff above the lake. Already it had pushed a salient down into the main valley, cutting off the long view. I burst into a run and it followed me, effortlessly keeping pace with my pounding feet and heart, down the next incline, along the tramway, down the path, and quite suddenly it was no longer there. The feeling had simply ceased. I was trembling at its memory, but no longer felt in the least threatened.

I carried on down, past the ruined farm, across the stone bridge, and along by the stream to the road. The rain fell steadily, I was wet through. Leaves on the roadside trees hung grimly down from the branches. Cattle hunched beneath them. A mile or two down the road, under a soft hillside and amongst the green land on the far bank of the river, the ruins of a large house rose like rotten molars from the encroaching rhododendrons, planted by former owners and now run wild, a demotic curse on the pomp of the place. Coming to the old church of Llanfihangel a farmer's story came to mind. All the houses around had been woken one night by the church bell wildly ringing. When sufficient people arrived at the church, they had gone inside, to find it in darkness, the bell still ringing. They ran outside, imagined devils at their heels, until a light was brought, and then returned to find a ram shaking its head with the bell-rope tangled in its horns.

I walked down through the graveyard into the church. A grey light seeped in through the leaded panes. The tiled floor was shadowy and the gallery above quite dark. Drops from the trees close by the wall pattered across the roof. I walked up the aisle. The altar was bare. In the pulpit a Bible lay open. Climbing the three steps, I began to read. My words reverberated strangely through the darkening church:

> "The voice said, Cry. And he said,
> What shall I cry?"

People came in through the door, filing slowly down the aisle, sidling into the pews, gliding along the gallery, silent and numberless, their faces downturned, listening as I read on. Quarrymen and farmers, maids and fieldwomen, shepherds, miners, woodmen, bodies bent and contorted to the exercise of their tasks, faces seamed against all weather—not a child in view, not a young face or a hopeful face amongst them as they uplifted now to hang on the resonance of a word. Not a face but that expressed a resignation, whether wearied or calm, patient, sardonic or sad; all borne down under a weight of acquiescence, the Word ringing out over them.

Grey light diminishing in the deconsecrated church. Outside the rain dripped incessantly. In the river behind the church, a sewin nosed its way upstream. I closed the Book and went my way.

East of the River Wye in Radnorshire are a group of hills which have no collective name, but which are among the most lovely in the country. These are the hills of which the Swiss mountain guide Jean Charlet is reputed to have said, "Mon Dieu, but the Almighty has forgot to put the tops on them!" In my early 'teens, when they were much less well-known than in these days of new roads and Bruce Chatwin novels, I chanced across a deserted farm amongst them called Ireland. A recent return visit there prompted some contemporary, and not particularly comforting, reflections.

Ireland, Radnor
The Guardian 1983

IT CAME INTO view as I breasted the hill. A few fields, emerald lapidary against the brown moorland, spoke of former cultivation. Thorn hedges white with may fringed the track, and a grove of ash trees all but hid the farm. No smoke rose from the chimney, no dog barked, and the ruts of the cart-track were grown with grass. I went up to the house, which stood four-square to the south, built from shallow blocks of browny-grey Silurian stone. Dark green nettles swayed by the door, which opened as if oiled yesterday. Entering I was met by a heaviness of damp, still air. To the right another door led off. Two broken chairs were the only furniture. In one corner the flower-

Ireland: "A few feet of cracked chimney breast maintained some pretence of uprightness"

patterned wallpaper peeled a little, and crumbs of plaster lay on the red-tiled floor beneath.

I had walked enough for that day, though still some miles short of my objective, so I put down my sack, investigated upstairs and down, opened a window to freshen the room, and thought to stay for the night. A makeshift repair to one of the chairs, then out to collect dry wood, lying about in plenty under the trees:

> Ash wet or ash dry
> Makes a fire fit for a king
> To warm himself by.

Soon flames licked and crackled in the grate of the black range, smoke rose from the chimney. I ate, then sat on the front step to watch the sun set round to the north of Rhulen Hill, sinking down far into the Elenith behind Mynydd Eppynt. Shadows of ash and hawthorn craved out over the green, shadows flowed down off Llanbedr Hill, engulfed Rhosgoch and Painscastle, lapped over the Begwns and the Black Mountains until an owl cued in the darkness and imperceptibly it had become night. A few more sticks on the fire, a candle on the range, I read a little from the battered, green-bound St Martin's Library edition of Yeats I had with me, swept dust from the floor, unrolled my sleeping bag, and settled down for the night.

No footfall from above, no clacking of latch or dimly-perceived whisper of voices from another room disturbed the lightness of my rest. No sound outside but the quiet sheep of the hills. Next morning I woke early as the sun slanted in through dusty panes, made breakfast of porridge on the range, packed and was gone—following green tracks over the hill to Glascwm in the glory of the morning, leaving nothing behind me but grey flakes of ash in the grate.

This was over twenty years ago.

We all know the peril of re-visiting youthful scenes—the disappointments, the shrinking scale, the ravages of time. Nostalgia is a Luddite and no memory can be dispassionate. In the anti-climax of the years we have all gazed on the face of a Flora Finching, whether embodied in a woman or a favourite hill, and felt then how nugatory is sentiment's simplistic assertion of the past's primacy. For all that, some things are worth preserving, or have deserved better fates.

The other day I found myself driving up a new tarmac road across Llanbedr Hill, linking Painscastle to Rhulen, its metal roughly quarried from the surface of the moor. Over to the right, under a knoll crowned by a gaunt, dead tree, was the ash-grove of Ireland. I walked over to see what changes time had wrought. A new, neat fence of wire and naked poles stretched round the old fields and the knoll above. It had all been ploughed and planted. From amongst a thicket of nettles, not so much as a rooftree stood proud from the mound of fallen stone. A few feet of cracked chimney breast maintained some pretence of

uprightness, but all else was rubble—no door or window, no shelter there now. I stood for a while in silence, then retraced my steps.

By the gate I met the farmer—one of those short, strong Radnorshire men, soft-voiced and wry. He voiced no surprise or annoyance at my being there:

"Been saying hello to the ghosts, then?"

"I suppose so. I remember this place when it was in a bit better state."

"Yes—we used to come up and play here when we were kids. Frightened of the ghosts we were—used to get down and away well before dark."

"You wouldn't think it could go to ruin so quickly."

"It was kids from those centres. They broke the windows, ripped it out inside. The rain got in, then the walls came down. They don't last long once the windows are out. No weight in the stones, see." He flicked a shard of rock from the path with his boot-toe.

"Your land now?"

"Yes—I bought it last year. Turnips and kale. Never seen a plough before."

Obviously I lament for the changes to Ireland and to Llanbedr Hill. For me these were holy places, little lovely landscapes unsullied by roads, unploughed, unpeopled. They associated in my mind with that stage in the growth of intellect when idealism is unperplexed by the contingent. That first encounter was entirely gratuitous in its magic, and earned my profound gratitude.

William Perrin on Llanbedr Hill; Ireland is amongst the clump of trees in the middle distance.

Modern farming and forestry—Mid-Wales

Thoughts like this possessed me as I walked along the new road. Two or three hundred yards from Ireland, amongst the heather, a woman and her small son were picking bilberries, her car parked nearby. She was about thirty, tall and quite slim, khaki shorts to mid-thigh and a mocking directness about her gaze:

"Hello there," she called out. "Are you out walking?"

"Trying to escape from the crowds," I said, with a grin.

"Oh yes, I often come up here from Hay to do just the same," she enthused. "It's so lovely up here."

She carried on picking her way through the heather, darting after the purple fruit with little, appreciative cries as we left her behind. No doubt but that the spirit of the place called as strongly to her as to me.

From the top of the hill I could see over Gwaunceste and Glascwm to Great Rhos, high point of Radnor Forest. Evidence of the plough was everywhere. In one huge, steep field three tractors worked simultaneously, spreading fertilizer from great heaps fed continually by eight-wheeled lorries. It was a scene of frenetic industry. I hold no brief against farmers. In their capital-intensive industry they have to survive. They must keep their eye on weather and the economic climate. Who can blame them for paying due regard to EEC Less Favoured Area directives, to grant-aid, to schizophrenic legislation which perfunctorily attempts to safeguard our scenic and scientific heritage whilst enshrining policies and offering incentives which aim to stimulate agricultural and silvicultural production—even where these can only lead to further surpluses to be bought up at high, guaranteed prices by the EEC Intervention Boards?

No one wishes the farmers ill, but at the same time what many of them are now doing seriously erodes the value, utility and amenity of the countryside for the wider community of this nation—and not for reasons which make economic sense to anyone other than owners of land. Nor is there likelihood of comment, confrontation or control by either of the chief government environmental watchdogs, the Nature Conservancy Council and the Countryside Commission, because executive positions in both these bodies are now heavily influenced or controlled by the landowning interest.

Lying in the heather on the common land of Llanbedr Hill, listening to the high, plaintive calls of plover and curlew, I wondered how long even this bowl of moorland would remain relatively inviolate. Beyond doubt, we are entering a new era of enclosure. Consider, for example, the following statement made by Mr Nicholas Edwards, Secretary of State for Wales, in 1982:

> . . . if we are to fully develop the opportunities that exist for further forest planting, and particularly this is true of Wales, we will have to find a better way of making use of the vast areas of common land in Wales, or land subject to common grazing rights. There are no easy solutions but we recognize the need for new legislation to make it easier to obtain better management of common land.

The ice-blue chill of Thatcherism pervades that message, which affects alike the walker, the smallholder and the hill-farmer. The countryside is fast becoming a major political issue, where the untroubled financial self-interest of the *haves* effortlessly prevails over the embattled recreational needs of the *have nots*. It is fatally easy to assume that the view of the environment as something worthy of protection is widely shared. It is not. Of course lobbies exist, some of them cogent and well-informed. A good example would be the Ramblers' Association under the secretaryship of Alan Mattingly. Their task, however, generally comes down to blocking on particular issues —yet for every hard-fought *cause célèbre* there must be a hundred quiet defeats against which the alerts were never sounded, or sounded far too late, or for which the energy and funds and expertise were simply not forthcoming.

There is a serious need for a wholly new and politically impartial appraisal of countryside planning issues whilst a countryside still exists for us to protect. To take a few cases to illustrate its urgency: Exmoor's wild land is now about the size of a municipal park; some of the most spectacular scenery on the Pembrokeshire coast is regularly shelled by the military, including German Panzer regiments; only this year, in the wake of the scandalous death of Mrs Sheila Wenham and shooting in a school playground of eight-year-old Emma Breen, a MoD spokesman opined that "increased fatalities could be expected amongst civilians wandering on to army ranges"—of which there are three-quarters of a million acres in England and Wales alone; the same Pembrokeshire coastal range mentioned above means that a designated long-distance footpath (the route of which significantly was negotiated by a government body, the Countryside Commission) has to forego the finest stretch of limestone coastal scenery in Britain and wander miles inland along roads and through oil refineries; on Plynlimon recently, Crown Estate land—to which there is unrestricted public right of access—was fenced and drained for forestry *before* permission was obtained from the aforementioned Secretary of State for Wales—an act of blatant presumption and illegality, and one wholly indicative of governmental thinking on the environment. Remember the leak in the early days of the Thatcher administration which stated that the government was aiming to "reduce over-sensitivity to environmental considerations"? Remember the chicanery over the recent Green Belt Land circular, which lay successively on the desks of Heseltine, King and Jenkin, for release only when a new term of Tory office had been safely secured? And what of the present bout of privatization-mania and asset-stripping from the Forestry Commission, which raises the question of all those rights-of-way ploughed up and destroyed by plantation, the proving of which now devolves upon the public, with the lengthy and costly procedure which that entails? Or again on the legal side, what of the fact that although rights of appeal exist against *refusals* of planning permission, no such rights exist against their *granting*, which is often neither disinterested nor well-informed?

With examples like these waging war on my peace of mind, I turned to leave Llanbedr Hill. Just then, at a stone's throw from the ground, an RAF Harrier screamed across the ridge, piloted no doubt by some skilful vainglorious boy. At the cost of a couple of these machines, or a few days' subsidy to the Falklands, planning controls could be implemented which would truly protect our native rural environment, safeguard it as a national heritage, and ensure that the statutory considerations as to amenity land laid down in the National Parks and Access to the Countryside Act 1949, the Countryside Act 1968, and even the Wildlife and Countryside Act 1981, disaster though the latter is, were consistently observed in detail and principle. But where, in the country of the blind, do our priorities lie? Remember the *Sun*'s motto at the time of the Falklands adventure—"the paper which supports our lads"? Where is there a single organ of popular opinion which can claim to support our land?

Readers of Welsh poetry will recall a resonant line from the Llywarch Hen cycle, spoken by the old poet mourning over the ruined hall of Cynddylan, where formerly he had known hospitality, culture, friendship, and which now lies bereft of roof, fire, or bed:

> Wylaf wers, tawaf wedyn
> (I shall weep for a while, then be silent)

Is that the best response we can muster against the ruination of our countryside?

The problems outlined in the above essay would not exist if everyone accepted the particular pieties involved. But they do not, and the articles of faith are as often written in terms of opposition as those of protection—a fact which the conservationists ignore at their peril.

Snowdon from Moel Siabod

Black Earth, Black Light
High 1985

THEY HAVE CUT a road into the flank of Moel Siabod. You can see it as you look out over the great marsh which stretches round to Skylark Pass. In the winter it is a black weal across the bleached grass, and even the encroaching bracken of summer cannot mask its disfigurement of this wild, wide hillside, nor cover over the place from which its aggregate was hewn. The National Park Wardens knew about it, of course, but what could they do? Reason with a man on piecework rates whose fist is clenched around the black knob by which he operates his digger? In principle, though not in this specific, the Countryside Commission would have known of it too—the outcome of the Uplands Debate they conducted a couple of years ago was that recommendations on the matter were made to the Government. But they were not accepted, and the grants for such roads go on, however slight their individual rationale.

I expect that when Moses came down from Sinai, the tablets of stone in his hand, and spoke out to his tribe what had come to him on that holy summit, they looked upon him a little querulously, as people do when they must needs recognize authority, and went about their usual tasks in their old ways, nothing having changed within. Perhaps they even felt more inclined, the power of "Thou Shalt Not" against them, to go out and do that which was newly forbidden. (As the good people of Islay might now go out to shoot the Greenland white-fronted geese of Duich Moss.)

Sunset and dawn are the great times to be on a mountain top. The physical world then settles itself down with all the sighing, rustling rhythms of darkness, or heaves and stretches itself into light. If there is one mountain I would choose above all others to watch these processes at their continual turn, then it is Moel Siabod. There are one or two better viewpoints in Snowdonia, and even a few hills for which I have a more intimate fondness, born of memory and association, but Siabod has a particularity on the face of the earth which recommends itself to me. And it has one of the best ways to reach a summit amongst all the Welsh mountains—the south-eastern ridge above Llyn y Foel, which is called Daear Ddu.

I suppose you aficionados of Welsh legendry will know all about Llyn y Foel and Daear Ddu, and their place in the epic tale of Hu Gadarn and the *afanc* (the latter ludicrously translated in most books on Wales as a beaver), which was dragged by Hu Gadarn's oxen to be drowned in Glaslyn. So profound were the oxen's exertions that one of them lost an eye pulling the monster over Siabod, and it rolled down to form a lake—Llyn Llygad yr Ych—lake of the ox's eye—nowadays more prosaically called Llyn y Foel. The fiery, roaring breath of the *afanc* burned the ground as it passed, and thus the ridge's name —Daear Ddu—black earth.

For all this scorched-earth pseudo-history, it is a magnificent way to gain the hill-crest. Whichever route you take to Llyn y Foel is fair enough—from Pont Cyfyng past the ferocious dogs of Rhos farm, through the old quarries where the deep green water always gives me a little *frisson* of terror as I pass, and over the shoulder of the moor to the quartz-speckled white rocks at its shore. Or through the resinous, sweet forest from Dolwyddelan, with the low hills rolling away behind you—they're both apt preludes to the ridge's orderly theme. You scramble up its sharp spine and the texture of the rock is dream-like. How can something so bubbly-rough be possessed of such gravity and precise form? It is over too soon, and it leaves you a few short, level paces from the hill's summit.

Because I like to sit on my hills at nightfall and dawn, I have often slept and dreamed up there. A patch of grass a little to the west, a few boulders for shelter, from which I once saw the black light. I suppose

the circumstances were significant, though I cannot exactly recall them. It must have been about thirteen years ago, for I had been living in London and escaped, as I then saw it, to Wales—just driven up with a few belongings in an old Ford Anglia (shortly to break in half on the road up to Cloggy) and vowed never to go back. Often as not that summer I would sleep out in the heather or on the hills, and this was such an occasion. I was sitting with my back to the summit cairn and facing east. It was an evening of absolute clarity and stillness, the sun was going down behind a shoulder of Snowdon and the cwm at my feet was inky with shadow. I was in that perfectly peaceful and harmonious state where you are so still that the gentle throb of blood around your body is as tangible, as audible, as the ticking of a clock. The whole outlook seemed of transcendent beauty—the green hills and woods and soft, low light. I was, in Simone Weil's phrase, "annihilated by the plenitude of being". There was an emerald patch of lichen on a rock catching the light, and when I looked up from it the shadow at my feet had spilled over with shocking suddenness and streamed out to the horizon. A second glance and it seemed to be pulsing back out from that point to the south-east, flooding the mountain with its sharp-edged, black light. You will understand the vision it suggested. I grabbed my rucksack, fled shuddering down the hillside to the west, and rested finally amongst some boulders suffused with the last of the western light.

"The shadow at my feet had spilled over with shocking suddenness and streamed out to the horizon"

"I . . . rested finally among some boulders suffused with the last of the western light"

Well, visions have their interpretations and I have brooded on this one long enough—it is full of darkness, this land of Wales where the sun dies, and I had witnessed the rising of the anti-sun. But these things shock you at the time and you only know them in retrospect.

There is a poem by Gwenallt—one of the four great poets who have written in Welsh this century—entitled "Rhydcymerau". It is a complaint and a harking back, a lament for the loss of culture and community and it sticks in my mind as few other poems do. It is also wrong-headed and chauvinistic, and misrepresented by those who use the occasion of a lament to traduce the humanity which is lamented. It links landscape and culture to project a vision of lost fineness. Down there, in the flow of the black light, in a chapel vestry, I have seen a woman of witch-like countenance, like her of the Salem print, one who would hold this poem as a holy text, stand up and hiss that "It is our landscape *and we will do what we want with it*."

So the farm tracks slash across the shoulders of Siabod and Cader, the road improvements gouge their curving, sinuous, insidious way through rough, gentle valleys, the plough cleaves higher than any financial return would dictate, and conifers thrust up through the drained land. But the people, the communities, the hopes and ideals, do not return. The black light of race-hatred, of unemployment, of ageing human stock left unreplenished, has overwhelmed them. Perhaps it is the same in all remote and wild places—I walked across a moor in the Ross of Mull the other evening. Former trackways and former houses were everywhere, the latter's walls still four-square against the winds, the turf of their roofs fallen in but the mortar, of sea-creature shells and silver sand, obdurately hard-edged where the window-frame wood had rotted away. On a pile of great abandoned blocks in a quarry above the sea, looking out to Iona, I watched the dappled play of light on the waters. They are a cleansing of the soul, these places, but when their communities are lost and the values which stem from social hope with them, then the remnants who inhabit there are left desolate, desperate, unremitting in their antagonism to those who would fondly dictate.

Politics apart, there is a release and liberation in simply being amongst the hills. Even if it is only for a snatched hour at the end of a grey day.

Up Here, Down There . . .
High 1985

THE OTHER DAY, with a rage of suppressed energy upon me and half an afternoon to spare, I burst out of the house and drove down to the Berwyns. Parking the car at Hendwr Bridge, my dog and I trotted and panted up the lane and muddy track which led past the stone circle and out on to the heathery spur of Cadair Bronwen called Trawsnant. There was a blustery wind in our faces from the south-east which carried with it a thin, niggling rain. Just beyond the ring of ancient stones, we branched off from the path and rested in the lee of a forestry plantation. It was four o'clock on an early December afternoon.

Off from my back came the rucksack, out came the flask, and with my dog nestling close for shelter and warmth—wearing her alert expression, ears cocked to denote expectation of food—I sat and looked out over the Dee Valley, saw the little lake of Mynllod on the opposite ridge glinting in the leaden light, watched the clouds massing over Bala and by Foel Goch, and felt ridiculously, inexplicably happy.

Why?

The place was beautiful, but not excessively or dramatically so, and the weather was foul with every sign of becoming filthy later. Robert Maxwell hadn't decided to make me an instant millionaire and there was still the dreary grind of repetitive, bill-paying hack-work to be faced when I returned to my desk down there that night. So whence the sudden elation?

I asked my editor about it. "What," I queried of him, "is the reason for the spiritual uplift you get from being in the hills?"

"Simple," he replied, "no telephone!"

That joking image does play a large part in the feeling I'm attempting to describe. To get up into the hills is to shed the connections of everyday life (pity the poor warden with his radio-telephone), for however brief a time. Thomas Hardy, who for this one piece alone should be considered one of the great hill-poets, encapsulates the mood exactly in "Wessex Heights". And particularly in the one echoing line, "But mind-chains do not clank where one's next neighbour is the sky", which I repeated to myself over and over again as I sat in the still shadow of my buffeted copse, sipping coffee and rubbing my dog's ears until she groaned with pleasure and rolled over to offer up her muddy belly for the same treatment.

I should tell you about my dog. She is a black labrador bitch, something under the usual size on account of having been runt of the litter. I took her on ten years ago when she was six weeks old and could fit easily into a large pocket. She is, after the manner of her sex and breed, unbelievably greedy, and a history of wrath-occasioning thefts has left her guilt-ridden about the same. She has a thin tail with the coarse hair rubbed away at its end from an excess of wagging against solid objects. She is alert and intelligent through every outdoor waking moment, brown-eyed, her coat shiny-black except around a now-greying muzzle, and although over the last year she has slowed up a little and climbs the stairs rather stiffly to her bed each night, she still brisks about the life in a joyous manner. Her name is Kigfa, and the simple, warm regard I have for her is one of the absolutes in my life. To watch her is an education and to walk with her in the hills a continual pleasure.

You may think I digress here but I do not digress; I am merely seeking another entry into my theme, questing for counterparts. "Down there", all is complexity, "the fury and the mire of human veins", "the mind-forged manacles", "sick hurry and divided aims", "the foul rag-and-bone shop of the heart". Up here it is uncomplicated, just such an uncluttered reciprocity as exists between me and my dog. Not only that, but you can see the *physical* delight of it in the way she—my dog—bounds about, stretching her muscles, careering along vibrantly alert to all the possibilities around her, unrecognizable from the constrained and dozing creature in her basket under the kitchen table at home.

I'm not really cheating here, because I had promised myself as we wound down from the Berwyns that I would introduce her fully in the next piece I wrote. But it has taken us a little distance from our afternoon walk. As I have said, it was 4 p.m. in December, coming on to rain, and though I had neither map nor compass and at best a half-hour of daylight I felt disinclined to go back "down there". After all, I had made good my escape and the hill reared up behind me. So away went the flask, I buttoned my coat, pulled my hat firmly down over my ears whilst Kigfa danced in approval, we turned into the wind and set our faces to the ridge.

There is a sensuality to be derived from all motions of the flesh, and walking uphill into a gusting, chill wind is no exception. If you detach yourself and observe it, so much is added to the enjoyment of a day out. I love the counterpointed rhythms of a rough walk, the strange calms in the wind's onslaught which cause you to lurch forwards from your braced stride, the piquant crackling wobbliness of joints scourged and ruined in a thousand jumps from boulder-problems or the starts of difficult climbs. On we went, the path a serpentine allurement, a siren-song of distance, Kigfa mincing along in front, round-rumped and cow-hocked, her ears flapping in the gusts. Out on the open moor we skirted a mire and ensnared ourselves thus in thick heather, from which we struggled back urgently on to the path. At the gate where the track up from Clochnant joined in, we were in the mist and it was thickening down to darkness, with sleet now sticking against the wet green of my jacket. I have to say that at this point my heart was definitely racing, and not just from the exertion. You surely know the feeling—that sudden access of fierce joy when a challenge emerges to confront the prudent choice? I had intended a short stroll, perhaps at most up to Bwlch Maen Gwynedd and down again. But somewhere up there in the mist and sleet, in the wild wind, were Cadair Bronwen, Arthur's Table, the couple of miles of splashy high ridge on the two-and-a-half-thousand-foot contour over to Blaen Llynor and the Nant Rhydwilym. How the wind rouses an exulting passion of opposition—what option is there ever but to go on, to seek out the bare, wild places in all their purity and obscure, howling loss? Set your shoulder, turn your stinging cheek, and press on, "for the desire of the heart always exhorts to venture forth". To be up there, in the night, in the storm, is an assumption into that elevated, elemental consciousness which the early Welsh and the Anglo-Saxon poets knew. Man may be doomed to loss, sorrow and desolation, but if he tries his strength and will, however briefly, upon the indifferent vast hostility of the elements, he rages against futility and asserts his right of being. The code of the warrior is at the heart of the mountaineer.

So Kigfa and I laughed and bounced and scurried along, taking decisions by instinct and confident in facing up to whatever their outcome might be. This way or that? The cairn loomed up, snow packing its crevices, but we did not stop, ran stumbling on, the path downhill now, no light beyond the faint grey glow of wet snow. The wrenching plunges into bog-holes, the slippery peat, the dips and rises of dark ground were seemingly endless, before the uproarious relief of coming out of the mist and hitting upon the track by the Wayfarer plaque at the Nant Rhydwilym, down which we turned towards home.

Strangely enough, with the pressure dissipated and it being full dark by now, we did lose the way on the descent. I wanted to keep on the right bank of the Afon Llynor but missed the fork in the darkness and crossed the stream by a bridge above the forestry. Determined to remedy the error, we took the first track we came across down through

Berwyn lower slopes—bare tree, conifers and phosphate

the trees, losing height rapidly along it and pleased that it was heading in the right direction.

A mile later we rounded a bend and saw our track stop short at the bank of a noisy, swollen and substantial Afon Llynor. We could have gone wearily back up the hill and taken the other track. We didn't need to wade this frightening rush of black water. But I put Kigfa on a lead and in we went, thigh-deep into its chill shock. Another six inches and the current would have been too strong for it to be waded. Once out, it was bouncing and barking, frisking and gambolling all the way down past Blaen y Glyn, the moon showing through gaps in the cloud, brilliantly edging the fretwork of trees, an owl dropping in ghostly white silence over us and gliding on across the stream.

The relief and the life of it! Back down in the dark valley and making for the car, the elation remained as a spiritual presence and a physical one too in the body's tingling weariness. It is a washing of the soul to get out into the simplicity of these hills:

> Down there I seem to be false to myself, my simple self that was
> And is not now, and I see him watching, wondering what crass
>   cause
> Can have merged him into such a strange continuator as this,
> Who yet has something in common with himself, my chrysalis.

It is not so easy, in all the hugger-mugger and hurly-burly of a difficult life, beset by the lies of politicians, the demands of vested

Berwyns—"the primality of all high places"

interest, the needs of friends and the necessity for work, to identify the essential qualities you must sustain to carry it on—the sensual awareness, the combative energy, the intellectual honesty and vigour. Up there it is all clearly set out to be seen, a freshness and a glory to the eye. It gives shape and definition to the primal qualities of character and remains with you, if you have gone open-hearted to its influence, throughout the dark days. I don't know whether you are any nearer to God on a mountain-top, but you can certainly come nearer to yourself. In Blake's view that *is* to bring you nearer to God. Perhaps that's why he wrote the enigmatic line, "Great things are done when men and mountains meet". I'm not much concerned to interpret things in that way, interesting metaphysics though it may be. But I know the strength and fullness of feeling the hills elicit from me. I know the need I feel for them. Let me finish with the first stanza from "Wessex Heights". The hills which Hardy mentions may be low ones in the West Country, but the feelings they invoke in him have the primality of all high places. Listen now:

> There are some heights in Wessex, shaped as if by a kindly hand
> For thinking, dreaming, dying on, and at crises when I stand,
> Say, on Ingpen Beacon eastward, or on Wylls-Neck westwardly,
> I seem where I was before my birth, and after death may be.

Does that come close? Do you need to come closer? And how glib and wan sound any attempts to explain the feeling away . . .

2: ON THE ROCKS

The sharp, pure experience of rock-climbing is the subject of this section. I have never really felt it necessary to address myself directly to the limp and jaded question of why we climb. Nevertheless, if that line of inquiry does appeal to any observer of the sport, then perhaps they will detect, at least implicitly, some of the reasons in the following accounts of climbs and escapades which have meant something to me. And I hope too that these pieces convey the diversity of the sport—its atmospheres and rock-types, its values, venues and approaches. The first of them takes a young beginner and initiates him into the Great Northern Mystery.

In Praise of Jamming
High 1983

WHEN I FIRST started to climb I had no idea about hand-jamming or its attendant arts of fist-jamming, wedging, and all the other variations on the central mystery of crack-climbing. As you may imagine, this was something of a disadvantage to a boy living in Manchester, upon whose doorstep lay the gritstone outcrops of the Peak District.

What I used to do each Sunday morning was race across Manchester to catch the 8.45 a.m. bus from Stephenson Square for the hour-long ride to Greenfield. I would sit on the top deck and peer along factory-lined roads to see who would be coming out today. Black Jack the negro, who had been seen to solo Waterfall Direct, and his friend Dave Featherstone might get on at Chadderton. Perhaps Len Chadwick would be waiting in the centre of Oldham, small, spare, and shabbily dressed, his white hair flying behind him and a spring in his step, ready for a 20-mile circuit of Pots and Pans, Holme Moss or Black Hill, to write up in his *Oldham Evening Chronicle* column the following Friday. Just up the road would be little Jack Landy, with whom you didn't argue, whilst Paul Fletcher and the Ripley brothers got on at Grotton, and our whole motley crew bumped and cursed and laughed along the road, hills and fields now swelling on each side, to be disgorged in Greenfield by The Clarence, whence we made our way up the steep hill, past the paper mill and scout hut, to Whimberry, or less frequently to Dovestones, Laddow, or even Upperwood Quarry for pegging in the winter. These moor-rimming outcrops, in all the thrust and jut of their smoke-blackened rock, were heart-thrilling to me long before I fully knew the fine intricacies their starkness bound.

To go regularly to Whimberry and not be able to jam was to work under a handicap, for the chief attractions of the place were the great crack-lines which Joe Brown had climbed in his nailed boots—the scratches were still reverently pointed out—just a few years previously. Coffin Crack you could layback, the Overhanging Crack you could

Opposite: Elegug Tower, first ascent, 1970. Peter Biven and Jim Perrin (photo: John Cleare)

Below: (photo: John Beatty)

Overleaf: Suicide Wall, Cratcliffe Tor (photo: Ken Wilson)

improvise around, but all the rest were fierce tests of your skill in jamming. Even now, over twenty years later, I can remember the peculiar combination of frustration and hypnotized terror with which I used to dream—actually dream—about the likes of Freddie's Finale, Blue Lights Crack, Ornithologist's Corner, and the Trident—routes guaranteed to gather a crowd the minute any leader embarked upon them. To stand at their base, to touch the cold, bulging granular rock, was to be faced with an aloof obduracy almost sufficient to inspire despair.

No one ever dropped the vital hint to me; the textbooks I avidly read had all been written by educated southerners without the first idea about it; as far as jamming went, I might have been born without thumbs. Quite respectably difficult routes were within my compass just so long as they did not rely on it for so much as a single move. It was my bête-noire.

The crowning embarrassment came one day when a climber we knew as Bill-the-Drill-because-he-was-such-a-bore (for such jokes God forgive all adolescents) took me up an ordinary Severe which involved jamming all the way. At the top, after the most desperate struggle, sleeves sodden with blood, I emerged with not a scrap of skin across my knuckles to huge cheers from the spectators. After that, scarcely able to climb, I skulked and sulked for weeks.

About this time I met Arthur Williams—known, for no reason I can remember, as Arthur Nirk.* He was court-jester to the Alpha Club and one of the best comics I ever met, with a continuous repertoire of anecdote and jokery, all delivered with dry wit and superb timing. He lived down the road from me in Fallowfield, with his brother Geoff, who was solemn by comparison, and his mother, who was amazingly forthright and even funnier than Arthur. At about 5 ft 6 in, with a lugubrious face, the palest complexion you ever saw and a Hitler moustache, he had a physique which made the seven-stone weakling look like Charles Atlas. For all that, he was a very competent climber, would have been about eighteen at the time, and owned a 500 cc Royal Enfield Bullet. One summer evening in my early 'teens he took me out to Helsby, the lovely outcrop of red sandstone near Chester, where we did the Pigeon Hole Wall problems (much easier in those days), Wood's Climb, which I liked and romped up, and finally Flake Crack.

I watched Arthur climb it. From the wide bridging position at half-height he reached up to place his left hand carefully in the crack. You could have drawn a perfectly straight line from his pointing toes through to his fingertips. With his right hand casually jammed a little below the other, he drew up his feet and with the knee angled out slipped his right toe into the crack, swung his hips to the right to allow

---

* Since publication of this article I have been reliably informed that he was called Arthur ('Alf a) Nirk because he wasn't a complete Nirk . . . ?

his left toe to jab in, and flowed up the rest of the crack in a smoothly mechanical and unhurried progress of stretch and gather. My heart sank.

Arthur belayed, took in the rope, and it was my turn to climb. The first section, on lay-aways, sloping footholds and sharp honeycombs, was in my favourite style but I was too apprehensive to appreciate it. When I arrived at the bridging position, I found the edge of the corner crack was sharp, swung into a layback position, and scampered my feet up the left wall.

"What you up to, youth?" queried Arthur. "You're not coming up this route unless you do it properly."

To reinforce his point he paid out a few feet of slack. I retreated to the bridging position.

"I don't know how to jam," I pleaded.

He peered down at me: "Like this," he explained, gesticulating towards the Runcorn chemical factories like a policeman on point duty.

"How do you mean?" I asked, obtusely.

"Look," he drawled patiently. "Shove your hand into the crack like this, flat. Get it to where it feels tight, then bring your thumb into the palm. Locking jams. Perfect. Me Mam could do this with her curlers in."

I tried it. It seemed to work. I eased my hand up and down the crack and where it felt snug, slipped my thumb into the palm.

"Just take it slowly, get your toes jammed as well, and get your body right and balanced before you reach for the next one."

I did as he said. Slowly, painfully slowly, and awkwardly, every muscle tense with effort and concentration, I edged up the crack, joints wrenching till I found the right angle at which to lean away before each jam went correctly in position. You could play with them! If you took the twisting action of joint and muscle into account you could rest without effort. As I heaved over the top my excitement was so intense I could only swear and giggle at him.

"Well done, youth," he rejoined. "Good job you didn't fall off —you can't even tie a sodding bowline."

He tugged at the rope round my waist, which promptly came undone.

This straightforward VS which I seconded over twenty years ago brought a feeling of achievement I've seldom experienced since, even on routes of infinitely higher standard. It was the key to many of the best moments in my later climbing. Even though it was only a simple lesson in a basic technique, I was lucky in having Arthur teach it me. For as a teacher he was kindly, patient, extremely funny, and perhaps most importantly he taught by example. His own climbing of the route was a model to which I could aspire. His attitude towards me as pupil was encouraging, but not soft or condescending.

Neb Direct, Ed Wood climbing

Previous page: Roger Alton on New Morning, Mowing Word (photo: Malcolm Griffith)

As we sat on top of Helsby that evening, looking out over the industrial towns all along the Mersey, the Clywdian Hills purple on the western horizon, he talked and I listened and occasionally questioned. The routes, the people, the crags, all came to life in my imagination. Over to our right, the vast bulk of the Pennines rose from the plains, lights glimmering here and there amongst its folds, brightening with the encroaching darkness, beckoning. We gathered up our gear, slid back down the hill, collected his bike from by the tennis court, and set off back towards them.

Most weekends in my first years of climbing were spent on the gritstone edges of Derbyshire, and these were what I set out to celebrate in this hymn to the gritstone experience, and to one of its finest routes.

Right Unconquerable: a Gritstone Paean
1971, published in Hard Rock 1973

IN RETROSPECT, STANAGE is for me the focal point in that Golden Age we all once knew when we first came to the hills; a pastel-sketched mood of mellow remembrance, the eastern sea-board of the Peak, west-facing over wave upon wave of moorland edge. Brown peat and purple heather, the rock so softly red in evening sunlight filtered through the smoke-haze of distant, unseen industry. So much beauty in those smoke-bruised sunset skies: violets and purples and violent reds, sometimes the Northern Lights flickering columnar over Bleaklow and Kinder, flanked by the lume of vast cities below the moorland night.

A time past, when the rocks stood about unknown to us, and eager and lustful we explored their every intimacy, climbed until the failing light veiled the crags with shadow and widowed them into night; and tired we would gather bracken golden from the slopes to sleep in sandy caves, our hands lacerated by the crystals of many a crack savagely fought. Early days, early struggles, our blood on the rock as an inextricable bond of friendship about which we built the flesh of our climbing career. The smoke-blackened surface of the rough rock, grouse croaking away and the fresh smell of wet bracken on a June morning; these are the reality of the place. Great nebs worn by the wuthering wind into stern, harsh forms. Rough rock, wild wind, and the reality of the place.

Gritstone has its own form of consciousness: quite simply, it posses-ses the finest and purest free-climbing ethic in the world. Every new wave in British climbing has gained its initial momentum from grit-stone's wild and prehensile freedom of attack. The keynote of gritstone climbing is aggression: the climbs are short and steep; characteristically they deal out inordinately large quantities of pain and fear. Torn hands, scraped knees, strained arms and a dry throat are all in a gritstoner's day: the cracks in particular are armed with vicious teeth. They have about them a degree of static malignity which it demands an equal display of controlled temper to overcome. It's not that climbing on gritstone is more difficult than climbing on other forms of rock, it's just that the defences are more systematically designed to disconcert: rounded holds, rough bulging cracks, and an overbearing angle; you just have to get used to them.

Stanage is the great crag; four miles long, and with over five hundred climbs. It would be impossible to get a consensus of opinion on which one is typical, let alone best. There are probably fifty climbs as good in their own way as the Right Unconquerable. But this one exemplifies the gritstone approach, and historically it stands at the beginning of an era—the last of the great cracks of Stanage to be climbed, and the first of Joe Brown's great gritstone climbs.

Brown and Stanage! Mohammed and Mecca and many subsequent prayer-mats. In 1947 the seventeen-year-old Brown came to the mountain long revered of his elders, and climbed it in unfaltering style, a rope attached to make the feat respectable. Since that time the climb has come to stand in much the same relationship to gritstone climbing as Cenotaph Corner to climbing in Wales; it is not so much a test of technique as one of approach, an initiation into the attitude of the harder climbs.

Relatively short, 50 feet more or less, it takes an overhanging flake crack running up the face of an otherwise remarkably smooth buttress. Round to the left it has a sister, who leads you on gently but clams up at just the wrong moment. She gave in a little earlier but isn't really as good, doesn't allow of the same freedom of movement and hasn't quite got the character of her right-hand twin. Possibly she requires a little more technique, but then climbing on grit is a physical thing.

There is a common start, a short crack which most people fall off before they realize they're not going to run up it. A step right and she stretches out above you. The first straight section of the crack is easily climbed, before the way is sealed by the base of a jutting flake. Above lie step upon step of overhanging flake, thirty feet and the crux at the top. There's a decision to be made, and not lightly because that's a long way to go on ever-weakening arms and what little courage is given to man; if you want it, you have to fight for it. Hunching your body fearfully beneath the flake, reaching high and out one-handed, suddenly you go, swinging right up on to the flake on huge layback holds, hooked hands, the crack sometimes closing, occasioning little shuffles rightwards, awkward hand-changes, anxious moments, racing up the flake to where the top layer juts disturbingly, and all the time on your arms, moving fast. If you do the climb at all, you do it quickly.

Mandy Glanville on Right Unconquerable

The top is rounded and frightening; you haul yourself over on flat hands in exultation. A race against failing strength and breath, fighting all the way, serious, yet an absolute joy in movement. The gritstone essence, living it fully over a few feet of rock. Let them be never so short, for me there are no better climbs in the world.

In the early eighties I went through one of those periodic bursts of enthusiasm for the sport which affect, from time to time, most people who have made climbing their way of life. But at times, when I relaxed from the training and rigour which the new-style sport demands, a sense broke back in upon me of those aspects of the activity which its latest developments seem to have left behind.

Whatever Happened to the Wet Days?
High 1982

SOMETIMES WHEN I sit watching the rain fall beyond a cafe window, or when I walk from a heated, steamy changing room along a slightly less warm corridor, and into a sports hall where all the sweat and clamour and intense rehearsal of movement of a climbing wall is taking place, a strange sense hits me of those cliffs out there in the wet and the dark, and the adventures that used to take place on them. Do people ever climb in the rain these days, I wonder? Or has the emphasis gone so far over towards merely engrossing technicalities that there is no longer any place in the designings of modern climbers for the odd dose of elemental struggle? Has the adventure gone from the sport, and does only the precise complexity of grade and number remain? I suppose the demise of the old adjectival system and its replacement by E grades and technical grades re-emphasizes the point—number holding sway over the flux, definition over flexibility, stepladder gradation over contingency and experience?

If I look back over my really memorable mountain days of the last twenty years, it surprises me how many of them have taken place on wet days, wet rock, and in filthy weather. They stick vividly in the memory—many of them on the classic Welsh routes: Main Wall, Fallen Block Crack, Pedestal Crack, East Gully Grooves, Bow Shaped Slab, Llech Ddu's Central Route, Mur y Niwl, were all routes I first did on dripping days when you'ld plod and squelch up to the foot of the cliff and the mist would wreathe and swirl, give you searing glimpses up into weird planes, cut-off and distorted verticals, the features amplified, thrown disturbingly out of context, the routes soaring or strangely disjointed, the sense of adventure thrilling in upon you as you approached their foot.

"A race against failing strength and breath" (photo: Ken Wilson)

Then there would be the ritual of garbing yourself for the ordeal —tightening up boots so that water squeezed out of lace and leather, selecting a just sufficiency of favourite slings, getting tied on and pulling your anorak through the rope a bit so that you could still stretch your arms to the full, and finally settling your rucksack comfortably on your back before you began to plot your way up the streaming rock. And straight away, as your fingers probed the ooze, cold, muddy water would begin its inexorable trickle down each extended arm, your shirt blotting up the first advances, gradually sogging down into a reservoir for the further waves which seeped on past your elbow, flowed shockingly cold into your armpit, spread down sides and back, soaking all in their path, until they met their final barrier in your bootsoles, whence they rose a little before escaping back to their temporarily halted progress down Mother Rock and scree, on by river and lake, and so to the wide sea.

Each move you made would be heavy, slow, deliberate—instead of friction, dynamism, balance, there would be a tortoise-like extension of neck and limb, but without any of that animal's quick retraction —just a ponderous, effortful placing of foot or hand out at awkward, grasping angles, allied to grunting shuffles, thrustings of the trunk, or a wedging of buttock, shoulder, or knee against this or that intruded, greasy facet, with the sole intent of placing as much reliance as possible in the frictional qualities of wet cloth rather than the flexed, athletic palm, hooked exiguity of a finger-end, or dry rand. Wonderful, inelegant stuff, prune-like fingers as often as not twining round a desperately-threaded sling as you gasped with cold and slumped with relief into whatever resting position presented itself in the vertical streambed of the moment. Then there was the shivering on stances as your second climbed, frozen from his soaking vigil against your laboured ascent, probably browbeaten into the situation in the first place, and now to be subtly dissuaded from any desire to take over the lead as you squatted in the least poured-over, most congenial of clammy cramped stances available, and fidgeted to get on with the route.

Afterwards there would be the warming race back down to pub or cafe, and all the joyful bullshit you could hurl at those who had been faced out by the weather as you sat there, vaporous, aching and content, over your pie and chips.

Of course, you don't just have these days on the bigger mountain crags. I've had as many memorable wet days on sea-cliffs, or on gritstone. There was the time John Greenland and I did the first ascent of Heart of Darkness on Mowing Word in a thin sea-fret turning to rain, with great waves crashing in below. You don't even have to do much climbing. I remember one bleak November day on Windgather in 1961 or 1962, when I first met my good friend of more than twenty years, bibliophile and stalwart of the Mynydd Climbing Club, Tony

Vember—the Drainpipe Crack
(photo: Dick Swinden)

Shaw. At the time we were both schoolboys of thirteen or fourteen, perhaps a couple of weeks in age between us, and a similar background of climbing experience. We did one route that day—the easy corner to the right of the cave on Overhang Buttress. The rest of the day we just sat and talked as the sheaves of rain winnowed against the crag, boasted of what we'd done or wanted to do, made tea on Tony's petrol stove with water collected from a drip off the roof—two kids in a wild place, huddled together, sharing a bicycle cape, backs to the wind and rain and their lives in front of them. I don't just mention this gratuitously. Friendships seem to me to be one of the things of inestimable value in this life—although nowadays if you say as much you're likely to be met with sneers or sexual innuendo—and I wonder if the very long-lasting friendship between Tony and myself would have been forged quite so firmly had we met as a couple of young rock-jocks competing on some sunnily anonymous 6a? The venue, the leisureliness of talk, the fact that simply to have been there and at that time denoted a real love of wild country in any weather, all to me now give a perspective to a friendship which is important to me, and which I and the friendship would be the poorer without. Could the same companionship arise in a sports hall?

Similarly with other adventures. Because these days of elemental hardship have so much stronger a shared component than the isolated endeavour of extreme rock, the comradeship is put more to the test. Sometimes it breaks. I can remember doing Black Cleft on Cloggy with an erstwhile friend of mine. Under ordinarily wet conditions Black Cleft is one of the great rock-climbs. If it ever dried out, it would probably be the most popular HVS in Britain—it's the best line in Wales bar none, the surroundings are superb, and the climbing is perfect jamming throughout, the crack conveniently widening as your hands bloat with wetness and suppurant slime. But it has a spring running down it virtually from top to bottom, so if you want to do it you have to be prepared for a thorough dousing, probably better taken in high summer than raw December.

When Rick and I did it on a wet day in 1968, I knew nothing about it except that Joe Brown had given me a tombstone smile when I asked him, and flatly stated that it was "the best route in Wales". So Rick and I set off, rather stupidly did the avoidable bottom bit, and spent the day swimming, gasping and slithering, socks over P.A.'s rapidly worn through, up this tremendous vertical watercourse. The crack was filled with a very luxuriant salad growth, most of which parted company easily enough with its nursery crevice to seek refuge on Rick's bowed head. He wasn't pleased, told me so, asked me to desist. I tried, but there he was in the line of fire and I wasn't so very controlled as to be able to aim away from him much of the time. Eventually, sodden, stinking and begrimed, we emerged from the top and Rick's not spoken to me since. I'm not sure that he didn't even give up climbing

Opposite: Charlie Fowler launches out on the Great Wall of Craig y Forwyn

completely after this event. But then, he was a gymnast, you see—a proper one, french chalk, jock straps, and all that. So maybe he was just ahead of his time, or maybe, in remembering all this, I've outlived mine. Who knows? Meanwhile, beyond the cafe windows, the rain still falls . . .

The surprise of the perfect jewel in the unexpected setting has always been for me one of the sport's greatest gifts. There are few more perfect—or more surprising—than the Great Wall of Craig y Forwyn.

The Great Wall of Craig y Forwyn
Unpublished 1981 (for Extreme Rock)

THE NAME IS almost an impertinence, or at best a loose tag, yet the route cannot fail to impress. Small is beautiful, perhaps? Does it matter that it cannot muster 100 feet of height, when its perfection is so blatant? It does not feel like a small climb. And, as so frequently in this odd sport, the joy of its climbing transcends the mundane or miserable in its setting. All this is to dwell on the abstract, which this piece of rock curiously inspires. Let me tell you more about it.

The approach, for a start: you drive up narrow leafy roads from the endlessly caravanned and dreary coast of north-east Wales, to find yourself in a pleasantly nondescript valley amongst low hills, with a suggestion of rock above the crowding trees. Good! You have found it, so now you kick up through thick trees and bushes on loose stony paths to emerge under a small, amiable limestone outcrop—nothing special. But walk along to the right, stooping under bushes, clawing through tunnels of thorns, stumbling beneath buttresses of gradually increasing height, and suddenly an angled wall sheers back into the hillside, high, steep and white. Forced in close against its foot by the encroaching foliage you crick your neck and gasp at its purity.

Nowadays it is laced with lines, almost every hold catalogued and recorded. The original route, our route, the Great Wall, was first climbed as an artificial pitch. There were a few attempts to climb it free in the early seventies, Littlejohn and myself on one occasion reaching the niche, but it was left to Livesey and Fawcett to make the clean ascent in 1976.

So—90 feet of rough, sound limestone, streaked black with lichen here and there, streamered in quiet corners with red, mauve and blue flowers of cranesbill, stonecrop or harebell, impendent, impeccable, immaculate.

They tell me it is E3 and 5c; perhaps my understanding of those terms is imperfect, but as a sight-lead it feels more than that. For one thing, the route-finding is not obvious, and for another the climbing is

strenuous all the way, resting is difficult, and the protection, since Livesey removed the pegs, is difficult to arrange.

Clean the mud from your soles, though, and step on to this pure rock. It is rough to the touch. The first moves lead off to the left and inspire confidence. Soon you are 20 feet up and a traverse line leads back right, so you swing across it and must then bring dynamism and friction into play as you launch out on cranked fingers into a scoop leading towards two long, stepped pockets. The pattern emerges. You search around at full stretch for some sufficient hold, then arch your back and strain upwards, feet angling in to gain friction from the glorious rough rock, till you can time or grab the next hold. (The grabs become more frequent the higher you get.) At the upper pocket, your feet on something indefinite, an old thread at throat level and a jam which can't quite pass for good to hold you in, you have to work out how to cant over leftwards across an incipient pillar to reach a flat hold which again you have to be in the right position to use correctly. It feels hard, is committing, by this time you're tired, and the protection so far is sparse. Eventually the right combination happens rather than is found; you pull hastily, land on big incut holds hidden above, and can almost rest, take a hand comfortably off the rock, fix a runner.

What's left is by no means anti-climactic. Above you is an incomprehensible flake, but since it doesn't move when you jab a toe behind it, you throw a nut in also, and eventually heave and stand on it to be greeted, panting, by a bolt.

I found the moves past this the hardest on the climb, motioned to my second to watch the rope, wished that he would not watch so closely how I climbed, so that I might cheat, pull on the bolt, but knew the misery of doing so, and so clawed past it gasping to the top and the thorny shrubs and flat, pavemented rock.

It is a leader's pitch, a perfect, arduous little journey through the intricate and the exigent, beyond exhaustion, to a sort of triumph as you take in the ropes and call on him to follow. There are routes which are better in situation, in context, but few where the climbing is somehow so complete.

Of all literary texts, the one which has afforded me perhaps the profoundest relief has been Whitman's "Song of Myself":

> *Do I contradict myself?*
> *Very well then I contradict myself . . .*

In part four there is an essay entitled "A Valediction", which my good friend Pat Ament labelled a "psychological retreat". Eventually I had to recant, and this is the result. The title is from Rilke's Duino Elegies, *and means "for staying is nowhere".*

"Denn bleiben ist nirgends"
Climbers' Club Journal 1976

THEY SAY THE male menopause occurs in about one's thirtieth year; and thus I feel worried, for here I am, entering my thirtieth year in a hot flush of new-found enthusiasm for climbing. I seem to have spent years in a fruitless attempt to give it up—for as long as I've been climbing almost I've been trying to give it up—yet here I am at the supposed changing point of a man's life, and the old symptoms back with me more strongly than ever. I sit by my fire in the evenings and visions of pieces of rock float past my mind; or I'll leaf idly through old copies of *Wilson's Wonderful World*, and a picture, even just a name, will cause my palms to sweat, my fingers to flex and unflex at the touch of each tiny imagined flake.

Yet, believe me, I've tried very hard to give it up. Oh yes, so very, very hard. And this stern moral overseer, whom I call my malefactor, implanted in me during a Catholic childhood whispers to me continually, "you must choose not to climb, it is mere hedonism, wilful, the self-destructive portion of man, the sin of Lucifer, Godless, and too much on a Sunday." And if it's not him it's soft-spoken Belial whispering, counselling, tempting with visions of Sunday mornings spent in slothful ease, toast and marmalade, the Sunday papers, a warm bed and a voluptuous woman, and believe me, that is a style of life which I would not affect to despise.

But still I want to climb these rocks.

Now as my best friends will tell you, I have little consistency, and for this reason I try to give my slightest inference the weight of a moral pronouncement—as with a certain heaviness one learns to spell, so it is on one's Odyssey. I think almost that I do not trust consistency; we look for life's essence in its fix or flow, and I would rather, in my own self, live in the flow. I love movement, especially movement on rock; not only my own, though this especially, but also that of others. Have you noticed to what degree you can tell a man's character from the way he moves on rock? Study it, and there it is in essence. Boysen for example: a languorous aesthete possessed of the most devastating polish of phrase—a sort of climbing Oscar Wilde, beauty for its own sake in his every move, and effortless as glass. Or Crew, so quick to grasp the essentials of a situation, yet with such a tenuous hold on them, such an infinite capacity for falling off. And then there's Wilson, muscle-bound and galumphing, the rock shuddering to his touch and a Rock-Ola jukebox on every stance. You could make a speculative science of it, like palmistry but more liberal. But this is to digress: I wanted to tell you how it came about that I couldn't give climbing up.

You see there are bad Catholics, like Joe Brown, Paul Nunn, and myself, and ours is the climb up to Hell; and there are good Catholics like Achille Ratti—theirs the kingdom of Heaven. So much is self-

Opposite: Andy Pollitt traversing the Great Wall (photo: Andy Pollitt collection)

Brant, Clogwyn y Grochan, Ann Hardwick leading (photo: John Beatty)

obvious; our solemn devils say to us "you must suffer" and therefore suffer we must, and devilish hard we find it. Joe Brown explained to me once that the routes you did were directly proportional to the size of your rat, the bigger the rat, the harder the route. I said to him "in my church there were no rats, only an Irish priest." I must tell you here that both he and I come from the poor areas of Manchester, he from Ancoats and I from Hulme; it's a moot point between us which area was the worse, but either way both were bad. Paul Nunn comes from Macclesfield, and Cheshire rats are relatively tame; to eat cheese makes one melancholy is a likely explanation. But to come back to rats, he began to explain:

"The rat is in your belly and it gnaws you into doing the routes."

"Is it like a wife?" I asked him, but he replied:

"No, because you're the rat who fills her belly and then she nags you not to do the routes."

I knew what he meant, but it wouldn't do for me; you see Brown's always been rather bellicose, and I've always had this secret desire for the soft and sensual life, peppered by the cerebral. Now this is where we tread the path to Heaven, strait is the gate and all that. One of my new climbs in Pembroke I called The Strait Gate, and a very good climb it is too, but of course they began to call it the Straight Gate, which made me irate, so that I had no reply but a string of witless puns. The Strait Gate? Oh yes; well one day it occurred to this implanted adviser, this malefactor of mine, that climbing was something I actually enjoyed. As soon as he knew this he took pains to conceal it from me, and would have it that I was a scared and jaded non-combatant, which like all unfair criticism contained the germ of truth. So he would have me give it up, and he deprived me of that sensuous touch of rock, that gross bodily awareness, that awful surrender to movement.

I had to creep back undercover.

On a winter's day I took myself down to Cader Idris and found myself, by chance as it were, beneath the Cyfrwy Arete. Oh shades of Arnold Lunn, the Pearly Gates on ski—package tours to Heaven; there's no getting away from the malefactor. If you're cursed with a memory like mine it will open up to you its files and memoranda at the most awkward possible moments. "You and the rock both in body are unsound" it told me, and proceeded to recount to me in loving detail the fall of that good Catholic, until finally it tailed off into incoherent ramblings about states of grace.

And I, I wanted the heights and the naked edges and the steep plunge of rib and groove, the splintered rock, wind-whistled and myself upon it. So up I went on that shattered hillside in company with a certain fear. It was so beautiful, I was lost. There were pinnacles and great drops; there were moves to be made and lakes far below, mauve horizons and I was unutterably alone; and the mountain did not shake me off, for I am not hubristic. It led me on like the eyes of a woman moving to her recline, and I could not but follow to the green slopes and grey-bouldered crown where I ate my sandwiches and drank my coffee, for I had come well-prepared, and watched ravens in the cold air above me. And do you know, those dark birds delighted in their flight! How they revelled on the wind, upturned and playing, and I thought, it is not a rat has brought me here but a joy, and I shall no longer listen to you, malefactor.

And so I began to climb again, though my muscles ached and it was hard. I called it an epiphany and I was very happy, though climbs which had once seemed easy now seemed hard. There is nothing hard about these new extremes, I told myself, doubtful at the moment of speech, and committed myself to one. I had not remembered that holds could be so exiguous, nor that overhangs could loom so; I struggled, and muscles twanged across the frets of my bones in the music of pain. But I did not mind, for afterwards I was alive and surely practice will make it easy once more. Where strength has been strength shall be again. Very good. What man has done, men will try to do; we live up to examples, their peaks fire our imagination, and the upward trek goes on . . .

In the mid-to-late seventies I went through a period of what I suppose in retrospect must have been mental breakdown: instability, broken relationships, isolation and paranoia. I did a lot of soloing at this time—not a recommended practice for someone who is not wholly in control—and used drugs, particularly cocaine and amphetamines, to boost my climbing standard. The crisis point was reached in an impressive situation.

The Latin quotations, which seem to have got many people's backs up, were inserted for another reason as well as the central and valid one mentioned in the concluding note (this latter was insisted upon as a condition of publication by a busybodying friend of the CCJ editor of that time). Their presence is also an elaborate joke which works (or in many cases obviously does not work) at two levels. In one way they are a challenge to an older generation who dismiss the sex-and-drugs-and-hard-rock style of life as one bereft of culture. In another they act as a moral commentary on the text, which latter is reinforced by the fact that they were also chosen by Dr Johnson to preface some of his "Rambler" essays, and the footnote translations are his. (I suppose too obscure a joke can't anyway be spoilt by explanation?)

Brian Wyvill and Sam Whimster on The Strait Gate (photo: Ken Wilson)

The Cyfrwy Arete

Street Illegal
Climbers' Club Journal 1978

YOU WOULD SAY I was not well. My life was in pieces and I was too shocked to recognize the case. But this is a broader perspective, and bye the bye. I had been on Romney Marsh for a few days, trying (and failing) to get into the bed of a girl with large, sensual hands and a calm manner. We had smoked a lot of dope, touched once or twice without vibrancy, walked in greening fields, and little else.

Posthabui tamen illorum mea seria ludo.*

It was a willed thing. Very early on a March morning I left, drove fast along the South Coast, stopped briefly in Salisbury for tea near the Cathedral, and dreadful cheesecake, then drove on to Cheddar.

I parked at the upper end of the layby beneath Coronation Street. This I thought a wise precaution. In from the base of my ribs there was a certain thrilling tightness. As if the day for it had come. You have a thing suggested to you, perhaps even years before, and you know with a sense of terror that one day you have to put yourself on those rails. In my case it had been seven, maybe eight, years ago, when I had first done the route with Frank Cannings. On top, he had said that it would be the great route to solo, and at the time he could have done it. I had just laughed, but really shuddered, really had been brought up sharp inwardly by the thought.

This day there was the momentum: I was down there inside somewhere quietly weeping, and all the while there was something inexorable going on. Firstly I put on my EB's, and fiddled with the laces several times to get the right balance between rigidity and comfort. Then I took two double tape slings and one shorter one, put them round my neck, checked my chalk bag, put it over my shoulder, made sure the tapes were not tangled.

* "For trifling sports I quitted grave affairs." [Virgil, Eclog. VII 17]

All this had been rather deliberately and slowly done, as if to wear down a bit of the momentum. I now sat in the car, took out the blanking plate where the radio would have been, reached in and brought out a tobacco tin. I cut myself two lines of coke on the lid—not too generous on this, I thought, take it easy—then snuffed them up, one for each nostril. Also I unwrapped a piece of silver foil from a cigarette packet, which should have had some speed inside; but it had got damp and soaked into the paper, so I ate the paper.

I now sat back, shut my eyes, and breathed in and out deeply to get relaxed. As I said, there was this part of me subdued and very frightened, and there was a sort of manic overdub on the basic rhythm of everything. I was really zapping along now and actually couldn't have given a fuck about anything; I was laughing. So I set off and steamrollered it, pretty quietly up through the ivied bits, but then very powerful and determined, out over the two bulges of the first hard pitch. On the bolt ledge I steadied my breathing, no more, just deeply in and out as I stood facing inwards, then up the crack and out, round the Shield. It was easier than I'd ever remembered it. Across the Shield I was so relieved I thought "Good, take a blow", clipped in two slings, knotted, adjusted them, and sat there. It was not a wise thing to do. Up to this point I'd been motoring, really moving fast and well. And now I broke the rhythm of the thing, sat down, and the subdued me broke back with a terrorized sense of the place I was in. I wept, I mean this literally. Once in the slings, with the car park 300 feet below, I was so scared that I wept.

Leniter ex merito quicquid patiare ferendum est.*

It was something of a grey March afternoon with a suggestion of dampness about it and a little seepage from the crack in the bulge above. I was sitting there blubbering like a two-year-old, wanting my coke, my dog, horizontal earth under my feet, in just about reverse order.

The need was, to get a perspective on something. The hysterics didn't last long, but once they had gone I couldn't get back to being fast and loose. I was holding myself very tight, very hard, using a lot of control. I tried to focus out but there was nothing vital to focus on. The greyness—rock, sky, road—was everywhere. Even the grass had a wintergrey sheen. Not so much as a woodlouse faltering out of its crevice. This frightened me a bit because if I just relaxed, I could relate to it, resign myself to it, and not give a fuck. I was letting myself down gently into being the objective correlative of a dead and inert world. Some part of me rose on an inner scream, which modulated into a vicious controlling anger. Out of my slings and working myself on to the rock again, it was all wrong. I was absolutely tight. My moves were bad—jerky, hurried and imprecise. It was like watching a poor climber who might just make it. I saw a climber once on Right Unconquerable

* "Let pain deserv'd without complaint be borne." [Ovid, Her. V 7]

and it was the same sort of thing. His runners were coming out, he was right out at the edge of control, you were aching for him to make it, but the thing was so fine, so nearly not. Curiously, pathologically interesting, yet distasteful, as I would imagine a dung-beetle to be.

The groove and sidestep bulge were prolonged as something out of a nightmare. At the bulge my fingers felt to be slipping in the crack. I took the crack above very slowly, lumberingly, feeling almost safe. The last wall was damp and protracted. I was beginning to expect to make it, and holding back. At the top I crawled and bit grass, laughing.

Ridetque sui ludibria trunci.*

After a little while I got up and made my way down to the road. I now felt desolated by it all. There was nothing cathartic in it. I felt worse than before. It seems odd to me that you, as readers, will evaluate it, say this or that about it, as though it mattered, which it did not. Just something, some sequence of psychic events combining with opportunity, produced it. Nothing changes by it. I doubt if I could ever do it again. Except that there are days when the rhythm builds up, the whole crazy edifice shifts, you cut loose, don't give a fuck, and you're away.

Dulce est disipere in loco.†

NOTE: Even before publication the above article has been very heavily criticized, and the criticism may well be justified. Three points seem to me salient: the drug references, the use of foul language, and the apparent intellectual snobbery of the Latin quotations.

On the first of these, my use of drugs, I can plead circumstantially that the time about which I write, immediately consequent upon my divorce, was one of emotional crisis. Some people find their outlets in drink or travel, work or suicide. My way out was, for a time, to become a habitual user of certain drugs. I have neither continued to do so, nor do I now excuse it; it merely was so.

With regard to the "foul" language—not my phrase—the writer has a choice—to present a version of, or to represent, the peculiar idiom and rhythm of his own thoughts. I apologize to those to whom my representation gives offence.

Lastly, the Latin quotations are not there to impress—I do not consider myself an erudite person and I do not wish to be considered as such. To me, these lines of Latin poetry have a currency; they comment, ironically, intuitively, humorously, upon situations in life of which their authors might not have dreamed. And by doing so, they re-affirm the ultimate community of Man. Contextualization, not snobbery, is their purpose.

* "And soaring mocks the broken frame below." [Lucan, IX, 14]
† "Wisdom at proper times is well forgot." [Horace, Od. IV, xii 28]

Most climbers of my generation seem to go through cycles of enthusiasm and decline, and have been fortunate in that advances in equipment and habituation have meant that on each new cycle they can attempt harder routes even than in their physical prime. I like to chart these comebacks, and enjoy the youthful company which they bring.

Taxation no Tyranny
Climbers' Club Journal 1980

I AM NOT a good psychologist and do not know by what springs fear works in us. Yesterday, for example, on a steep little piece of rock in Llanberis, there it was . . . I'll tell you how it came about. Martin, who is young and headstrong, and I had gone out on a warm Sunday to try a new route. It was on Castell Cidwm, and to be quite frank we got nowhere on it. It seemed to us scarcely feasible, for there was not a hold we would have defined as such in view. Also, the day was one of those when you get up late and the car breaks down and your EBs, still wet from yesterday's sweat, slip on as easily as an elephant down a mousehole. It was a day of the aching muscle and the wrong decision, the ill omen and the throbbing toe. I was even frightened walking along the grass terrace at the foot of Cidwm to our projected route. Fear elicits from me the intensest desire to get my backside on the ground. I have sidled thus quite happily across the steepest grass in Wales, when on my feet there would have been only a good whirling, toppling dose of vertigo. Some day some kindly and inspired equipment manufacturer will invent the pantseat crampon, and usher in the era of first backward ascents. But this is the merest rubbish. We ran away from Cidwm.

He said, "What shall we do now?" with the day half gone.

"Where's near, and what have we not done?" said I.

At a certain stage in a climber's life he enters the phase where everything which he has not done, he has not done for a very good reason. Either that only the most intense effort of fitness will carry him through, or evil reputation adheres, or at best, the route has never caught his eye. I cannot tell you which of these reasons covers yesterday's choice. But he, this youth, Martin, had decided to do Spectrum and I had to tag along. "No hardship," you may say, "not hard at all." And it may be so, but last year I watched someone fail upon it, and therein lies the point. By subtle illogic I had convinced myself of its unattainability. In my imagination it had become a feat, something in the order of tumbling into bed with Charlotte Rampling, Shirley Williams and Marjorie Allen all at the same time. Which would economize on your vocal cords, but could leave your performance in some doubt.

*Above: Hardd, Carreg Hyll Drem
(photo: Malcolm Griffith)*

*Opposite: Left Wall, Dinas
Cromlech. The author with Barry
Ingle (photo: Malcolm Griffith)*

Where was my theme? Oh yes; the point is, I had seen someone fail at a particular point on this route, and was convinced therefore that it was beyond me. So strange an emotion is apprehension. We arrived at its foot and Martin, too eagerly for my taste, volunteered to lead the first pitch. In an anxiety situation, you make the evidence fit. Instead of realizing that the pushy young bastard was actually grabbing the supposed hard pitch, leaving the easier top pitch for his grandad, I thought the opposite. When he fell off his pitch, twice, with all the aplomb of youth, I suggested he should come down and let me do it, for I could see what he had not seen and treacherously, competitively, miserly, was not prepared to tell him so. But he would not, and was spurred on, and said, "Watch the rope whilst I jump", which he did. And when I came up I used my secret hold and could reach what he could not reach, so that it fell easily to hand. A tactical point you might think, but not so, for it confirmed my view. I gathered his gear and quaked, and set off up a thin crack. "Oh," I said to myself. "You have climbed so little these last few years. You are fat and lack finesse." So this thin crack, where all should be ease and pleasure, was fretful tribulation to me. I put in a runner, and then another, and stood up a little, and explored it tentatively, became rather engrossed, stretched inquiringly after a hold and when it slid beneath my fingers pulled on it, though it was less than it appeared, and slubbered a foot over a piece of slimy blankness till it stuck in a groove, and the net result of all these manoeuvrings was that I was caught with my runners twenty feet below, an overhang at eye level, and little choice but to carry on —which I did, and then I was 30 feet from a runner, and frightened, and not relaxed. So there followed a period of squirmings and contortions and the dropping of karabiners and fumbling with ropes and similar ineptitudes at the end of which a point of security emerged, and a smile re-emerged, and fear went to hide itself again for a while.

I moved up to a ledge. Ledges are hard to leave. I recognized this one. The poor man I had watched last year struggled to leave it for an hour or more before he came down. Chalk marks went off right into the gully. Again, I totted up the evidence. Looking round the corner the sun shone in my eye and I could see nothing. So I groped, and could feel nothing, and I dabbed with my feet and they would stay on nothing. "Where does it go?" I wondered. "Can it really go out there where it is so blank and steep?" Such rhetoric is good: it makes you put on more runners. I leered down at Martin and told him how frightened I was, hoping that beneath the assumed quaver in my voice he wouldn't detect the shrill, dry undertone of fear. He merely told me that I was a cowardly old fart, which I knew anyway. Now a little more groping revealed a large, sharp hold, and the next thing I knew I was up it. Then the rope jammed, so quite blasé by now I put a tape on a flat spike and climbed back down to free it. Nothing so easy as a known quantity. Which is all to labour a point about the duplicity of fear.

I shall tell you another story or two. At Easter I was in Pembroke. It was the time when Ken Wilson found the perfect venue for his new-found fascination with war-games, but as usual nobody would play with him. It was also the time when a far-back Sandhurst-type complained to Dave Cook that the place was full of people-who-didn't-know-how-to-do-as-they-were-damned-well-told, and to me that these bally-climbers who came on the bally-tank-ranges were bally-irresponsible and might bally-well-damage the archaeological remains, which I suppose has something to do with blowing up one's credibility. To come to the point, Littlejohn collared me, probably mistaking me for Friar Tuck, and carried me off to do a route with him. Or rather, to hold his rope, which I did with utmost unctuous competence, and when he put a runner above his head I thought to store up riches in heaven, or rather a tight rope in the near future, by holding the rope subtly but distinctly tight. But instead he shouted at me and told me not to cheat, and I quaked with fear. When he had been on it an hour or more he arrived at the top, and this not without some difficulty, and then he was all smiles and told me, great ironist, that it should be called The Pleasure Dome. No one seemed to be crossing the water from the direction of Porlock, so I climbed it, in a state of near-panic. Some people I have known climbed like this all the time. It fills you with good resolutions about getting fit and climbing more and the like, all of which hurt. The best one-liner I've ever heard in this area was from Warren Harding, who told me, without leaving his preference in any doubt, that he had either "gotta climb a whole lot more, or just a little bit less."

When I had climbed just a little bit more, I wound up the machine called pioneering instinct, and focussed it on a slippery little crack sidling through the first belt of overhangs on Mewsford Point, which I think Pat must have wanted to do, because he half-suggested that it had already been done, which made me suspicious. So I had a weekend in Derbyshire, where strong arms grow and, since it was still vacation-time, co-opted Jim Curran and drove down to Pembroke on the Monday. We called in at Pat's on the way, to check on the truth of this route rumoured to be in the vicinity. And actually enough it turned out to be nowhere in the vicinity, and Jim and I were all glee, and Pat said we were bastards because he had to go up to the Lakes to do some guiding, and anyway this route would be too hard for me. Next day we slept late, abseiled in, and looked at it.

Mewsford is a big, complex, and quite wonderful cliff. At the top is a band of shaly degeneracy, and at its base is a narrow channel between the cliff and a tilted slab of rock, which clears at low tide, but through which the water races furiously from half-tide onwards. My little crack was just what it seemed to be: an easy entry to what lay above, overhanging, but on big firm holds. Forty feet up I took a belay and brought up Jim. As I watched him tie on, the zeal of the convert rose in

me. All the slapdash habits of ropework which had sufficed for years were now repugnant to me. But I kept silent and tried covertly to adjust a few things, then set to work on my pitch. There were sundry traversings left and right and soon the one way, and the one way only, became apparent, and it was hard. "How long", I wondered, "since I did a 5c pitch on this end of the rope?" No answer from the mists of time. I vented my terror on Jim. I lectured and wheedled and nagged; I gave him my Sticht plate and fiddled with his belay and he, most long-suffering of men, grew distinctly irritable and told me how long he'd been climbing and so on. The more he protested, the more finicky I became, and the sun beat down upon us. When I'd got everything to my liking, it was not to his, and he complained, and I complained, and the sun baked as the sea crept in. The route was not getting done and Jim was saying Hail Marys, so finally I tried this smooth little groove, and came down, and tried again and wobbled up for a few feet, got frightened, fixed a runner, moved on, got elated, climbed fast over a bulge with big holds, found myself miles from a runner with no prospect of another, climbed on to where I could fix four or five, worried about how much rope was left, and ground to a halt beneath the collapsible top. There were wafer-like flakes of some loosely-compounded aggregate. There were monstrous blocks of pure, incomprehensible detachment and poise. I pulled dragging rope through, and shuffled breathlessly past. What I threw off by now plopped into deep water. I reached the top with just enough rope to sit on the edge without a belay. And Jim leant heavily on the rope. This, I thought, is a *volte-face*. As soon as I could, I crawled over to secure myself to a military flagpost. Jim came up, and it was all apology and exultation. We waggled our toes in the sun and lost an abseil rope in the sea, but it didn't matter. A week or two later I watched a razorbill wavecutting erratically out over the wide sea which stretches to America.

On it flew, dipping and veering, finally lost to view somewhere out on the rough, cloud-dappled plain of waters. "Yes," I thought, "it is a joke, of sorts, or the work of a cosmic joker, who gives to each of us his battle, to each his clamorous victory."

The leading question which most non-participants will ask is "What's the best (hardest? highest?) climb you've ever done?" You can never really give an answer, for it depends on so many factors: company, anticipation, quality, place. For me, there needs also to be an element of exploration, of probing into the miniature, unexplored vertical landscapes of the rock-face. And there was one occasion on which all these combined to perfection.

The Gate of Horn
Mountain 1980

"There are two gates of sleep; the one is made of horn they say, and affords the outlet for genuine apparitions."

Virgil,
Aeneid VI, 893/4

THERE WAS AN inauspicious feel to this day. It began badly. All the jollities of the previous night, all its jousting and shrieking and lechery had brought down on us the exceedingly polite wrath of the Vicar, in whose field we were camping. He requested that we leave. Even Mrs Weston in the Bosherston cafe was something less than her friendly self. The Sunday papers had no report on Boycott's century in the Roses match. It was a sunny morning and we all felt ill. Dicky Swinden and I had been climbing together all week, gradually getting so mellow that by now we'd almost ceased to move. Where the momentum came from to get us to the Cauldron I don't know, but that was where we went.

Of course, we'd had great ideas. There was this line right of the groove and we'd put it together, wow them all, show them who was the pedigree team. But when we saw it in the clear light of morning all we could think was, "What the hell . . ." Dicky and Kath lay in the sun. Ben and Ken and Dave threw ropes down here and there and ploughed down them. I fretted and mooched and eventually thought, "Oh, well, I'll go down here."

The Cauldron is a huge hole in the headland, something over 150 feet deep. At the bottom the sea comes in through an archway on one side, and through a great cleft on the other. The pool at the bottom is at most 50 yards across. Today it was still as emerald and glinting with reflected sunlight. Until they started gardening, that is.

I tried to put in another belay stake for my abseil. It wouldn't go in. The others sloped towards where I wanted to go. I tied them off and tried to make myself think, "So what if they do fail?" Three bits of wood, two of them splintered broomhandle. I put a rope to the edge, tied the abseil rope to it, and threw it down the arete. By this time Ben and Ken and Dave were making the sea boil, whooping and cheering and crashing. Formation gardening. In this amphitheatre my head felt like a stricken submarine with depth charges being laid all around it.

The route lay down a groove just right of the arete of a tower on the landward face of the Cauldron. Within ten feet I knew it wasn't on; it was just too loose and too scrappy to be worth doing. I carried on down, kicking and prising off the odd block in a desultory sort of manner. My 150ft rope ended twenty or so feet above the sea and I'd forgotten to tie a knot in it, so after 100 feet I stopped and muttered across to Ben, 30 feet away on the far wall, that I wasn't going to bother, shit route, not worth doing, going back up, and got my prusikers on the rope. On impulse I looked round the corner into the cleft. I hadn't remotely considered the possibility of a route up this wall, which overhung at a constant five or ten degrees beyond the vertical for over 170 feet straight out of the sea:

"Jesus Christ!"

I was dumbstruck and juddered my way back up the rope as fast as I could to the top. I rearranged the belay, threw the rope down, and set off. Within a few feet I was hanging right out from the rock in the middle of the cleft gazing at a perfect, sound, straight crack. Not even a crack really; a plumb line of weakness with pockets and holds leading down to a cave and kittiwake ledge. Beneath that a crescent line of holds curved down and round to the sound lower section of the arete. I slid down and set myself swinging in the middle of the cleft until I could grab hold of the rock. Letting go, I almost hit the far wall, and this time made a total mess out of getting from the Sticht plate into the prusikers. Back to the top I went, with the rope tangled in everything. I couldn't believe it. What would it be like? How would those holds feel when you were on them? Could you get to them from round the arete? I pulled the ropes up and ran round the top to Dicky.

He was somewhere between sleeping and waking.

"Well I'll go down if you want to go down, but I feel really sick."

I said maybe we could do it tomorrow and that it was stupendous and that I just had to go for a shit, I was so frightened. And I was, so I ran off, leaving it at that, and ran and ran, and crouched behind a bank and shat. After that I felt better and ran along the track, and all the time I could imagine myself launching out across that wall, so I ran a bit more till my chest wasn't so tight and I was breathing easily and I ran over to Dicky.

"Let's go for it now."

He came along. There was no sullenness or condescension about it. We both knew how each other felt. I knew he was feeling stale, tired, and a bit delicate, and that he'd rather lie in the sun with Kath, but that he'd come along and blast in there, supremely competent, and be happy to have done it. And he knew that I was on some sort of high and gripped out of my head and on to something big. So he brought round his gear and I was obsessive about big nuts and Friends and scrounged some of his chalk and he set up the rope and went down first whilst I fretted about how cold it would be down there and should I wear shorts or Polar pants. Then I followed him down. He was belayed beneath a little groove we'd seen in the base of the arete. I'd sort of bribed him on top by saying I'd go for the middle pitch and the rest would be easier, and though I was under a compulsion to go for that pitch, I was thinking what a good climber he is, and how much easier it would all be for him. But off he went up the first pitch, a 60 ft slim crack, steep and solid. I was cold, belaying, and really worried, thinking I'd get stiff and tight and not be able to do it. But he wasn't long; he just drifted up it in

Opposite: Gate of Horn; the first ascent (photo: Dick Swinden collection)

his easy way and got belayed. I came up to join him on his pedestal:

"We must go round the arete somewhere about here."

I bridged up past him, very awkward and intimate, hoping I didn't smell too badly after a week in a tent. Above his head I got a couple of nuts in a crack, and felt around for holds on the wall. Bridging wide, I could get some, smallish but good. The wall overhung as much as the one round the corner. I peered round:

"Oh, shit! Oh, Jesus!"

"What's up?"

"It's just incredibly beautiful."

"What?"

"The colour of the water."

He shrieked with laughter.

"What's up with you?" I asked, a bit peeved.

"There you are on a 6a move and all you can think about is the colour of the water."

"It's not 6a," I said, "I just make it look that way. It's about 5b. Anyway, have a look."

He did. Through the cleft you looked out into the bay beyond through dark green walls, and out in the daylight the water was an incandescent glow of green, more emanation than substance, shockingly beautiful, visionary, an acid trip of sunlight.

Back bridging in my little corner, I was cowed and scared. The wall round there was unbelievably steep. I had another half-hearted sally out on to the arete. It was really tiring. I told Dicky to watch me and set off back. The top runner came out just as I was thinking of jumping off onto it. I was shaking:

"Oh fucking hell, Dicky."

"Cold down here," he said laconically, shivering in his vest. I had to make the moves. I put the runner back and another by it, moved back to the arete, groped across for a hold, and shuffled then swung down and round. The runner I tried to get in was the wrong size. There was a voice in my head saying, "Go for it. Go for it." Outside and over there I could hear Ben on his route talking to Dicky.

"He's powering up it. Christ! It looks fantastic. The holds must be incredible."

They were! I stopped to put in a wire, and a Friend just above it. It was all so cool and good. I was so strong and concentrated, and the ledge came almost before I wanted it.

"I think he's OK now. He's at a ledge."

"Oh Jesus, Dicky, this is so good."

I sidled into the cave. It was flat, deep, and comforting. There was a big thread. I tied on and shouted down that I was safe. The place stank of birds. I kicked off a rotting, precarious nest, and underneath insects crawled and squirmed. The nest hit the water with a dull flack. Dicky's turn now. He was a bit apprehensive:

"Watch the ropes. I've just taken the runners off and I'm moving across."

He was round on the wall, grinning and gurgling:

"Incredible . . . unbelievable . . . it makes Deep Space look pathetic . . . This Friend's really good . . . Oh, Man! It's so bold . . ."

He was up with me, clipped into the belay, and so happy. He could hardly wait to get on the top pitch. You could see it in him, he was hungry for it as he sorted out the gear and half-listened to what I'd seen about it. Then he was away:

"Oh God! God! I don't want it to stop. This is so good." He was playing with the crack, delightedly. Ken peered over the top.

"What's it like, Dicky?"

He was climbing slowly to make it last, every move in exquisitely considered slow-motion:

"5a and fantastic," he shouted to Ken. Then he was up and tied on and I followed up this soaring line out of the cleft with the wall dropping away green and shadowy beneath. At the top his eyes were shining. We were inarticulate. I believe we so far forgot ourselves as to hug each other and scream with laughter. And there it was, a supreme fiction, an experience lived through together which all the memorial words, all the splintered shards of definition we vainly tried to gather could never approach. Something quite beautiful, searing, and beyond. That evening Ken and I left to drive to Bangor. All the way he talked tawdry politics, but my head was singing:

> . . . like a black globe
> Viewed by sons of Eternity, standing
> On the shore of the infinite ocean,
> Like a human heart struggling and beating.
> The vast world of Urizen appeared.

Before I slept I was hanging there again in that great cleft, watching the sun on the water as though, waking, I had passed through the Gate of Horn.

One of the delights of the sport is just wandering about, watching what's going on, musing on characters, histories and anecdotes, perhaps doing a little bit of climbing here and there as the mood takes you. Or not, as the case may be.

The Land that Time Forgot
Crags 1980

EACH SATURDAY THEY roll into the car parks or laybys beneath the Milestone or by Ogwen Cottage. Clearly labelled as venture groups or outdoor clubs, from Hemel Hempstead or Swindon, they spill out of their new transits or old ambulances, Bedford buses or Sherpa vans, assemble behind their breeched and bearded leaders and stride or shamble off into the hills. You see them from time to time—a little trail of orange across a rocky hillside, or a gaggle around a summit cairn, as regular in their habits and regulation in their garb as any city gent. Come Sunday afternoon, they take to their buses and set off home-wards down the old A5. Ogwenites—lest we forget.

I feel unashamedly fond of the Ogwen valley. Like most other climbers of my generation, my roots in Welsh climbing were planted here. At Easter 1961, I first camped by the stream between Gwern y Gof Isaf and Helyg. In my Timpsons boots were tricouni nails which I had bought from Ellis Brigham's old shop, somewhere at the back of Ardwick Green in Manchester. I had put them in myself after cutting away bits of the commando sole, just as it told me to do in the book I had read about it. All but two of the nails fell out during the course of the week and for all I know they may still lie scattered and rusting among the rocks of Tryfan.

During our week we did all the climbs a beginner was supposed to do: the easy Milestone routes, Chasm Route on Glyder Fach, the Original Route on the Idwal Slabs. We did boring slab routes on the Gribin Facet, and the horrible Monolith Crack on the same cliff. One day we went over to Craig yr Ysfa to do the Amphitheatre Buttress and Amphitheatre Rib; another day was spent on the Gashed Crag and Pinnacle Rib of Tryfan's East Face, and yet another scrambling round the North Ridge and Bristly Ridge and down the Gribin.

We had the inevitable 100ft hemp rope and we didn't have a guidebook, but people told us what was what. I remember seeing Soap Gut and thinking that it must be Cenotaph Corner, because that was the only Welsh climb of which I had heard at the time, and Soap Gut was the only corner around. It never occurred to me that there was another valley with other cliffs. All climbing life was surely here? If you finished climbing early you could walk down to Bethesda and its cafe, with meat and potato pies of enormous size, with gravy for 9d, or 1s 3d with chips.

Once, at our campsite, we were berated, as a band of filthy, young rowdies who were camped rather too close to Climbers' Club property for their comfort, by a pompous military gentleman whom I only later came to recognize as a doyen of Boys' Clubs, Good Works, Himalayas and the Public Face. Not that we took much notice of his outrage, with half of us hiding behind a boulder, giggling, and the other half playing simpletons. We'd seen him earlier in the week having an immense amount of trouble on a Diff we'd already done, so respect was out of the question.

In Dorothy Pilley's enchanting book of reminiscences, *Climbing Days*, there is a memorable description, only a sentence long, of

*". . . the group dynamics of mixed
adolescent parties"*

meeting a party of just such incompetents as we were then, on the Milestone Buttress. "The storm of jolly burst upon us like a spring gale." To me, that has always seemed the quintessential Ogwen mood—friendly, humorous, expansive.

The valley itself is so much broader than the parallel Llanberis Pass. It spreads itself amply between shapely mountains. There are always stretches of water, wide perspectives, sculptured outlines to tempt the eye. The climbs here, the climbs we did in our first week, say, are all perambulations between broad galleries or cosy nooks, with little entertainments on the way. You can gather and gloat and laugh together, and none of it seems too serious.

Dorothy Pilley again: ". . . how perfectly hand and foot holds are apportioned to the climber's needs . . . a peculiarity of Tryfan rather than climbing as practised by modern experts." Even the look of the rock differs between Ogwen and Llanberis. I wouldn't say Ogwen rock is better to climb on—although it can be as good as any rock in Wales—but it is certainly more pleasing to the eye. There is nothing more drably depressing in the rain than the vast bulk of Dinas Mot, its dolerite sodden and dank; or Craig Ddu or Clogwyn y Grochan, with their acres of featureless hillside above. But when the rain comes to Tryfan, the rock gleams silvery and the least touch of sun makes it glow and ripple with light. The same is true of the Glyders, or the Slabs, and if the Gribin Facet looks shabby and the Kitchen cliffs positively infernal, they still serve to counterpoint the shining sweep of rock, the longest expanse in Wales, which lies between.

I drove up to Ogwen the other Saturday to compare notes with my memory. Up the track to Idwal I went, nowadays a constructed and maintained footpath and not the marshy boulder hop it used to be. I sat on a boulder as a platoon of schoolchildren marched past, to study glaciation or vegetation, sheep or the group dynamics of mixed

adolescent parties, all of them no doubt equally well tabulated, defined
and dismissed without the need for further thought or resonance, on
fact-sheets entitled "Cwm Idwal Nature Trail", "The Great Performing
Landscape Extravaganza", or some such. Meanwhile, groups of climbers clad as I have not seen climbers clad for years stumped cheerily
past on their way to the shingled green tea-shack by Ogwen Falls.

At the bottom of the Slabs I sat down and looked around. Nothing to
hold my attention at first. I was musing at the credulity of the medieval
ship's party sent by their captain from the coast to discover whence the
clouds boiled up, who fled on seeing the Devil's Kitchen, thus giving it
its name, when the Irishmen arrived. I have no idea how many of them
there were. There was no way in which number could have held sway
over the flux of this party. They proceeded to climb the Idwal Slabs on
a single rope. You will notice that I do not say that they climbed any
single route on the Idwal Slabs, because they did not. They climbed
them all, in a single rope, spreading, fluctuating, sweeping, laughing,
they moved up the whole length and breadth of the Idwal Slabs like
nothing so much as a vast fishing net with bobbing corks in between.

At some point Minerva appeared. Minerva and the Irish have
nothing to do with each other apart from their near-coincident arrival.
Minerva was a lithe blonde-haired woman of magnificent bodily
charm, a little creased at the corner of her eyes in a way that denotes ill
weather or frequent laughter, and she held herself in such a manner
that a susceptible man might have fallen in love with her there and
then. She wore floppy baseball boots, faded corduroy jeans and a
chequered Norwegian sweater. Behind her, as she trotted down from
somewhere up towards Cwm Cneifion, leggy and fawn-like came a girl
of ten or eleven, obviously her daughter. The two of them padded a
zig-zag course up, down, and across the first 50 feet of the Slabs, came
to earth with a toss of their heads and not the suggestion of a jolt, loped

". . . she held herself in such a manner that a susceptible man might have fallen in love with her there and then"

off across the short turf to the far side of the lake and were gone. I saw them later, sheltering from the rain under the trees in front of Idwal Cottage, looking like nothing so much as two deer, and half-expected them to flare their nostrils, stamp their feet and skip away at my approach. The Irish army of occupation, meanwhile, had reached somewhat over the halfway mark when it began to rain. I will not dwell on what happens when a rope of between six and 37 Irishmen scattered across a belay-less cliff at a point some 250 feet beyond its base decide to retreat! Suffice it to say that the essential geniality remained.

Perhaps it is because Ogwen has never been in the forefront of Welsh climbing that it seems so relaxing a place. It has its bad points, of course. The vigilante mob of badge-toting vultures and self-appointed guardians of public safety who pose on the wall outside Ogwen Cottage any fine weekend for the tourists' benefit, would never be tolerated in any serious climbing area, but here little heed is paid to them and their ghoulish presence is accommodated.

Never at the forefront of Welsh climbing? I wonder why that should have been? It was one of the very earliest climbing venues in Wales, the Williams brothers having climbed the North and South gullies on Tryfan's East Face in the late eighties of the last century. Throughout its history it has been visited, often regularly, by the leading climbers of the day: Archer Thomson, Steeple and Barlow, Ivor Richards, Waller, Longland, Kirkus, Edwards, Hargreaves, Cox, Preston, Harding, Brown, Boysen, Livesey, Fawcett, have all left their mark here.

I suppose the most likely explanation is that there is really not very much steep rock in Ogwen. There are small areas which, added to the general charm of the place, prove sufficient lure to the fanatical eye. There are even some very good steep miniature cliffs, so we get pockets of harder climbing on such places as Carreg Mianog, Clogwyn Du, the Terrace Wall, Drws Nodded, Gallt yr Ogof and Suicide Wall.

But there is no single steep major cliff where the lines for a certain period coincided in their difficulty with the highest standards of the day—as they did on Lliwedd before the Great War, or Cloggy from 1930 to 1955, or Gogarth from 1965 to 1975.

This is not to say that Ogwen has not from time to time produced some remarkable routes. Jack Longland's Javelin Blade (E1, 5b), climbed in 1930, certainly remained the hardest route in Wales until Chris Preston climbed the original route, Route One (E2, 5c), on Suicide Wall in 1945, which in its turn was probably the hardest route in Wales until well on into the Brown era. At the present time Chris Shorter-Herbert's Cobalt Dream (E5, 6b) on Drws Nodded is cert-ainly the biggest, and may well be the hardest roof problem in Wales.

But in general, Ogwen rock rambles rather than runs to difficulties. The North-west Face of Glyder Fawr, from the Upper Cliff to the Idwal Slabs, the cliffs of Glyder Fach, the East Face of Tryfan, these are archetypal Ogwen cliffs and they are not majestic imposing precipices—not even their most devoted admirers would ever claim them as such. But they are still something worthwhile. Each of the three cliffs I have mentioned is a big cliff, of good rock, possibly by its very nature lacking in good continuous natural features other than amorphous ridges or unpleasant gullies. It is seldom very steep. It tends to dry rapidly after rain. Above all, it is generally very clean and free from the more glutinous mud and decaying vegetable matter of other easy-angled cliffs in Snowdonia.

I don't know why this should be, but the general run of cliffs around Ogwen are very clean. There are some which are not, of course—Gallt yr Ogof or Clogwyn y Geifr are as dirty as any pioneer could wish—but most of them are quite sparkling. I am sure this is not just a matter of the traffic they now receive. Perhaps they were extremely well gar-dened to begin with, before climbers started to have qualms (and quarrels with the Nature Conservancy) about that sort of thing.

E. W. Steeple and Guy Barlow, two of the most prolific early pioneers in the Ogwen district, were reputed to have left "white gashes, where mats of turf had been cut away", wherever they went. I don't think, however, that Steeple, Barlow, or Capability Brown himself could have cleaned up these cliffs to their present extent without a considerable natural allowance at the outset. Perhaps there is a simple botanical explanation to do with soil types?

I wonder if this cleanliness forms any part of their attraction for women climbers? I don't know of any other place in the British Isles where women form so strong a part of the climbing tradition of an area. Hope, for example, best of the routes on the Idwal Slabs, was first led by a woman, Mrs Daniells, during the First World War and was originally named Minerva, "to mark the fact that it came from feminine skill and prudence". Pat Kelly, founder of the Pinnacle Club, died on Tryfan in 1922. The shade of Dorothy Pilley lies softly across

Tennis Shoe (photo: Ken Wilson)

Holly Tree Wall. Elizabeth Coxhead's immensely likeable novel, *One Green Bottle*, is set at Idwal Cottage and much of the action takes place thereabouts. Connie Williams of Idwal cottage fame and Gwen Moffatt were also true devotees.

About ten years ago I guided a 45-year-old newspaperman from Venezuela, David Nott, up Great Wall on Clogwyn Du'r Arddu. It was damp, it was his first climb for over 25 years, and he had very little difficulty with it. In the pub that night I asked him how he had become interested in hard climbing. He told me that in about 1946 or '47 he had been camping by the side of Idwal Cottage and had conceived a violent passion for the girl in the next tent. He had, naturally, propositioned her and she had replied, "Only if you take me up Lot's Groove tomorrow". His sole climbing experience was two or three Diffs and this was, with the exception of Suicide Wall, the big name climb of the day. He got up it and that night claims he was duly rewarded for his efforts. You might think this story is far-fetched, but a month or two after David had gone home I met the lady in question and passed on his regards to her. I swear her eyes went quite dewy.

"Ah, David," she sighed. "Oh yes, I remember David."

The history of this place isn't simply a macho catalogue of stirring male deeds, and it is all the more attractive and humane for not being so. Hence, perhaps, the pleasure I felt in the latter-day Minerva and daughter I spied at the foot of the Slabs.

From the feminine aspect to the misogyny of Helyg, last of the Climbers' Club bastions of male exclusivity to fall. I suppose each of Ogwen's places of hospitality has its own character. Willy's Barn, at the back of Gwern y Gof Isaf, is a wonderful enough place, as I'm sure Ogwen Cottage was under the watchful eye of Mrs Jones (not watchful enough, however, to stop Archer Thomson from purloining her coal hatchet to hack away at the ice of the Devil's Kitchen for eight or nine hours during its first ascent).

But Helyg has more clutter of redolence than either of them, or anywhere else in Wales for that matter. It was the epicentre of Welsh climbing in the inter-war years, the constant haunt of all the best climbers of the time. The place itself is spartan, at times little removed from the "wretched hovel" stigma with which George Borrow branded it, but the outlook is the sheerest luxury, out and across and down the Nant y Benglog. Its logbooks read like a pre-war hall of fame; all Kirkus's and Edwards's first ascents are here.

And, of course, there was the Helyg boulder. It is really not very much to look at. It is probably 15 feet high, composed of very smooth rock. It has a crack problem which is sweet and utterly straightforward jamming, and which had a reputation for extreme difficulty until about 1930. It also has a wall problem of Menlove Edwards's which is probably 6a. Edwards's least known and most amusing guidebook is to the Helyg boulder. It is an odd sort of guide. It consists of a diagram on

"Helyg has more clutter of redolence than . . . anywhere else in Wales"

which all the holds are numbered and an inventory by the side of all the uses to which these holds can be put, all the crazy sequences of moves that can be devised. It doesn't take much imagination to extend this logic into a computer and set programmed robots to work on places like Harrison's Rocks. I don't think it would ever work in Ogwen. The number of holds would send even the most advanced computer awry.

Earlier this week I walked up to Bochlwyd Buttress and soloed up its marvellous miniature Kirkus route, Marble Slab, originally described by its author as "a delightful climb of great delicacy and beauty of technique on perfect rock". It is one of two Ogwen climbs which I regularly include in an evening's soloing round, for a quality which you can only call charm.

The other is Edwards's Direct Finish to Wall Climb on the Milestone: "It overhangs a little and is unutterably adolescent but it quite graces Tryfan." Two routes which do not quite make 100 feet between them, yet which embrace a whole world and typify the place. To come back to Marble Slab, and this week: I did my climb, whistled to my dog to run round from the bottom and walked over to Llyn Bochlwyd, where I sat on a flat boulder by the lake for maybe half an hour, watching the mist play up and down the gullies on Glyder Fach. It then began to rain. I hurried down and, on the steep section of path above the bog which lies before the Idwal path, I came across an old man belatedly struggling into his waterproofs. I do not know how old he was, but eighty would probably have been a conservative estimate. We exchanged a few quite inconsequential words:

"Your dog likes this, at any rate."

"Oh yes, she's a water dog."

"Well there's enough of that about."

And then he laughed. I swear he laughed for no other reason than for the joy of being alive, and in a place such as this, no matter what the weather. Rain seamed down his old face and spattered across his sunken cheeks as he stood there on the path, rocking with laughter. To see him was a beatific experience. "An appetite, a feeling, and a love" still present at his age, and still invoked by that landscape.

Later, I stood by Llyn Ogwen. The rain had stopped. Gusts of wind sent little chasing opacities across its surface. I looked around at the familiar things which I have surely known for over twenty years: the mountain ash with its red berries and the alder by the stream, the great square boulders, the little alluvial promontory thrust out into the lake, may-green lichen mottling a wall and the faint intermingling smells of myrtle and sphagnum moss.

Any of these at any future time without a moment's notice could bring back with startling clarity this instant, when I looked across a windy Llyn Ogwen to see the upper rocks of Tryfan shot through with a fading gold.

They do not signify, these landscapes of the mind, with their shocking instants of awareness. They merely resonate, like the chemistry of lovers, through our solitary lives. And they fall as richly into the gatherings of the imagination here, in Ogwen, as in any place on God's earth.

The way of looking at the climb as an allegory has always attracted me, and I attempted it in this story. As far as the fiction is "about" anything, it deals with ageing and the adventitious, and its acknowledgements at the end are to Wordsworth's "Matthew" poems, the Book of Isaiah, and Menlove Edwards. The two climbers may be read as aspects of the same personality, and the story, the imagined setting for which is Mewsford Point, was suggested to me by an accident which took place on Gogarth some years ago. The one character who has any objective reality is the woman. After the story was published an incident occurred which seemed to underline its point. Coming back from Derbyshire to Wales with Dicky Swinden one weekend, we stopped on a wet, dark, Sunday night at the Cerrig y Drudion cafe. She was there, came across to our table:

"You could have done, you know. You should have said . . ."

With which she smiled, and disappeared into the night.

Fictive Heroes
Crags 1980

HE AND I were very close: make of it what you will, but of all the myriad possibilities I can say no more than that. And on this day we kept company, in an odd sort of scenario. We set out, quite early in the morning, the tide well out, slack water and a sea of no great roughness; a white crest here and there neatly counterpointed by a very few delicate riffs of white cloud.

The path we took lay along flat clifftops, across land used as a gunnery range. Shattered tanks from mock battles rusted down into the pitted earth. Twisted scraps of metal were scattered around, bright, powdery, or flaking and brown. We picked them up and thought it a great joke to toss them about, starting in mock fright at the imaginary boom.

Lest it should sound too desolate a landscape, let me say that the grass was short-cropped, dotted with bugloss and little round mushrooms, that skylarks sang and the sun shone. Also, in our minds we were happy. There was an expectancy there, and a longing too. We knew where we were going, for we had a couple of lines in mind. We had seen them, fleetingly and from a distance, had talked about them, enthused about them. We had even openly wondered about their probability, but had bolstered up each other's confidence.

He had said, "You do that crack, you're good at cracks, and I'll do the wall above."

Each to his own abilities. What he said made me strut along the track a little more confidently, and if I got up my pitch then from our first stance and those hoped-for good belays, I would concentrate on him, pay out his ropes, ready myself for the urgency with which he would tug them through to clip each of his runners, play with him an infinitely caring game of watchfulness and consideration.

So we went along, sauntering, boasting, darting about after object or perspective, and soon enough arrived on the terrace above the cliff. There were other people there, some of whom I knew. A girl I'd met a time or two in a pub. Looking at her as she lay unconcernedly in the sunlight, I felt a certain desire for her, a wish that she and I might lie together, taken out of time and responsibility for a little warm-hearted relaxation under a gentle sun.

But he was busying himself about his equipment and I changed, reluctant to put aside this imagined interlude. We passed over to the abseil point. I belayed the rope on two long tape slings, and threw it down. Then there was the process of sliding over the edge, the cautious deposition of faith and bodily weight on to the belays, the relief of letting out rope and the lessening anxiety of the descent.

At the bottom I skipped across boulders, dodged waves and sat, in a beautiful calm of minutes, on a slab beneath the cliff waiting for him to join me. There was, for a time, no urgency about it. There were other climbers over to one side on a more broken wall. There was the necessity for choice, but the tide had barely turned and would not be running over these sea-worn slabs for an hour or two yet.

So we sat and toyed with this line or that. What would they be like? What holds would there be on that little facet of slab which seemed to slip by the biggest of the overhangs? How wide was the crack in the corner by that rib, and what gear would it take? How steep was the wall? How sound was that block? You might say they were idle musings, but they were not. Into each situation, imaginatively, we could put ourselves, and our hands would sweat as though we were there. But imagination was not enough.

However happily we engaged in the creation of these fictions, their insufficiency was wormwood and gall to us. Our fictions became our rulers, compelled us to consider them in the forms of reality. What could we do, so long as we had the capacity, the energy, the active will, but resign ourselves to their realization? What could we do but acquiesce?

"Let's do the one on the left," he said.

So across we went to the foot of the crack. He uncoiled his rope, I mine. I tied them into my harness. He took them and put them in his Sticht plate, smiled, nodded.

The block above my head was rough and sharp. I pulled on to it awkwardly and squatted, untangling a clump of wires on my rack. To get it right, not to feel too heavy, not to be too accoutred, but to have the right thing for the right place; an ideal to which we seldom approximate.

The crack slanted out left around a prow before straightening up and bulging a little underneath a ledge. I stretched up for a hold, pushing up from the knee, getting my body arrow-straight to curl my left hand around its edge. When it was there a quick exhalation of breath, a little should-I-shouldn't-I spasm over what was already decided, a swing out, hanging from one arm in a squat, a slight roll of the shoulder and foot-push to get the other hand on a hold. And a panicky sort of Oh-God-I'm-in-it-now giggle as the left arm went probing up again and felt, then flexed on to a hold. From which all the automatic adjustments of the body moved around a single point—the away movement of hips and shoulders, the up-kick of the leg, the turning out of the knee to get the toe just so on a squarish little block of limestone. The instant of hanging there, viewing what was above, sizing up, coiling, and then the long timed move up and past and through, and the awkward half-secured tentativeness of a hand searching a crack for a jam. And relief when it eventually, however tenuously, slots in.

A runner, and by the ease with which the right rope comes through, you know he's with you, and you look at him, he smiles and your reply is a little snigger of complicity before you push air out of your lungs and

Megalith, Newton Head, Pembroke.
Keith Robertson climbing

immerse yourself in the rock again. It was not a hard crack, however it may have looked. I felt almost as if I had cheated. Overhanging, yes—seemingly difficult—but the holds were there, and I was fit enough. I didn't really even have any doubts, which is why it seemed like cheating, why I almost felt let down.

I had known, even down there, that whatever abilities I possessed comprehended the problems of this crack, and so it was not enough, just a glib ending where I wanted an apocalypse. He was glad, though. He wanted to get on his track and this was just a thing in the way. He was glad that I was there and tied on, and that he could leapfrog over and beyond.

He was sitting on his ledge, well belayed, looking a little furtive in his squint-eyed avoidance of the sun. It was hot. There were no shadows on this south-facing cliff. He was sweating; he had climbed the crack with a heavy competence, not the climber he'd once been, the moves at their completion were jiggling and hurried now, where once they would have been ice-smooth and casually precise.

But he'd done it and there'd never been any question but that he would. From time to time there'd been a ghostly memory of authority about his moves. And now he sat on his ledge in this curious avoidance of the sun, looking slightly diminished. The other took from him what gear he might need—put the bandolier over his shoulder and sorted out the rack, which was in a mess. The next pitch really worried him. He was edgy, uncommunicative. He found the attempted jokes irritating and the slight, high edge on the first man's voice made him nervous too. He stood at the bottom of the groove, one hand keeping balance and the other fumbling in his chalk bag. There was a small and awkward foothold at shoulder height; nothing much for the hands, a smallish layaway, a sloping fingerhold. He tried them, tried a little move on them. He could just hold on, but could he hold on enough, put in sufficient power to get his foot up there? He stepped back down to the belay ledge.

"What's it like?"

"A bit thin. I don't know what the holds are like above."

"Ah, well. You can do it."

He traversed left and spent a minute or so craning his neck about to get different angles on what he imagined was a hold over a bulge. From one angle it looked perfect, but from none of the others could he make it fit. He stepped back beneath the groove, shook out each arm in turn, then committed himself to it. It didn't even seem very hard, with all the impetus he'd built up. His feet edged perfectly on to little holds, or smeared across a particular rough area with complete precision.

It was all-in-control, well-back-from-the-edge stuff, and he stopped after 25 feet to fiddle in a couple of good wires. The bulge above came easily. There was an obviously good firm hold and he wound himself up for it, went, got it and carried right on through until he was standing on a slab—quite a large slab, stretching up for 25 or 30 feet to the next steep section.

He looked around for a runner; nothing much came to hand, but he jammed a hex in a crack as a gesture and carried on. As he moved past, it lifted out of its crack and slid down the rope. There were some clouds moving in from the west and it was colder now. Beneath the wall above the slab was a good foothold but, sloping slightly from one end to the other, it made his calf ache. Looking up, he felt a spot of rain on his cheek.

He scanned the wall anxiously. Thirty feet above, and over to the left, an easy groove with samphire growing there led to the top. On the wall between there seemed to be very little. A few small fingerholds to start, a thin crack and what might be a good hold to reach the bottom of the groove.

He looked to place a runner by his feet, and cursed for the hex that had slid down the rope. There was a slot which would surely have taken one of that size. The next size down waggled about, held in place only by fretted, thin edges of rock. He left it there as a token, and chalked up.

He dabbed chalk on the fingerholds so that he would be able to see them clearly when they were needed as footholds. Moving on to the wall, the lack of protection frightened him. He felt for the first moves, came back and tried to rest his leg on the awkward foothold.

It was definitely beginning to rain now. He let his mind run on from thoughts of a fall to a grey, nervous, uncaring state. He sized up the thin crack and sorted out the wires on his rack. The first move up was dynamic, a long reach for two fingerholds, his body flattened on the rock and pointing like a ballet dancer on his toes to get an extra inch or two of height. A ripple of tension ran down through his body. He kicked his feet out and ran them up the wall to edge with his left foot on a tiny flaky hold. Locking off on his left arm, he reached for a pocketed finger-jam at the base of the crack, laying away off it, swivelling his left knee out and rolling his hips over the foothold so he could stay there and fumble a wire off its krab. He slipped it into the crack, clipped in a krab, tugged on it gently and clipped in the rope.

Whew! He felt safe. A runner above his head. Another reach for the hold and the route would be there. He straightened up on the foothold, still not quite able to reach. His right arm was pumped solid with the strain. The runner was at eye level. All his hopes centred on this one hold. He moved his right foot awkwardly on to a little flake near his left thigh, eased his left foot off and canted his leg out to keep balance, leaning right out on the crack. Every scrap of timed awareness went lunging for the hold. His fingers snatched on to it. It was flat, but rough. Not very big. Should he go on it? There was a foothold out left if he could change hands.

(What should have happened here? He was strong; his momentum had carried him thus far. He had one move to make and had already attained the holds which, for a few moments of time, had been the focus of his aspirations. But just then, something entirely adventitious happened.)

His right foothold snapped. He grabbed for the security of the runner. It pulled; the one below likewise. His limbs cascaded down on to the fretted slab, headlong. The lancet rock carved his flesh as its bulk crushed his skull and thrust him raggedly outwards. He seemed to float in the air as he came within sight of his companion, but he was bound inexorably beyond help, limp and silent in his flight.

The tide was coming in fast. There must already have been six feet of water in the channel below and each fresh set of waves brought it a little higher. I felt worried for him up there and tried shouting, but he would not have heard me above the sound of the water. When I looked up, rain dabbed at my face.

Some of the blue rope pulled through, so I guessed he had a runner on and felt a bit easier. I was wishing we were back on the clifftop and running for the cafe. Then the ropes went slack. I heard a thud and he

Meshach, 1963. The author cheating (photo: Ken Wilson)

was in the air above me, grotesquely spreadeagled and the rope snaking down.

I tried, hopelessly, to take in the slack but he was past me and came on to the wires in the groove. The top one pulled; I was jerked upwards. There was a splash as the bottom one held. A wave sluiced gently up the slab where we'd been sitting. Everything went silent.

I didn't know what to do, hardly daring to look down. The rope was holding him on the surface of the water and there was blood coming from his head. I knew he was dead.

I sat above, shocked, morose, and strangely uncaring. The tide hung about the full, timelessly, and the rain spattered down. No one shouted or saw. As the daylight faded, the tide came to ebb. The sky cleared; points of light glinted far away on the other coast. A ship passed, out at sea. The channel grew shallow, splashier, then drained and dried. I let him down, unfastened from the rope and pulled it through his runner. I slid down, untied his corpse from the ropes and pulled it up above the high water mark.

Above us the cliff was patterned with shadow. Great areas were now impenetrable. All intimacy of detail was lost in its vast loom. I turned a corner and went away.

The abseil rope was still in place. I climbed a crack by it in the failing light. Forty feet below the top I pulled it up and tied on to it. A little groove led upwards. I climbed it, testing each hold, stiff and fearful. At the top I coiled the rope and went over to the sacks. It was all just method, memory, routine. I sat down, stretched out my legs, put my head on a sack and slept.

I woke in the darkness. Its intensity, the strangeness of familiar forms, made things seem urgent. I sat up, hearing the sea, put a sack on, the rope across my shoulders, then the other sack, and thus burdened set off. On the range, lights were coming towards me. I blinked as they shone in my face.

"Where's your mate?"

"He's dead. I left him on the slab."

"Are you sure he's dead?"

"What happened?"

"Does anyone know where they were?"

I couldn't think what to say. A case of unrealized aspirations? The cost of living like this? Over on the far coast a lighthouse winked. Mechanism or conspiracy, I wondered. Back there, a wave had already licked him from the slab, carried him through the channel, released him to current and fathom.

Somehow I thought it must be so, the lightness, the deftness, the pearls of his vision clammed down into fearful depths, clouded, rotting, devoured. Cost and contrast and a seeming grasp, all those witty rhymes, all our fictions, quiddities, and vapidities, all coming down to this.

Out over the sea, clouds lumbered from the west. Perhaps we would evade them. The horizon was ill-defined, the water an oily presence, sucking, crashing and booming around the base of the cliffs. I lay down to rest among the withered flowers and my mind confounded the moon. After many days they visited me.

"What are you doing?" they asked.

"Climbing," I replied. "Climbing up the walls of my mind. Trying to get out."

I could tell they were not happy with such a reply.

"This is all very well, but, you know, those walls do not exist," they explained patiently. The clock chimed. I was ravenous.

"Let's do the one on the right," he said.

Silly Arete. Matt Fisher seconding

3: THE HUMAN FACTOR

In writing about any human activity, we should surely stress the human side of it as much as the activity itself. Indeed, it has always been the characters you meet through the sport who are its chief attraction for me. Most of the subjects of this group of essays and sketches are (or have been) people I have known. Some have been close friends. All have had an influence on the way I think about, or look at, aspects of the mountain experience. We start with an appraisal, written early in my acquaintance with him, of a man who had a more profound impact on me than any other person I have ever met. I first encountered him in the little hut-shelter on top of Cader Idris one snowy Boxing Day in the mid-seventies. My dog and I had arrived there by way of an easy snow gully on the north side of the mountain. He arrived from I know not where, and grimaced at finding he had company. His outdoor clothing and equipment were a little shabby and very old-fashioned. He squatted in a corner of the hut and took out a pipe and tobacco, which my dog eyed alertly in case they were edible, causing him to curse her roundly but at the same time chuck her gently under the chin, shaking her jowls playfully. I offered him coffee, and he accepted, grumbling aloud that this was a place that of all places he thought to have had to himself on a day such as this (a favourite joking taunt of his, I later found out). I laughed and called him a miserable old sod. He lit his pipe and drew in smoke between pursed lips, the corners of his eyes puckering in amusement at the insult. I saw him occasionally thereafter, usually at his house near Barmouth, and grew almost to revere him. To this day, the service to mountain writing of which I am most proud is that of having edited, and seen back into print, his Seven Mountain Travel Books. *But for the moment, here are my early impressions of H. W. Tilman.*

In November 1977, shortly after this piece appeared, Tilman was lost at sea somewhere in the South Atlantic. In his eightieth year, he was heading for a mountainous Antarctic island. Nothing is known of his fate or that of his companions.

Chaplin as Mountaineer: H. W. Tilman
Climber and Rambler 1977

"I FELT I could go on like this for ever, that life had little better to offer than to march day after day in an unknown country to an unattainable goal."

Opposite: Stennis Head; Ben Wintringham "resting"

H. W. Tilman

It takes little imagination to identify the author of the above quotation—H. W. Tilman—but it takes more imagination than most people possess to comprehend the breadth of his lifetime's achievement. I must confess to a bias: I'm as addicted to Tilman's writings as other people are to, say, Chaplin or Buster Keaton films. I see in them an image of man's ingenuity, resilience, sadness, comedy and greater humanity; though I must say that such an airy list of abstractions would not weigh heavily in Mr Tilman's scheme of things. Take the closing shot of a typical Chaplin film—the tramp shrugging his shoulders and setting off down the road to adventures new—and you have Tilman in essence: something a little more sad, fine, considered, and enduring than the Keystone Cops of Mack Sennett or the present-day Himalayan circus of Chris Bonington (the latter of whom he upstaged so consummately, albeit unconsciously, at the Buxton Mountaineering Conference of 1976).

Harold William Tilman was born into a solidly middle-class family in 1898. His father was on the Liverpool Docks Pilotage Committee, and they lived in Wallasey. Tilman, as I suppose we must call him, for his is an austerity which brooks no easy familiarity, was educated at Berkhamsted, and at the age of sixteen, on the outbreak of the Great War, went to the Royal Military Academy, then at Woolwich. In 1915 he was commissioned into the Royal Artillery and spent three years as a subaltern on the Western Front. Unlike most subalterns he survived the war, though wounded, and in doing so won the Military Cross and bar. (It's perhaps working on the wrong tack to wonder what part luck played in his survival, for throughout his life his luck has been too consistent to be just that.)

After the war, in a lottery for officers, he won a square mile of British East Africa, Kenya as it now is, and thither he went by steamship in the October of 1919: "I knew nothing about land and less about farming it."

But nevertheless he set to with a vengeance, bridging rivers, building houses, making roads, levelling the bush, and eventually (after financially devastating experiments with flax) planting coffee at the rate of 30 or so acres a year. He was there for ten years:

For those ten years, except for an annual shooting excursion and one brief visit to England, I had kept my nose to the grindstone. I saw no-one except at week-ends, so that, in spite of the efforts of kind neighbours, there was some danger of my becoming as mossy and as difficult to uproot as some of the bigger trees which had taken us days to stump.

After ten years of this solitary life he sold up, and in partnership with another planter—an arrangement which gave him more leisure—began the process of creating a farm again some 30 miles further from the railway and encroaching civilization. There is a quotation from Dr Johnson which is central to Tilman's thought and consequent achievement: "To deny early and inflexibly is the only art of checking the importunity of desire."

With our unquestioning post-Freudian emphasis on the ill-effects of repression, we would tend to dismiss such a thought. Tilman embraces it gladly. He gave fifteen years of his life, more or less, to creating a situation wherefrom he could spend the rest of it in one of man's great enquiries into the physical world around us. To do so, and in doing so relinquish what are commonly regarded as the "best years of one's life", argues a stringency of self-control which few possess.

He began climbing with his sister in the Lake District on trips home to England in the twenties and by 1930 had taken a couple of seasons in the Alps. In 1929 another young planter by the name of Eric Shipton had made the ascent of the lower of Mt Kenya's twin peaks. An account of the climb was published in the *East African Standard*, and thus Tilman came to write to Shipton, almost ten years his junior, to ask him for advice on East African climbing. As a result of the letter the two met:

> On the last day of February 1930 S. and I forgathered at Nairobi, whence we left by car for the mountain. S., who like myself was a coffee planter, had a farm north of the railway about 160 miles from mine. In the middle of it was a great tooth of granite which soared up for about 200 feet—an eyesore to a planter, but to those of the faith better than water in a thirsty land. S. had worked out several routes up it to which I was later introduced.

On this occasion the two climbed Kilimanjaro in thick weather. Obviously they found each other's company endurable (though they were perhaps too different in character for it to be absolutely congenial), for later in the same year Shipton conceived the ambitious plan of a traverse of the twin peaks of Mount Kenya, by ascending the unclimbed West Ridge, and descending the 1929 route. This they achieved on the first of August: one of the major and least-celebrated feats of British mountaineering before the war. The West Ridge is still regarded as one of the classic courses in African climbing, and one of the most serious ways of reaching Batian's summit. Now graded V and 3,000 feet in length, its first ascent as part of a complete traverse of the mountain, in a day, starting from Shipton's Cave (much lower than is usual nowadays), by two relatively inexperienced climbers, its then remote setting and the icy conditions they encountered on the rocks amount to something of a magnitude comparable to the greatest achievements in the Alps at that time. Tilman's account of the climbing is so low-key that the reader could easily imagine it to have been little more than an easy day out on Great Gable.

Shipton's Himalayan career began on Kamet the following year, and Tilman was left to his African devices of planting and hunting, eked out with an expedition to the Ruwenzori in 1932. "More by good luck than good management", Tilman and his companion made ascents of all the area's major peaks. In his account of one day, in the course of which they climbed Semper Peak (15,483 ft) and Edward Peak (15,986 ft), there occurs a very telling little passage:

> From the col we would drop down to the unnamed valley between Mt Baker and Mt Stanley, on the south side of the Scott Elliott Pass, returning to the Bujuku valley and our camp over this last-named pass. It meant a long day, and was rather a shot in the dark, but it took us into fresh country and, in spite of the prudent adage, we preferred the unknown to the known. . . .

To my mind, what makes Tilman a great travel writer, apart from his considerable literary skills and astringent humour, is this absorption in what lies around the next corner, in where a particular feature fits into the landscape of his imagination. Few writers have dwelt with such voluptuous interest on the far-flung view, on the great apron plains below a mountain or the sinuous valleys threading its bulk. The old fustian question "whither bound?" becomes with Tilman a Faustian prayer for knowledge.

Tilman gave up farming in 1933. For a while he prospected for gold by Lake Victoria, but found little. He climbed Kilimanjaro alone, sleeping in the summit crater, and there decided on his best way home. If Whillans's motorcycle ride back from Trivor is worthy of remembrance, so too is Tilman's bicycling from east to west across Africa. Tilman was not a cyclist, at least not for pleasure, but it seemed to him the logical means of reaching the West Coast and a port where he could embark for home. His bicycle "was an ordinary English make, costing £6. I might have had a Japanese one for £2." His map was torn out of the back of a magazine, his diet was eggs, often bad, and bananas. The 80-or-so page account he gives of this journey, in *Snow on the Equator*, is a masterpiece of clarity, comedy, and curiosity. One wonders what General Amin would have made of him?

His mountaineering began in earnest in 1934 when he and Shipton made the great lightweight reconnaissance into the Nanda Devi basin. For the next fifteen or more years the Himalayas became the focus of his aspirations:

> To the mountaineer they furnish fresh evidence, if such were needed, of the wise dispensation of a bountiful providence. For lo! when the Alps are becoming too crowded not only with human beings but with huts, the Himalaya offer themselves to the more fanatical devotee.

H. W. Tilman with the bicycle he rode across Africa. (Taken outside Bod Owen, May 1977)

In *Snow on the Equator* he complains of the spoliation of Mt Kilimanjaro by huts and visitors' books. Twenty years later he was to look afresh at the Himalayas and say of them:

> The Himalaya are extensive, no less than 1,500 miles in length, but a quiet man might well shrink from going, say, to Katmandu if he thought he was likely to meet there eleven other parties with their 5,000 porters.

There is a story, quite possibly apocryphal, though the words are in character, of his inadvertently stumbling across the base camp of a Patagonian expedition, and saying to the first person he saw (in the story it's Whillans, who for once is left speechless): "I thought this was one corner of the Earth, damn it, where I could have hoped to be alone."

In 1935 he took part in Shipton's Everest reconnaissance; a high-altitude climbing holiday in which members of the expedition, after the survey was completed, climbed 26 peaks in some 60 days, Tilman himself going up seventeen of them. He didn't go on Everest in 1936, perhaps because he had seemed to be badly affected by altitude the previous year. Instead, in company with Odell he climbed Nanda Devi, the Goddess Nanda, at 25,645 feet the highest peak then climbed by man. The incident which everyone remembers about this expedition, of course, is the reaction of the two climbers on reaching the summit: "I believe we so far forgot ourselves as to shake hands on it."

Which is a fair example of Tilman's laconic humour. In fact the point is significant; here is a moment for which no apt or adequate expression can be found, therefore let the slightest gesture suffice: "After the first joy in victory came a feeling of sadness that the mountain had succumbed."

The Ascent of Nanda Devi, to my mind, is the most fully achieved account of an expedition yet written; it's subtle, modest, humorous and respectful. If mountaineering has a literature this is a classic of it. Thinking about recent expedition books by way of comparison, they bring to mind a cartoon of Jules Feiffer's, in which the usual puny mannikin strives manfully after the seduction of a beautiful woman, eventually achieves it, and in the last caption can only think, "Just wait till I get back home and tell the boys about this!"

The Everest expedition of 1938 was led by Tilman, and failed because of bad weather at 27,200 feet, to which height Tilman climbed without using oxygen. It did at least produce the only modest *and* readable account amongst the many of expeditions to that mountain. The following year war broke out, and Tilman at once enlisted: "I was forty-one," he said, "and they thought that too old for a Second Lieutenant." So "they" promoted him and sent him to France, the Middle East, Tunisia and the Western Desert; and parachuted him behind enemy lines to organize resistance groups in Albania and Italy. He did a little climbing, less ski-ing, won the DSO, was made a Freeman of the City of Belluno, and finished the war as a Major. Afterwards he served in Burma as British Consul at Maymo. In 1947 he was back in the Himalaya, attempting Rakaposhi with two Swiss mountaineers, Muztagh Ata with Shipton, then British Consul to Sinkiang, and finally walking down the Oxus from its source into Afghanistan and imprisonment. Needless to say, he contrived to get himself freed (by going on a hunger-strike), and reached Chitral. The story of this year's wandering is wryly recorded in *Two Mountains and a River*.

We pass over his Himalayan perambulations of the next few years in order to get him to sea, in the elderly Bristol Channel Pilot Cutter which he bought in 1954, called *Mischief*. It's fair comment that Tilman married once in his life, and married a boat. When they met he was fifty-six and she was a sturdy forty-eight. She was a working boat, without gimmickry or gimcrack devices. For fourteen years he sailed her, across every ocean of the world, through ice, storm and inhospitable waters. She was his way of life and when he lost her off Jan Mayen Island, inside the Arctic Circle, in 1968, she was more deeply mourned than all but the dearest of wives. Ostensibly she was his means of travel to remote mountain areas; in reality she was more than that. She embodied a new realm of challenge and exploration; he had to learn to navigate, to learn the elements of seamanship, and obviously he learnt fast and well. His first voyage took him across the Atlantic to South

America, through the Magellan Straits to Peel Inlet. Here he landed and with two companions, one of whom fell ill and the other of whom could speak no English, he made the first ethical crossing, a double crossing in fact, of the Patagonian ice-cap. His homeward route took him through the Pacific and the Panama Canal, a total distance of some 20,000 miles.

The rest is cruising, almost always with mountains and ice in view; tiny islands in the Indian Ocean, the rim of Antarctica, the West Coast of Greenland, have all come within his compass. After losing *Mischief* he bought *Sea Breeze*, another Bristol Channel Pilot Cutter of 1899 vintage; in 1972 he lost her and bought *Baroque*, of the same ilk, built in 1902. She now lies in Reykjavik, waiting to be sailed home, for last year her crew mutinied and left her in Iceland. I can understand why; Tilman's is a rare austerity which few can take. He wrote, after a crew member had left him on another voyage:

> His real grievance was that we had no distress signals and carried no liferaft. In my view every herring should hang by its own tail.
>
> Anyone venturing into unfrequented and possibly dangerous waters does so with his eyes open, should be willing to depend on his own exertions, and should neither expect nor ask for help. Nor would equipment of this sort be of much use in Drake Passage [between Cape Horn and the South Shetland Islands], where the chances of being picked up are so slim as to be hardly worth considering. A yacht is supposed to carry distress signals, but is not overmuch reliance placed on them by owners of small craft? Yearly around our coasts so many calls are made upon the various rescue organisations that by now the average man should be ashamed to think of adding to their number. The confidence that is placed, and successfully placed, in being rescued fosters carelessness or even foolishness, and condones ignorance . . .

It need scarcely be pointed out how succinctly apposite this is to the whole distasteful business of mountain rescue. And yet it seems curiously symptomatic of our culture that such a statement as this can foster among us a form of assent which yet does not imply actual credence. Though we would all be brave men and great explorers, facing hardship with equanimity, we cry out for the impetus of sponsorship, the assurance, or nearly so, of safety, and the world's acclaim:

> Activity can be instilled and competence acquired, but the right attitude must be ingrained—the cheerful acceptance and endurance of small privations and wearisome duties and the unquestioned belief that the success of the voyage and the care of the ship is what matters most: "This ship, the ship we serve, is the moral symbol of our life."

Thus Tilman, a man growing old, not far from his eightieth year. He lives in a house looking out over the Mawddach Estuary, to Ruskin the most beautiful walk in the world, and across to Cader Idris, perhaps the most beautiful mountain in Britain. He's surprisingly small, and almost frail, but as upright and dignified as the values by which he lives. Menlove Edwards said of him: "He looks a formidable man, a campaigner who loves campaigning and has no use for perplexities; an expert at direct living." Yet he has a quiet humour which is all-pervasive, self-effacing and reflective. The absurdity and sometime nobility of man's travail in this great world are, I think, clear to him; as clear and reasoned as they were to his beloved Dr Johnson. And as Dr Johnson is now largely unread, so too does Tilman's example go largely unheeded. I find it immensely sad to see this fine old man alone in the home of his retirement, if he can ever be content with such. And I feel that my generation, through the actions consequent on slipshod values and shallow beliefs, through too easy a submission to personal gratification, have in large measure betrayed him, and not once but time and again, through action as direct as mutiny and as oblique as commercialization. He's a cultured and civilized man, unembittered though finding it hard to comprehend. He in Barmouth, his boat crewless in Iceland: the moral symbol unmanned: should this be the way it all ends?

When I first suggested to the editor of a climbing magazine that it would be interesting to do an article about Pat Littlejohn, his immediate response was "Surely not—what's he done?" Obviously a man of very high standards (a year or two later he took me on one side and congratulated me on a book I had written, but then queried whether the subject was worthy of a full-scale biography), even he seemed satisfied that Littlejohn deserved to be written about when the catalogue of his achievements dropped on his desk.

The Craftsman: Pat Littlejohn
Climber and Rambler 1981

IT IS A flawless spring day. The limestone glints in the sun. Sky and sea vie in their tints of blue. I am sitting on a rock ledge above the water, holding two ropes, paying out or taking in, fixing my attention on my leader, who is 80 feet away on an overhanging wall. Methodically he moves up to a bulge, probing, arranging his limbs this way or that beneath, around, across it. Each movement adds something to the pattern. After a while, he takes it back to the bench. Or rather, he climbs back down fifteen feet to a foothold, where he rests. The process fascinates me. This foothold in the middle of a white wall, and him standing on it, his body arched into the rock, one hand at a time hanging down by his side, shaking out. I watch him carefully. The impressive thing is his absolute quietude. He is staring fixedly at the piece of rock in front of him. From time to time he changes the angle of his head but gazes at the same place.

Quite suddenly, he looks back down at me, nods, I take in, he climbs back to the bulge. His left foot goes up, left arm on an undercut; from this triangle of forces, rock, foot, arm, a dynamic extension; his right hand clips on to a hold, right foot angles out on the bulge; a pause. The trailing foot moves to balance out the geometry. A few more adjustments and he's ten feet beyond the bulge, resting, fixing his attention on something I cannot see. Again, there is an eerie, fascinating aura of quietude about him.

I follow. It is very hard and strenuous. I have to move quickly, I cannot rest where he did, but he keeps the rope tight at the bulge, and I cannot come to much harm. I reach and grab and heave. At the top he asks, "What do you think of Pleasure Dome as a name for it?"

"Good. Great. What a route! Desperate!" I pant.

"What did you think?" he asks.

"6a."

"Well," he says, "Maybe . . ."

Pat Littlejohn (photo: Chris Howes)

The scene repeats itself throughout the day. I'm left wondering about these patches of quiet in the rhythm of his climbing. Eighteen months later, we are sitting in a room in his Cardiff house. Darkness outside, the rain beating down, as well on the street as on the cliffs we have climbed together. I question him:

"Come on, Pat. When you're climbing there are these times when you just seem to go off into a trance, sometimes for ten, fifteen minutes at a time. What goes on? Is it like, say, meditation?"

He starts talking about his route Tiger, Tiger (E5, 6b), on the Space Face of Mother Carey's Kitchen:

"There was this hole. It was like a helmet that was much too big for me. Above it the rock was incredibly steep and I spent ages just trying to work out the moves. And then I'd come down and stick my head up into this hole. It was a fantastic strain on the back of my neck, and a weird position in the middle of this wall, but, you know, if you asked me now, I could draw you the inside of that hole in exact detail."

His hands sketch the outlines. Another snatch of his conversation comes back to me. He is talking, quite humbly, about his capacity for appreciation, and the thing that comes over is a sensual awareness of the textures of rock. His hands gesture to describe it, and they are motions of delight.

Next day, on my way back to North Wales, I stop off to see my friend John Greenland at his workshop in Hay-on-Wye. He makes traditional things, furniture, writing boxes, in wood, and he makes them supremely well. He shows his stock of wood to me, describes its qualities with his hands. From under his bench he pulls out two pieces of rosewood and lays them down, then talks about them—with his hands. The shock of recognition comes to me that he and Pat are talking the same language. Driving on, musing, it suddenly occurs to me that it must be so—the journeyman in rock or wood can do without it, but, for the craftsman, this fine sensual awareness of his medium and its potentialities is both bond and consummation of his craft.

Pat Littlejohn at thirty is at last beginning to look his age. When I first saw him, in the sixties, the only possible description for his appearance was cherubic. He was short, fresh-faced, and naive. Add to that a broad Devon accent, and you could easily have a figure of fun, a butt for jokes, or a put-upon apprentice. He was no such thing.

Pat comes from Exeter, which was not, in the mid-sixties, anything like a traditional climbing area. He had no friends who went climbing. In those days there were no centres, school departments or courses in Exeter. His introduction came by way of reading a couple of books, which stimulated a desire to go caving. He and a friend of the same age, Geoff Jones, with no more knowledge or information than knowing the location of a couple of caves, started exploring the Devon caving area around Chudleigh and Buckfastleigh. They had carbide lamps, and a wire ladder which Pat made out of stays discarded from his father's boat. Cunning from an early age, he got Geoff to try this out first. It broke. On another trip, into the caves at Chudleigh, all their lights failed at the bottom of the cave. They groped back until the faintest glimmer of light could be seen, climbed towards it, and emerged two-thirds of the way up a 100ft limestone cliff. That day, or perhaps another day round about the same time in 1965, they saw two climbers pegging a route, and decided to take up climbing. Geoff purloined a grappling hook, which in reality was a yacht anchor and was no use when they tried it. Pat appropriated the main guy from the biggest marquee at Exeter Flower Show, and the pair of them headed for the rocks.

They first tried the classic V. Diff at Chudleigh, Wogs, but it was very open and exposed and they didn't get up it. Unabashed, they were back the next weekend to try another route, this time Barn Owl Crack. Geoff had a peg, Pat had his father's hammer, the one was applied to the other, the rope threaded through, and the route overcome. All this is no more than the usual apprenticeship stuff, and the Exeter Climbing Club quickly took them in hand. Within eight months Pat had led his first Extreme, Oesophagus at Chudleigh, and was marked out as a young prodigy. Peter Biven began to take an interest in him. Biven, until his tragic and horrible death in the Avon Gorge a few years ago, was one of the more interesting characters to grace the British climbing scene. He had been, in the fifties, a leading gritstone climber and later had moved to Exeter, where he was a focal point in local climbing. He was assertive, intelligent, cultured and involved, extremely good com-

Opposite: Deep Space, Mother Carey's Kitchen. The author and Roger Alton climbing the classic Littlejohn route

pany, and still a fine climber. His influence on Pat was considerable and they began to climb together regularly. But Pat soon found himself leading the hard pitches all the time. And Pete perhaps clung on to Pat as a way of retaining a toehold in the sphere of extreme climbing, whilst committing his main energies elsewhere. There was a third party, Frank Cannings, from Exeter but then at university in Bangor.

Cannings was probably the dominant figure in South-west climbing in the late sixties. He was an extremely impressive rock-climber, certainly one of the best of his time. Pat says of him that he was "the neatest and most precise climber I have ever seen—you could never tell how hard anything was that Frank did, because he made himself climb well even on easy rock, and his footwork was superb." Frank was almost certainly the major influence on Pat in the sixties. When he was in Exeter, they began to climb together regularly and Pete, slowly and a little resentfully at first, began to fade out of the triangle. Pat had already become intrigued by new rock when climbing with Pete, and had produced a large number of routes on the crumbling limestone of Torbay, including such classic lines as Moonraker (HVS) on the Old Redoubt. Climbing with Frank, the list began to lengthen and the quality became more consistent: Dreadnought, also on the Old Redoubt; Interrogation on Hay Tor; Omen, Zarathustra, Desolation Row in Bosigran's Great Zawn. And finally Liberator, Pat's name and a joint concept, but a route on which their climbing relationship fell apart. I think it was a case of the established star, Frank, having to channel his energies into a demanding career and slowly losing confidence in his ability to keep ahead of Pat's youthful ambition and energy. The example Frank had so diligently set became that against which he was judged, and against which, as the situations they spurred each other into became more serious, he was finally found wanting. He dropped by the wayside too, whilst Pat left Exeter with the pioneering obsession firmly implanted, and moved to Bristol to take a course in Town Planning.

If the latter half of the sixties were the formative years of Pat's climbing career, the first half of the seventies were the rich harvest. During this time he emerged to widespread acclaim as the most prolific explorer and pioneer of new routes on British rock since Joe Brown. Robin Collomb, writing in 1972, stated that "a new concept of what constitutes bad rock has enabled young Pat Littlejohn to power his way up incredible new lines, often of very unusual character, on such high and forbidding cliffs as Tintagel Head, Pentire Point, and Blackchurch. Littlejohn . . . must now rank among the top ten climbers in Britain today."

If anything, this was uninformed understatement. In the early seventies Pat was putting out routes which, in technical difficulty, were equal to anything of their time, and which, in seriousness, frequent lack of protection, extreme difficulty of approach, and sheer commit-

ment required, went well beyond anything else in the British Isles. America on Carn Gowla, Il Duce on Tintagel, routes on better-known cliffs such as Crow at Cheddar or Pagan on South Stack typified his output. He was putting a new challenge into British climbing at a time when, in the traditional areas, it seemed to have become moribund. And he was thinking it out quite logically and quite consistently. Ordinary outcrops or safe mountain crags did not spell adventure to him, whereas on the chiefly unexplored coastline of his own South West England, the opportunities were legion. Biven had scratched the surface before him, but Biven's ethics had been those of the backwater —if it got hard, pull on a peg. Pat saw no reason why mainstream climbing ethics should not be applied to remote and committing situations. By the early seventies he had found the perfect foil to his own enthusiasm in the madcap Keith Darbishire. Keith was very much inspired by the same things as Pat: he had few qualms about launching out into serious, savage, or intimidating positions; he had an almost unlimited faith in Pat's capacity to climb technical rock; and he was always ready at a moment's notice to do the most expedient thing. A good example of this, on the first ascent of Il Duce, was his manner of seconding the second pitch, which involved climbing a huge overhang. Keith quickly realized that this was beyond him, took out Pat's runners at the start of the roof, and then simply leapt off, taking a 60ft pendulum before prusiking back up the rope to join his bemused leader. This new element of derring-do took the two of them quite frequently into desperate situations: for example, the stormy day on which they decided to traverse from Trebarwith Strand to Backways Cove. Above them were 150ft cliffs of overhanging shale with no lines of escape. At one point Pat was swept off and thought he would die. A rope move and rising tides had made retreat impossible. They had no option but to finish the traverse along a completely unknown stretch of cliff. A single impassable zawn or blank stretch of rock could have been the end. Enterprises such as this were optimistic almost to the point of foolhardiness, but they were explorations which brought their due in the form of new routes in unlikely, unseen, inaccessible places.

Thinking about it, one thing becomes startlingly obvious; which is that not many people who have stuck their necks out in this fashion are either still alive or still pioneering at a high standard. There has to be something beyond mere technical skill or an instinct for survival to account for those very few major figures in climbing who go on producing great routes year after year. Motivation? But then, what is that, beyond a sufficient desire? If you ask Pat why he manages to grab the routes which other people have had their eyes upon, longingly, maybe for years, his explanation is disarmingly simple—he says he just wants to do them enough not to be put off by the things which put other people off. Routes like Pagan, or Hunger, his superb climb on the main cliff at Gogarth, were certainly looked at by very able climbers before Pat did them, but, according to Pat's almost simplistic theory, they didn't want to do them enough to come to terms with their steepness, looseness, seriousness, or whatever. It's probably true . . .

I suggested above that the early seventies were a richly productive time for him. During this time he was, without knowing it, putting out a few climbs which were technically of a new order of difficulty. Routes which spring to mind are Madrugada and Caesar at Cheddar, both of which are now graded 6a. But at the same time rumours were filtering down to the South-west of the climbing revolution taking place in Yorkshire and masterminded by Peter Livesey. Ken Wilson, climbing's version of Warwick the Kingmaker, phoned Pat in about 1975 to put it to him: "There are people climbing two grades harder than you in Yorkshire. What are you going to do about it?"

In 1976 Pat went on the International Meet at Plas y Brenin, and had the opportunity to see Livesey and the young prodigy Ron Fawcett at close quarters. I remember meeting him in Tremadog car park during this week, and finding him profoundly impressed. He was struggling, whilst the others were virtually running up routes grades harder. Added to this, Livesey had recently been free-climbing aid routes or aid sections of routes, amongst which were some of Pat's—Darkinbad and the Brightdayler at Pentire Head, Dream and Liberator at Bosigran. But this meet, which could have been a mental disaster, thrusting him back into his shell, in fact gave him the key to the new approach.

Livesey delivered an immensely revealing lecture on the bases of the new order—training, the importance of finger strength, the ordered and analytical use and preparation of equipment.

"They laughed at my gear," Pat says. But when he went back to Cardiff, where he was now living, the edge of his motivation was honed to a new sharpness. He started going out bouldering on the dock walls at Cardiff: "My standard improved by a grade and a half in two months." He went back to repeat his own routes without aid. Four years ago, when Arni Strapcans profiled Pat for *Crags* magazine, Pat had climbed over 400 new routes. Today the total stands at over 800, which seems like an adequate response to Ken Wilson's question.

I remember an afternoon—it's probably ten years ago now—which I spent with Pat bouldering on Fachwen. There were several of us—Martin Boysen, Malcolm Howells, Dave Potts, I think Peter Crew may have been there. We were all climbing at more or less the top standards of the time. Pat was a bit younger than the rest of us, and very quiet. It was all very noisy, boisterous, competitive. Except that when Pat had done the established problems the rest of us were gabbling over, and done them in his neat, controlled, inexorable style, instead of standing back and barracking and jeering, like the rest of us, he simply got back on the rock and started working on new variations and problems of his own. He wasn't being competitive, at least I don't think so, it was just that his appetite for rock was greater than ours. By the end of the afternoon everyone, including Martin, who at that time was generally esteemed to be the finest virtuoso performer on British rock, had been thoroughly burnt off by this methodical, precise, forceful young climber.

Al Harris used to tell another bouldering story about Pat in Yosemite. Pat had just discovered the virtues of chalk, and brashly stated that since his discovery of the stuff he could do any problem Al cared to show him. Al took him on for a bet: "Ten dollars you can't do Bachar's Lunge."—This being one of the harder problems around at the time. Pat took the bet, tried, and failed—miserably.

"Not my style of climbing," he excused himself. "Find me a finger crack."

"O.K." said Al. "Double or quits on Bacharcracker."

Pat took the bet, tried the problem, failed again, and was so disgusted with himself that he paid Harris the bet in full.

If you've read this far, ask yourself now how much you know about him? I've known him for quite a long time. I would consider him a friend, someone I like and respect. I could tell you much more about him: that he has a wife and daughter, towards both of whom he holds out a sort of kindly, grappling, and serious-minded affection; that he was an English teacher in Weston-super-Mare; that he now works in what is partly his own business, Outdoor Action in Cardiff; that he is 5′ 7″ tall and has huge forearms. I could tell you something of what he feels about the present climbing scene, and what he sees as perhaps an over-emphasis on athleticism to the detriment of the fuller experiences available on rock. I've told you nothing about his Alpine, Norwegian or American climbs and first ascents, or about his ambitions in the direction of Alpine-style ascents in the Greater Ranges.

Presumably, in a climbing magazine, we want to see him only as a climber, and maybe even only as a British climber, and ignore this, the wider context.

But for all that I could tell you about him, and for all the judgements you are likely to put upon it, perhaps you would learn more if you were to set foot on some of his routes—there are enough of them, in all conscience, to choose from—Pagan, say, or Crow, Il Duce, Antiworlds, Deep Space, or The Andromeda Strain. No bad thing, in judging, to find yourself judged. You might find yourself agreeing with me in considering him to be one of the perfect masters of British Rock. In one of his articles in a climbing magazine he wrote:

How many routes could the two miles of solid sea cliff at Carn Gowla provide, or the half-mile at Tintagel, or the miles as yet unexplored? The existence of climbs such as Il Duce, Eroica, and Darkinbad had so far tended to channel attention to certain parts of certain cliffs. How much more might be found if more parties decided to look around the corner?

Opposite: Jill Lawrence on Tower Face, Stanage

I suggested to him recently that with climbers now managing 6c and 7a, perhaps we could finally write him off. He grinned.

"Well," he said. "Maybe . . ."

Eight hundred new routes, and you ain't seen nothing yet . . . ?

The Guardian *asked me, rather chauvinistically, to contribute an article to their Women's Page as one of a series on women in sport. Writing for a non-specialist audience was in itself an interesting exercise, but the most amusing facet was the response it aroused from some of the climbing fraternity (not sister-hood!). All their incipient sexism burst out into a great howl of protest and derision at the suggestion that Jill Lawrence's movement on rock was more aesthetically pleasing to watch, more rhythmical, fluid and akin to dance, than that of some very good, or even great, men climbers. Whether they were simply disbelieving, or threatened and jealous, I don't know, but the article is reprinted here to re-affirm my belief in the point made.*

Role-Model: Jill Lawrence
The Guardian 1983

AT THIRTY-TWO you can easily be over the hill, for rock-climbing is generally a young person's passion. But Jill Lawrence, the best woman rock-climber in the country, is that age and still improving.

The sport's image blurs in with that of mountaineering—a host of Boningtons waving ice-axes aloft as they grit their teeth behind ice-encrusted beards and straddle the summit of Terror Peak. Rock-climbing isn't like that. These days it is practised as a distinct sport in its own right—sunny days on rock in shorts and a tee-shirt, free-form gymnastics. It is attracting ever-greater numbers of women into its ranks.

There is no organized competition in rock-climbing—that takes place within the individual and against objectively graded scales of difficulty. Jill Lawrence's particular skill is at leading—going first on the rope—the core-experience of rock-climbing. The leader is the one who takes the risks, perhaps even the falls, who faces up to the weaknesses in her or his own character and whose personality wins through. To go second on the rope is very much second-best—a more secure, circumscribed, and safeguarded experience. Many women who come to climbing are attracted or dragged into it by a bullying or pleading male who wishes to impress on her, through the sport, his own manliness. Thus the recurrent syndrome of the eternal female second, time and again taken on to climbs beyond her experience and developed capabilities.

Jill Lawrence on the Left Unconquerable

Jill came into climbing in 1973. As a student at Bingley College of Education, she was taken up a severe climb on the Yorkshire gritstone outcrop of Almscliff: "At the top I nearly bounced off the edge of the crag. I was so excited," she recalls. At Bingley she came into contact with Peter Livesey, then the leading British rock-climber and a lecturer at the college. She was soon following him up the hardest climbs.

Although in many ways this was a good entry into the sport, it fostered in her technical ability rather than independence of approach. The prestige and intrinsic interest of taking part in the first ascents of some of the country's hardest climbs held her for a while, but she quickly realized the direction in which she wanted to go, and more and more she started to lead on less difficult climbs with people of her own standard, drawn from the supportive community into which she had been introduced. Her climbing improved and her ideas on it clarified: "I became much calmer about it, and instead of rushing at a series of moves, knowing I'd be all right if I fell off, I would consider them, work out how to use my body, conserve my strength, and stay relaxed. It became a much more complete and interesting experience."

College over, she instructed for two years at an outdoor centre until 1979, when she took up a post in Barnsley teaching ESN children. She travelled widely to different climbing areas—the French and Swiss Alps, the Dolomites, Baffin Island, the Yosemite Valley. This summer she resigned her teaching job to become "a full-time rock-climber, till I run out of money." She plans to organize courses, based in North Wales, with female instruction for women who would like to climb. But she hopes that these will not merely develop the obvious and relatively easily acquired skills. She believes that through the activity of climbing, women can acquire self-confidence, resourcefulness, aggression, honesty, and insight which will help them in other social situations.

The particular quality of excellence Jill Lawrence's climbing displays is her style. "Style" in climbing has two senses. "Good style" is a code term for climbing without recourse to any of the little tricks which many climbers use to lower a route to their own standard—artificial aids, tension from the rope, and so on. In this sense, Jill is a very honest climber—she does not cheat against the sport's unwritten and unenforceable rules. The other aspect of style is an aesthetic one, and it is here that women possess some advantages over men. There is something akin to dance in the actions of a supremely good rock-climber. The moves are rhythmical, perfectly balanced; their stretch and flow, gather and release are, at the best, a joy to watch. At present there are probably no women in this country capable of leading routes of the very highest standards of difficulty, where strength of fingers and arms becomes paramount. Come down just a little, put a good woman and a good man on the same route, and the woman will often give the appearance of greater ease and awareness.

I was out on Stanage Edge, one of the brutishly steep gritstone outcrops in Derbyshire, with Jill Lawrence a few weeks ago. In the course of a full day's climbing I did not see her make a single false move. The delicacy and poise, the easy swing of movement with which she overcame climbs that, for a previous generation, had been the hardest of their time, was a continual delight. Climbers like Joe Brown and Chris Bonington, even in their prime, could never have approached its type of elegant perfection. When questioned about her style, she simply says, "I'm not as strong as the men, so I have to be more careful in the way I use my body to get up climbs."

The point holds, even among absolute beginners. Girls are generally more precise, economical, and considered in their movements, and in consequence at the outset of their career are often able to get up technically more difficult climbs than boys. Rock-climbing is perhaps a unique activity in the dialectic it mounts between self-analysis and controlled action. Independence, resourcefulness in the face of hardship and physical danger, consideration for others and an ability to cope with your own fears are undeniably useful traits to acquire. Jill Lawrence possesses them all; there can be few better climbers to emulate.

John Redhead

Working on High *magazine gives me the opportunity to fill out bits of space, where and when it proves necessary, with brief character-sketches. These are two of my favourites thus produced—of very contrasting personalities, though each has a similarly attractive quality of vitality about him.*

Two Sketches: John Redhead, Robin Hodgkin
High 1985, 1984

1. John Redhead

"DON'T YOU EVER train?" I ask him.

"No," he replies.

"Then how come you're fit enough for the routes you do?"

"I'm not fit, but once you've done a few of them you can get up 6b's anyway, and 6c's with a fall or two."

He states it quite matter-of-factly. With anyone else, I wouldn't believe it, I'd yell them down, screech "bullshit!" at them, but I know with him that he doesn't climb from one month's end to the next and yet can blast straight back into the hardest things around.

"So do you just get off on the adrenalin?"

"Yeah!" A great, spreading smile, huge rolling eyes, manic laughter.

"So that's your obsession with Great Wall?"

He snickers with delight at the mention of it and starts to talk cryptically about *the* line.

"And it's possible. I've been down it. Looked at it. It'll go. But it's death . . . there's nothing!"

A great open vowel sound for the last which leads him back to wide-eyed laughter.

I just watch. Believe me, this is the strangest cat around. I have seen him poised elegant, relaxed, grinning, where there *was* nothing. And the moves! Pollitt is playful as a puppy: bounce, gambol, plunge, scurry back; Fawcett is the great ape, all free-swinging elasticity; but Redhead is the big cat. There is no one like him in the climbing world today.

"The painting comes first," he tells me, and I think of his vast canvases and their tiny, intricate, detailed beauty. You could say Richard Dadd, half-imputing a fine madness, striving to identify a tone and style, but it's a faint echo and he's his own man. You could state an absolute professionalism and technical mastery of perspective, colour, form—but it's bald language, thin soil for the grasses to grow.

A warlock with a loping dog, a night-creature, sleeping in stables, yet his house glows with a gentle green.

I know Redhead. He is a master, of rock, of design. He can both represent and create. There is vast egocentricity in him and humility too, lapping oceans of unsureness; deep, rushing channels. He wanders, then suddenly bounds spring-heeled quite out of your sphere. I know and do not understand. His routes—Margins of the Mind, the Disillusioned Screw-Machine, Demons of Bosch—amaze. For him, they are out there on the Way of Weird. He is some sort of distant brother to our humanity, watchful, wolfish-visaged, beast-taut. If, one day, he sprang clean beyond our comprehension or just disappeared with a puff into the ether, I would not be astonished.

2. Robin Hodgkin

A gentle old man sits under a Spanish chestnut tree in the garden of a house in South Cornwall. His wife serves China tea in robust pottery cups whilst he talks about their involvement in the Society of Friends —the Quakers. He grips his cup between thumb and first finger joint—the other joints, the other fingers, are missing.

A week or two earlier, outside a pub near Oxford, David Cox is talking: "Robin Hodgkin was the best natural climber I ever saw. Even after Masherbrum, without his fingers, he could climb better than I could with all of mine."—this from the man responsible for the first ascent of Sheaf, and the solo ascent in 1938 of Sodom (Spiral Route) on Craig yr Ysfa—still graded HVS.

The conversation in the Cornish garden continues: "Our Oxford generation—David's and mine—was terribly affected by the death of

John Hoyland on Mont Blanc in 1934. We did, though, manage some worthwhile things." He talks about a small trip made to the Caucasus in 1937, when they climbed Mount Ushba: "Do you know of anyone having been there from this country? It's an extraordinarily beautiful mountain, like the Matterhorn but higher, more dramatic, more . . . difficult." The last word is rolled gleefully around the tongue and he bursts out into a smile when it's delivered.

Masherbrum? "Oh yes—there were two of us up at 24,000 feet and our camp was avalanched. We got out, and rescued an ice-axe between us. I was the lighter one, so that went to my companion, which in a way was lucky for me—of the two of us, I was the less badly frostbitten." He recounts the descent in a storm, the distance and time to the camp, the retreat, hands and feet turning gangrenous, from the mountain, then, as if to say "enough of this heavy talk", thumps you playfully in the ribs and suggests a walk. The path to the coast is tunnel-like, sunken and dark. He moves lightly down it, spare and vigorous as he comes up towards his seventieth year. "They patched me up well in Edinburgh, saved what they could of my fingers, and then John Hunt was terribly kind to me. He invited me to the Lake District and got me climbing again. Once I got back to Oxford it was decided that I should be shipped off to the Sudan." He worked there as a teacher and educationalist throughout the war years, and did some climbing (see Tony Howard's piece on the Jebel Kassala in the May 1984 issue of *High*). Did he miss the mountaineering society of his time? "Oh no, not much. If a man's not got some new direction to channel his energies into by the time he's in his thirties he's likely to end up as a pretty boring fellow."

When he came back to Britain, Jack Longland urged him to apply for the vacant headship of Abbotsholme, then a shambles of a "progressive" school. He reorganized it, made outdoor activities an important part of the curriculum, stayed a decade and when his contribution had been made, and the school's reputation established, he left: "As progressive schools go we were probably a bit right of centre—we believed in structure and a degree of ritual as necessary to education." After a sabbatical of a couple of years to order his thoughts, he finished his career as an Education don back at Oxford, served on the Mount Everest Foundation, helped with the Hunt Report on Mountain Training.

Walking along the cliff-tops he reminisces about his climbs of the thirties in Wales—the new routes, Sunset Crack and his variations on Pigott's and on Glyder Fach's Direct Route: "David and I and the Mallory sisters were camping for a week under Cloggy. Ken Wilson has it firmly in his head that something must have been going on and keeps asking us who was sleeping together, but we really were very innocent. The Mallory girls were there with us simply because they liked climbing . . ."

Opposite: John Redhead on Cock Block, Clogwyn y Grochan (photo: Redhead collection)

Above: Al Harris

Opposite: Harris bouldering on Fach Wen (photos: Malcolm Griffith)

He talks about friendship, and the importance of same-sex friendships—in particular his own lifelong friendship with David Cox—in a person's development. The kindly respect, the affection and lovingkindness which flow out of the man are uplifting, yet there's nothing sanctimonious about him. He's a thoroughly down-to-earth, sensitive and practical Christian. But also sly, puckish, humorous, bullying even if you let him get away with it. He fences and bickers, though not with animosity.

We halt above a cove and he suggests we turn back to be in time for dinner: "A pity," he says. "If we'd got farther we could have gone trespassing. I love doing that!"

The next morning, as I'm leaving, he shakes hands then thumps me playfully in the ribs again. And a little hesitantly adds, "When you come down again, put a day aside and take me up a route. I haven't been on a rock-climb for four years . . ."

Waiting for me at home is a letter from Kevin FitzGerald: "If you didn't know Hodgkin you will by now have met one of the really great men in the mountain world, or any other world come to that. We all ought to be Quakers."

I'd go along with that . . .

When a particularly close friend dies—and amongst the inner circle of climbers this is a terrifyingly frequent occurrence—there are times when a formal obituary is somehow not the thing required, and when more properly an anthem, a celebration of the way they have lived, is what is needed.

Prankster, Maniac, Hero, Saint and Fool: Al Harris
Crags 1981

YOU SIT DOWN and try to write about your friend of so many years, wishing that the words would flow as freely as you wish your tears could flow, and knowing they can do no more than gesture towards the man you knew. Al Harris dead! I suppose we all thought he could keep up his clown's act on the thin edge forever, that he'd always be there playing that manic, exuberant, jestful balancing act of his; that you only had to arrive and enthuse and it would be "I'm ready—let's go for it." Except that latterly the troubles had been falling thick and fast and somehow he was fighting them all the time or just keeping them off, and he never did seem ever quite to get on top. So we all stood back and said, "Harris is trying too hard these days," and what we didn't give credit for was that he was having to. And these last few years were about fighting it off and surviving on his own path, as we all stepped aside into our little niches in the tunnel, watched fate's train go rushing by and wondered what we were doing there anyway. So that on the last late October night, when he set off on another drunken, desperate dash from haven to haven of warmth, energy and movement, only a couple of kids would get in with him and race down the dark, wet road, zapped and smashed and cutting it right down to the quick until Fortune could take it no longer, breathed out, looked away, and he crashed himself dead.

Then for a week all the philosophers dismembered his memory until his coffin sank from sight and we writhed within, knew that he'd gone and the cost of living like this.

There was nothing very original about Al, and when he curled his lip into a wintry, gratuitous sneer you sometimes felt there was nothing very good about him either. But there was something beyond any of that and compensating for all of it: liberated energy in superabundance, inspirational. He was the world's best playmate. Everything he did was noisy, gleeful competition, a restless search for the newest, the biggest, the fastest, the loudest sensation to be experienced and shared with the rest of us.

My first memory of Al is of him riding his scooter up the Llanberis Pass in the winter of '62–'63, when the Pass was blocked and the road was ice-glazed and hard-packed snow. He rode like it was a speedway, digging his heel in so the snow flew. Time and again the scooter would slither away and bounce off a wall and he would be sliding down the road shrieking with laughter, would pick up the bike, rev it up, and go through it all again. He went where the play was, and wherever he went he added to it; came from Croydon, started climbing on southern sandstone, and none of that matters; boasted that anything Crew could lead he could follow in winklepickers, and proved it on Zukator; ended up at his cottage, Bryn Bigil, which became playshrine and focus for a generation and more; ran a Llanberis cafe for a few years; was as widely known and loved in America as over here. And that was it—you couldn't help but love him. He might irritate you like hell, use you, abuse you, challenge you, and let you down—though never when it mattered—but you would still love him for the grace and life of it all, and you'd suffer with him too in his moments of black misery and collapse that came all too often in these latter years.

He was a good climber, frightened and emotional sometimes but very good, brilliant on boulders, enormously competitive, muscular, and all the time laughing, gibing, playing. He had enough ability to have been among the best of his generation but it never meant that much to him—good to while away a sunny day, but not to get in the way of play and laughter and lightness. Modern climbing wasn't much in his way of things—all the training and the rigour and the calculated cool spelt out what he was set against—if it wasn't an instinctive, joyful outpouring of energy it wasn't really for him. It strikes me now, when I look back over all the good times I've had with Al, that what I shall miss about him most will be his spontaneity—if he didn't like, didn't

feel, didn't want to do anything, out it came straight, direct, no deceit, no hiding, no ulterior motives. And if there was something he wanted or liked or felt for, likewise he would come through with it and you would know. He was a great argumentarian with an odd and utter honesty which endeared him to most, got him hated by some, but let all and everyone know where they stood. Rude as hell, living totally by his own rules, didn't give a damn, but put yourself up alongside him and see if you come out as honest and straight as he did in the end.

There are the stories as well: the falls, the parties, the jousts, the crashes, all the texture of twenty years on the wildest shores of the climbing community, all the madcap come-and-go characters and bit-part players that he'd known and who'd seen him as some sort of centre and focus and special genius: all the tales that he'd told to Lucy Rees, for her to put down in their novel, *Take it to the Limit*, but that novel doesn't get near to what he was, to his freewheeling, manic, promiscuous, style, style, style—it gets Harris down as an admiring adolescent might, and he wasn't like that. He wasn't a simple sort of American super-road-hero straight out of Kerouac or *Easy Rider* —oh, he could play those parts, but that was it—they were parts to be played, roles in accord with what his needs were, outlets for all that demonic energy, or times when Al could lose himself somewhere between tight-rope artist, ringmaster and clown.

His funeral was extraordinary. It was more than just one of the climbing world's periodic closing of ranks. When the preacher of the place had rattled off his standard remarks—"I will lift up mine eyes unto the hills. I have chosen this text especially for Alan"—I do not think any amongst the hundreds of people present so much as breathed an Amen. The established order of things had never seemed, even in his life, so far away from a true assessment of Al's character as it did in his death. It was oddly quiet, hushed; I think only his last mistress wept audibly. Why? Was it the tragic inevitability of it all—this cat whose nine lives must have gone ninety times over, this Icarus who flew so much higher and wilder than us before the feathers fell from the wax? Were we silent as for an elegy read over the embodiment and associate of our own youth? I don't know. I only know that a world without Harris is a little meaner, darker, poorer and more quiet than it was with him around. I only know that his is a hard act to follow and that if you go out there on the brittle edge for as long as he did your life is a charmed one, and probably a short one too. His death has aged us all.

But we have our memories. Of driving along the motorway in the dead of night, blowing a joint, changing drivers at 110, playing to the hitch-hiker we'd just picked up; of climbing through friends' windows at four in the morning and jumping gleefully into bed with them; of keeping going on speed for days on end, boozing and partying and whoring and soloing around on crags here and every-damned-where there were people to be played with and get revved up about this or

"Oh, fuck, no, he's done it!" The Atomic Finger Flake (photo: Al Harris)

that; about sharing a bed with the same reluctant girl, hands continually converging on the same objectives throughout the night, and sticking it out to see who would be first to leave in the morning; smoking endless joints on the stance of a climb and his voice drifting up out of the depths: "Oh, fuck, no, he's done it!"; about tipping cars into quarries at dead of night and madly useless robberies and driving his Champ up absurd inclines and leaning into the wind of a hilltop on his scrambles bike and all the falls and all the broken limbs and the too much dope and mushrooms and joints and the too many miles for the mind to stay out and free and cold from the phantasmagoria of it all. And then the last night, when for once he couldn't get the timing quite right; the oncoming lights in the rain and a rib pierced his heart and the picture was torn apart—unpardonable, reckless, and thank God alone that no other was badly hurt.

Oh Al; it is such a fragile thing, this life, and you never gave a damn, not an ounce of compromise with it; you just kept on in there and it was your special magic saw you through. We crouch in our retreats and know your passing. You no longer there to apply a poultice to the blister of conformity and draw the wildness from us all; us no longer able to creep back exhausted and quietened into our safe burrows, with you out there to link us to our losses. When I first heard, a couple of hours after, it was no surprise and I did not think then that the desolation would be so vast—but it is, it is worse. There is a hollow space now in all our lives, and the boundaries have moved in. At first we shrugged it off, hid from it. Now we can only grieve for the heroism and the loss, for your having stuck it out there for twenty mad years that enriched us all—prankster, maniac, hero, saint and fool . . .

I sit here trying to write about my friend of so many years, and can do no more than gesture towards the man I knew. God rest and save him: with our thanks . . .

What began as a promotional article for a book about Scottish ice-climbing here turned into something quite different—a plea, really, for the quality of the writing *about mountaineering to be appreciated, as well as the importance of the events being written about.*

The Ice Climbers: A Literary Discourse
Climber and Rambler 1982

THERE WAS A time, before the studied inanities of the early *Mountain* magazine and its attendant checklists of collectable experience coarsened our responses and devalued our sport, when climbing seemed capable of producing a worthwhile literature. There are signs that it may be so again, but more of this elsewhere. For the present, I offer up to the disinterested reader an extended and retrospective review of work by a group of authors who are as good as any we have in post-war mountain writing.

There is no obvious explanation as to why post-war Scottish climbing writing should be so richly diverse and excellent. It could be that the *Scottish Mountaineering Club Journal*, under the successive editorship of Geoffrey Dutton and Robin Campbell, has something to do with it, but in fact most of the pieces about which I intend to write do not originate from the *SMCJ*. Of the authors I have in mind, their backgrounds and outlooks are as different as can be, so no joint factor can be isolated there. The simple common bond lies in their subject matter—Scottish winter-climbing—a sphere of action every bit as evocative, resonant, heroic and eventful as Arctic exploration, the Alpine Golden Age, Himalayan first ascents, or any of the other great sagas of adventure and elemental hardship.

In this last is the key. It is easy enough to write gilded contemplations of sunny days on rock. But in the strange sub-Arctic of the Scottish mountains in winter, the climbers probing up in the half-light, sketchily belayed, uncertain as to route, conditions, or even possibility, the narrative takes on an intense thrust and urgency. When this is allied variously to humour, expressive skill, or a wise detachment of mind, the results can be quite magnificent.

The writers I want to deal with here—Tom Patey, Robin Smith, Jimmy Marshall, Dougal Haston, and Bill Murray—are by no means the only ones in the field. There is an embarrassment of riches. I could equally well have chosen, say, Hamish MacInnes, Tom Weir, Len Lovat, or Dutton and Campbell themselves. Or I could have singled out some later outsiders writing on the same theme—Geddes and Rouse, or the sesquipedalian comedy of John Barry, for example. But the five above suit my theme, and I will start with the man who, for many, is the favourite—Tom Patey.

One Man's Mountains, the collection of writings and verses which Patey put together shortly before his death in 1970, and which was published in 1971, is an uneven book. You often hear it said that if Patey were alive today he would make mincemeat of the latest obiter dicta of Secretary Gray, or that cycle of eternal recurrence which gave us Citizen Ken. He probably would, given such easy targets, but I don't think that is where his real strengths as a writer lie. The section entitled "Satire" is the weakest in the book. The hits are palpable, but they are also obvious. He has none of McNaught Davis's pungency, or the subtle lancet savagery of Robin Campbell. Something kindlier than vitriol flows from his pen. His gift is not for satire, but for comedy, and more especially comic characterization. It is the characters we remember. If Nicol, MacInnes, Grassick, Bonington, Whillans, had never done anything other than appear in Patey's essays they would still live on in our consciousness:

> Hamish was satisfied with his "shift" and prepared now to rest on his laurels. "It's the interesting stuff that gets me, I'm afraid. I'm not much of a hand at step bashing," he said, indicating the rest of the gully with a lordly gesture."

There you have the quintessential Patey—a delicious and warm-hearted exaggeration of character, the art of comic deflation, a delicate sense of the inherent absurdity in all our actions.

This is not to suggest that Patey is limited to a single tone. He is also master of a more rumbustious, slapdash style of comedy—essentially that of situation. In "Appointment with Scorpion" there is the delightful scene where the four climbers all become stuck "at different points on the face between 50 and 100 feet from the ground," which leads, later in the same essay, to the following incident:

> Grassick had been heaving himself up the fixed ropes to the accompaniment of much grunting and hoarse cackles of laughter. Now for the first time we could see his face, distorted with a horrible fixed grin, appearing over the lip of the overhang like some strange monster from the deep. At that moment, with a long-drawn-out howl he dropped from our sight. The rope to Mike went taut, and simultaneously the snow stance he was occupying disintegrated, leaving him dangling from his belay. I glanced at Nicol in dismay. "It's all right," he assured me. "We're not tied on to them anyway."

Patey's essays, the memorable ones at least, are finely honed. It seems almost at odds with his popular image as the roughcut, scrabbling and improvising individualist, but his best essays give the impression of having been worked over, polished, and brought as near to perfection as their author could manage. They begin and end well

—Patey's endings are an object lesson to any young writer—and the points of characterization are handled with a deft economy: " 'Somebody's left a boot here,' I shouted to Don. He pricked up his ears. 'Look and see if there's a foot in it,' he said."

In a conversation with Tom Weir only a few days before his death, Patey remarked that he had "worked damn hard on these pieces". His labour was well rewarded, and he leaves us a cast-list which shambles with comic magnificence into the legends of the sport.

Patey's better work, with a couple of exceptions (notably "A Short Walk with Whillans", which is his best essay) is concerned with Scotland and the Scottish winter. It is interesting to speculate on whether the colour, variety and humour of his writing drew its initial awareness from the throng of characters and individuals amongst whom he had his roots, and who are described so well in "Cairngorm Commentary". If so, why did not more good writing emanate from the school of Grassick, Nicol, Taylor, Brooker, et al? There was one other writer, naturalized in Aberdeen, who might well have developed interestingly had he lived. As far as I know, Jerry Smith wrote only one article. Entitled "Sestogradists in Scotland", it was published in the 1958 *Climbers' Club Journal*, and describes the first winter ascent by Patey, Brooker and Smith of Parallel Buttress, Lochnagar, in February 1956. It is a pleasing evocation of the winter-climbing scene of the mid-fifties, and draws a mischievously affectionate portrait of Patey. Smith is particularly good—probably better than Patey—at conveying the engrossing technicalities of a climb, and he does this in a style far removed from the ugly "tools, terrors, and placements" jargon of modern ice-craft. But Smith died in an abseiling accident on the Peine a year after its publication, and apparently nothing else of his remains.

There is a little group of essays about climbs on Ben Nevis in the winter of 1959–60 which is quite unlike anything else in climbing literature. Robin Smith's "The Old Man and the Mountains", Jimmy Marshall's "Garde de Glace" and "The Orion Face", and Dougal Haston's "Nightshift in Zero" have been quoted time and again: certain passages from them appear to be the equivalent of the True Gospel to any aspiring winter climber; they have given new words to the climbing vocabulary (I lose count of the number of times subsequent writers refer to their crampons "scarting about in crumbly holds"); they have the intrinsic gossipy interest of revealing what their respective authors thought of each other, and the routes described have inspired generations of climbers. All this conspires to make them attractive to a strictly literalist approach, but I wonder, looking at these essays again, whether their literary quality, as divorced from their content, justifies their influence? The climbs, of course, were momentous: the Orion Face, Point Five, the route on Gardyloo Buttress, the night escapade by Smith, Haston, and the novice Wightman in Zero. As a catalogue of major climbs in a brief period of time, this outdoes anything that Patey or Murray can put together. But there is perhaps not very much in these pieces apart from their narrative content. Robin Smith's literary persona has an attractive ingenuousness, though verging at times on the arch, and there is a persuasive quality of enthusiasm and energy about his writing. Marshall's accounts are refreshingly direct, as in this passage:

> Following up was like walking on eggs, the dark pit beneath our heels sufficient warning to take care; a short step of ice above Wheech led on to the high snow slopes which form beneath the terminal towers of the Orion Face. Here the expected respite failed to materialise; knee deep and floury, they whispered evil thoughts, threatening to slide us into the black void and extinguish the winking lights of the CIC Hut.

Haston too contributes his own sly, streetwise humour to the group. Taken together, they are a remarkable comment on state-of-the-art ice-climbing circa 1960. Taken individually, as I do not think they should be, for they gain much in their grouping, they seem pretty pale and plain journeyman accounts of the deeds which ushered in a new winter-climbing era.

To turn from Smith, Marshall and Haston to Bill Murray is like putting down a volume of Lamb and taking up one by Hazlitt. The difference in quality is as immediately obvious as if we had suddenly moved from a minor to a major key. It has become fashionable in recent years to debunk Murray's writing, about which at times there is a stiffness which gives ammunition to the attack. Robin Campbell, in a forthcoming book on ice-climbing, mercilessly lays into the "Bill Murray brand of German Romanticism", and even Patey jibed gently at him in his "Ballad of Bill Murray", though a comment earlier in the book, about routes "so well described in Bill Murray's two books on Scottish mountaineering as to render further comment superfluous" leaves us in no doubt as to Patey's true attitude towards his mentor.

To my mind, Murray's two books on Scottish climbing, *Mountaineering in Scotland* and *Undiscovered Scotland* (now happily bound together and published as a single volume), would alone place him amongst the greatest mountain writers—Tilman, Mummery, the underrated and overprolific Frank Smythe, or the doyen of them all, Leslie Stephen. They are certainly the two best books ever written about British hills.

We have one of those curious accidents of biography to thank for the quality of Murray's work. The conditions under which he wrote his first book, *Mountaineering in Scotland*, are well known and were chronicled in a moving article published in a magazine some years ago (and later included in the anthology *Mirrors in the Cliffs*). *Mountaineering in Scotland* was written during three years spent in prison camps in

Czechoslovakia and Germany, after Murray's capture in the Western Desert. I have little doubt that the qualities of impassioned wisdom, detachment, humility, and scrupulous self-honesty displayed in his writing were developed during those years.

There is an account early in *Undiscovered Scotland* of Murray's capture by a German tank commander, and it differs quite considerably from the later magazine account. Being slightly sceptical by nature, and I hope this does not offend a man whom I admire above all other living mountain writers, I wonder at the anomalies—not from the point of view of the author's veracity, which I believe to be absolute, but from the point of view of his literary technique. The second account is both fuller and yet more restrained, more effective and dignified than the first. In the same way, *Mountaineering in Scotland* has the feel of a text which has been meticulously worked over, its events balanced and considered in their description, a fine sheen imparted to the writing. I cannot quite bring myself to accept Murray's implication that it was delivered rough-cut virtually from prison-camp to publisher, and thus let through to us the public. It seems to me probable that, in the interval between his return from Germany and delivery of the manuscript to Dent, he worked at it thoroughly, polishing, refining, increasing the dramatic effect. As a very small example to support my view, which may well be entirely wrong, there is at one point a complex quotation, correct in every detail, from Hazlitt's "The Indian Jugglers" (one of the three finest English essays—both the others are by Hazlitt—and perhaps the only one which will stand comparison with Montaigne's "Que philosopher, c'est apprendre à mourir"). There are two possible explanations here: either that Murray's memory is extremely powerful—that he has total recall—or that on his return to Britain, as would be natural, he carefully sifted through and revised his manuscript, checking facts, dates, quotations. All this is to labour a point;* Murray patently not only has an extremely powerful memory, but he is manifestly also a dedicated and conscientious literary craftsman. Writing of his quality is the product of excruciating labour. In the magazine article he describes the quandary he faced when he first sat down to the task of writing the book:

Without diary, maps, or books to refresh memory, I feared I should lack detail of the climbs, which could not be spun out to chapter length. I was right, but the daily concentration of mind in trying to remember, continued day after day for weeks, gave at last a most astonishing result. Memory began to yield up what it held more and more freely, until it came in a flood. Every detail of experience was suddenly there, and in full colour. Nothing had been forgotten. I discovered that memory safely holds all experience in minutest detail, and that what fails (from disuse) is the ability to pull the

* In which I appear to be in error. Bill Murray tells me that a volume of Hazlitt's essays was amongst the books given by the Red Cross to one of the concentration camps in which he was prisoner.

record out of its pigeonhole. The deprivation became a gain. Every climb had to be relived, which in writing terms meant re-created.

He does re-create the scenes of his climbs with an astonishing vividness. Here he is belaying Mackenzie on the first ascent of Deep-cut Chimney, Stob Coire nam Beith:

> I glanced down at the sun-bright cup of the corrie. That plain view of the sweep of the snow-fields between the torn crags is stamped in my mind with peculiar intensity. I can recall it clear and sharp at will, visualize a fragile snowflake on the wall and the sinuous curve of a drift in the corrie . . .
> The confined space of a gully may appear at a disadvantage, but within the smaller field of vision, whether the sun shine upon a filigree of frost, burnish a further crag, or flood some distant moor or river, one observes a quality in sunlight that cannot properly be seen in the open; one sees a peculiarly rich and mellow glow, which in open country is absorbed into the landscape and lost to the eye.

The movement of this passage is typical of Murray's method. There is a progression from a minute and particularized description of the immediate landscape to a quietly reflective statement upon the qualities inherent in that landscape. What Campbell defines in Murray as "German Romanticism" is in fact no such thing. It is the very English quality of our Romantic Poets—a step through Blake's "Doors of Perception", or a surrender to the power of the Wordsworthian formula, "emotion recollected in tranquillity". Throughout *Mountaineering in Scotland*, the better of the two books, there is a sense of implicit dialogue between Murray and Wordsworth's "Preface to the Lyrical Ballads of 1800". It reaches overt expression in the following passage from *Undiscovered Scotland*:

> The full action of meditation is usually made difficult or impossible on mountains by wind and weather, time and company. But our observations can be made for later and more effective use in privacy. We should then recall the forms of beauty, visualizing each until our love for its beauty is aroused, and end with the greatest beauty known to us—it may be a sun rising or a sun setting, or a night sky or mountain, the beauty for which no words can be found. Encourage unreservedly the awe and wonder to which this last gives rise. These feelings of the heart give nourishment and life to the will and mind, which all acting in unison raise consciousness to a new state of awareness.

I should say that this is only the first section from Murray's clearest exposition of his philosophy. There is nothing very original about it—it derives from Wordsworth and before him from the empiricist Hartley—and anyone well acquainted with "Tintern Abbey" will already be familiar with much of the vocabulary. I do not think that matters one jot. The philosophy which underpins the work may be borrowed, but it is nonetheless deeply felt and informed by the fine qualities of the author's mind. And he synthesizes it majestically in these two books of linked essays on the theme of Scottish hills with the best descriptions ever written of these particular landscapes, with exciting climbs, and with a series of character portraits which may be slightly larger than life, but with which I would seek no quarrel. If your theme is the potential dignity and worth of human consciousness—as it is with Murray—then it is only right to accord dignity of motive, character, and action to those who inhabit the expression of that theme. You could say that Murray strives too hard at times to define the undefinable; you could say that he invests his set-pieces too richly and too often with a roseate glow; you could say that his attempts at humour can be a little solemn and ponderous. For all that, along with Tilman, whom he knew and with whom he climbed, he is my favourite mountain writer, and the best of them all on British themes.

What, you might ask, has all this to do with mountaineering—all this stuff about Murray and Wordsworth? I can imagine the question being posed, and I think it is a sad one—one that too readily might pass the lips of those who have been nurtured on the newsreel melodrama, banner-headline-claptrap, and Second-Division-football-reportage style which came in at the end of the sixties with Ken Wilson's *Mountain* magazine. The answer is quite simple to give. The everyday skills of mountaineering, the techniques and mechanics, do not amount to much. Year by year they change, retaining at best only an historical interest, and are forgotten. It is for qualities beyond the mundane descriptions of events that we remember great mountain writers: Menlove Edwards at grips with the psychomachia in a climber's mind; Patey's human comedy; Murray's lively reverence for mountains as the supreme symbols of order and beauty in Creation. It is the good fortune of post-war Scottish mountain writing that it can claim two of these writers as its own, and that the two should be so different yet so complementary: Patey the clown, whose human insights entertain us so crisply and so joyfully; and Bill Murray, the High Priest, whose prose can sing. I end this review with another quotation from the latter. The scenario is once again a winter climb. The passage describes the aftermath of an ascent of Crowberry Gully, on the Buachaille, in February 1941, just before Murray went to join the Middle East Forces in Egypt. It was thus his last climb before internment. Whether you label it as adrenalin-induced, religious mania, or a mystical experience, I do not know, but I doubt if there are many who have not felt something towards this state, or whether there is anywhere a better description of it. It is the essence of the mountaineer's world:

> We stepped on to the open mountainside at seven-fifteen p.m., and came face to face with a cloud-racked, starry sky. The ring of low crags under the summit, the ground beneath our feet, and all the rocks around were buried deep in fog-crystals. Although night had fallen, yet up there so close to the sky there was not true darkness. A mysterious twilight, like that of an old chapel at vespers, pervaded these highest slopes of Buachaille. We stood at the everlasting gates, and as so often happens at the close of a great climb, a profound stillness came upon my mind, and paradoxically, the silence was song and the diversity of things vanished. The mountains and the world and I were one. But that was not all: a strange and powerful feeling that something as yet unknown was almost within my grasp, was trembling into vision, stayed with me until we reached the cairn, where it passed away.
>
> We went down to Glen Etive for the last time, and I fear we went sadly. The moon shone fitfully through ragged brown clouds.

John Hoyland in 1934, a month before he died on Mont Blanc (photo: Rachel Gilliatt collection)

As a period of Welsh climbing the thirties have always fascinated me. The great men of that time—Colin Kirkus, Menlove Edwards, Jack Longland—were all three interesting personalities who deserve to be written about at length. John Hoyland might have joined them in the Pantheon had he lived. As it is, he constitutes a sort of footnote to climbing history, and a sad and necessary reminder of the risks and ambivalence of our sport. (The title is from a poem by another mountaineer, William Empson.)

The Missing Dates
High 1985

> If things are as you fear, I can only say that I looked on John as potentially the best mountaineer of his generation. There is literally nobody of whom I hoped such great things, and to whose development I looked forward so intensely. I doubt if there has been any young English climber since George Mallory of whom it seemed safe to expect so much . . .

THESE CHARACTERISTICALLY GENEROUS words were written by Jack Longland—himself outstandingly the best all-round mountaineer of his own generation—in mid-September, 1934. They were addressed to John Hoyland's father as the latter set out with Frank Smythe to instigate a search for his son, who, with his companion Paul Wand and with the intention of bivouacking on the Col Eccles before ascending the Innominata Ridge of Mont Blanc de Courmayeur, had left the Gamba Hut on 23 August of that year and had not been seen since.

Let me scatter on the floor a few more pieces of the mosaic. There arrived on my desk the other day a small, grey volume, limp-bound and fifty-years-fragile, simply entitled *John Doncaster Hoyland*. There is no date on it, but it was probably printed in the autumn of 1934 and put together by John Hoyland senior, who was at the time Warden of Woodbrooke, the Quaker college in Selly Oak, Birmingham. I already knew a certain amount about its subject—knowledge accrued over the years, tabulated, silently stored away. Then came this memoir, and snatches of conversation, moments of experience, came drifting back to me. You know how a mood can attach to a name? Well John Hoyland for me was redolent, I suppose, of high, colourful summer. I first heard his name from an old Quaker friend, David Murray-Rust (the man, incidentally, who introduced Wilfrid Noyce to climbing) during the time that I spent at Woodbrooke. I knew that John Hoyland was related to the Doncasters who had made, in the twenties, that exquisite little VS (one of my favourite ways up or down the crag on the glowing June evenings when Stanage is at its best) which now shares a start with Goliath's Groove. And that distantly, therefore, he was related to a friend with whom I'd shared many memorable, if often prickly, climbing days. I was aware, too, that his cousin was Howard Somervell, of those muted and haunting mountain paintings. And I also knew that his name was the opening bar in the litany, "John Hoyland, David Cox, Robin Hodgkin", which, when chanted, brought back all the freshness, enthusiastic endeavour and bright optimism of mid-thirties mountaineering, when the balance between romance, risk and achievement was so perfectly held.

So I set out to discover a little more about the man. First stop, and one which is always a pleasure, was with David Cox in Oxford:

"John? Oh yes. I first met him on an OUMC meet at Helyg in March '34—he must have come up in October '33, which was a year after me. Nobody'd ever heard of him and he turned up on about the second day. In those days the OUMC's level of performance wasn't very high—Idwal Slabs, North Buttress of Tryfan, Gashed Crag if you were lucky. There was quite a lot of snow down and we were loaded up with ice-axes, taking about six hours over Gashed Crag. To our surprise John Hoyland appeared that evening having done Cheek Climb on the Terrace Wall and also the Direct on Glyder Fach—in these conditions—which in those days was one of the hardest climbs in the Ogwen area."

David inspected his pipe carefully, as though searching for a clue, smiled, and off he went again:

"He'd taken a boot off in order to do the final crack and he'd dropped it, couldn't find it, and he'd walked back to the hut through the snow with just a stocking on his foot. His foot was very cold but he didn't seem to be making much fuss, and we thought, really, this fellow seems to be upsetting the standards of the OUMC just a bit. However, it was interesting to talk to a chap who was obviously serious about his climbing . . ."

The subject of Jack Longland cropped up at this point, and David remembered that John Hoyland knew Longland and had with him a description of his climb on Clogwyn Du'r Arddu: "And he actually wanted to do it, which we thought absolutely barmy, particularly since it was March, with quite a lot of snow about." After a day or two spent on Dinas Mot, where Hoyland led a party up the Cracks, attempted the Direct Route in the rain (having to retreat from high up on the long second pitch), and "mucked about over on the right-hand end, but didn't do a definite route—it was mucky and wet and raining", the OUMC group was inveigled into going over to Cloggy:

"There were four of us with the intention of climbing, and two or three other OUMC chaps came along just to muck about and walk, and it turned out to be a jolly good job they were there. We didn't start up the thing until about 12.40—and then we did that fearful thing at the bottom which nobody does nowadays—the Middle Rock—it was an absolutely dotty thing to do, but you see Longland had done it and there it was . . .

"We got into the most frightful trouble higher up . . ."

More smiles and musing on his pipe. I prompted him to continue.

"We got benighted on the cliff and had to leave the fourth man, Anthony Seraillier, below Faith and Friction. He was on the stance there for nine hours, had to rope down in the dark, and we hadn't known whether his rope was long enough to reach the bottom. Two of the walkers had to come round to the top and pull us out on a rope, so that was rather a shambles.

"We were all a bit surprised to find that the first slab was not all that difficult, nor even particularly exposed really. When we got to that little perch below Faith and Friction, it was very wet and cold, with a lot of snow up above. John took off his boots and dropped them at that point—yes, he did make rather a habit of doing that on this particular meet—and it took him a long time to get across Faith and Friction, which I gather is one of the pitches whose currency has greatly depreciated—I think they go further round these days. My recollection is that Jack, on the original climb, made a very delicate step across on to a rather nasty and sloping hold, whereas if you'd taken a slightly wider circle you could have gone round more easily.

"Well, we all found this jolly difficult. I took off one boot, I think, and the third man did it in nails. We were all terribly slow and very impressed by the exposure there, and by the time the third man was over it was getting dark—short days and all that. Anyway, that was all a bit of a shemozzle and we got home to Helyg about four in the morning, I suppose."

In a letter to his father, John Hoyland reveals how much David Cox—who had never, it should be remembered, been on anything harder than a V.Diff before this holiday, is playing down his own part. He takes up the account above Faith and Friction:

. . . after climbing an easy pitch, there came another hard one, and I found I could not do it under the conditions, but Cox very gallantly undertook to lead it, and much to our relief just managed it before it got dark. It was a really magnificent effort, and . . . has showed me more than anything else the worth of a good upbringing and education, as two people I was climbing with last Christmas who were physically just as sound, cracked up completely under far less trying conditions . . .

Cox now finishes the story of this epic first encounter. A day of rain has intervened:

"We'd left stuff all over the place—John's boots and I think my boots as well were at the bottom of the cliff and the rope Anthony had used to get down was still in place, so two days later John and I went back. It was the last day of the meet and the others were all cleaning up Helyg.
"We were supposed to be collecting all this equipment but it was rather tempting to do the climb."

Which is what they did: "We took a long time, three or four hours, because we were loaded down with equipment—boots, ropes and so on—and there was still a good deal of snow around. But the way John climbed those two crucial pitches—Faith and Friction and the final overhang—was magnificent."

This was on the 27th of March. Four days later Hoyland was again on Cloggy, this time working his way up Pigott's East Buttress Route ("harder but less exposed than the West" was his verdict on it). Jack Longland, Paul Sinker, a Professor Turnbull of St Andrew's, and A. B. Hargreaves were climbing Longland's at the same time. Jack Longland tells the story:

Opposite: The third ascent of Pigott's Climb, Clogwyn Du'r Arddu, 1928. Ted Hicks leading

"In those days we used to climb the open groove below Faith and Friction facing outwards, legs and arms splayed. Okay provided you knew what your feet were doing. Turnbull was about two-thirds of the way up when he placed his right foot smartly on thin air beyond the edge and nose-dived over the overhang guarding the Black Cleft. Paul Sinker, anchored on my original piton, held on nobly. I had a poorish flake about 12 ft higher up, so that if his piton had gone—it bent through about 40 degrees—I think we should all have been over the edge.

"Turnbull was left swinging about 12 ft away from the crag, relatively helpless. I shouted across to John Hoyland to come and help. He must have abseiled down rapidly, as he was very soon at the start, had lassoed the wretched Professor, and drawn him in to safety. John asked him whether he took any precautions against such happenings, and he answered that he always carried a small flask of brandy. Challenged on whether he had used it now, he gave the splendid reply, 'Oh no, I keep that for real emergencies!' Realistically, we were all very lucky to be alive, and ABH never forgave the tumbling Professor."

Which latter offered the opinion about John that "from the way he moved about on the cliff it was obvious that he was a wonderful climber and full of joyous adventure." This particular adventure over, Hoyland went back to his East Buttress route to continue the ascent of Pigott's, in the course of which he made the first lead of the top crack—an awkward 5a off-width which still causes consternation to many leaders. At the end of the day's climbing he returned with Longland and company to join Geoffrey Winthrop Young's annual Easter party at Pen y Pass, where he met "all sorts of great men—two Everest men and the son and daughters of Mallory among others. It was very interesting and great fun . . ."

Term-time in Oxford, far from the mountains, quietened his activity for a while. But David Cox remembers one outing from there:

"John Jenkins wrote—in the most ridiculously exaggerated way —about some piffling little crags in Shropshire called Pontesford Rocks. There was a thing called the Pontesbury Nose which he said hadn't yet been led and was harder than anything on Gable's Eagle's Nest Direct—which in those days was thought to be quite a climb. John, when we got there, led this thing without even a rope. That was where I fell off and that was very unfortunate because that was the last serious occasion on which I climbed with John. Except . . ."

There appeared a broad, boyish grin, his eyes creased about with laughter lines:

"D'you know about the Indian Institute and the elephant? No? Well next to my college in Oxford was the Indian Institute, on the roof of

which, on top of a little dome, was a handsome bronzed weather-vane in the shape of an elephant, on a long spike. It really involved no climbing, because I had rooms on the top floor and you just got out of my window, walked along the roof and climbed the dome, which was about 20 feet high and rather smooth.

"Anyway, we roped up and while John was about halfway up this thing a trapdoor opened in the roof and out came an Indian caretaker, looking very sinister in the dark. John got down as quickly as he could and we ran back along the roof into my rooms. I was the only man in the college who enjoyed climbing, and my rooms were rather adjacent, so I came under suspicion. But then I had this accident at Pontesford and later developed an abscess where my head had been cut, and had to go into hospital. So John and Paul Wand, knowing there was no risk of my being suspected, repeated this effort, with very much the same result, except it went a little further this time. He got the elephant off and slung it round his neck with some rope—it was surprisingly heavy, I remember, because I had dealings with it later on. Out at this point popped the caretaker, and by John's account got hold of the rope. Paul Wand roped down into the street somehow on another length of rope and John, with the Indian between him and his escape route, had to rope down into the college on yet another length of rope—why they should have had all these lengths of rope or whether they'd cut one in half I really don't know.

"This all left John prowling around in a strange college at about two in the morning. However, he found a way out over some rather awkward railings in one quadrangle which land you in the garden of the Warden of New College. He climbed over these, not knowing where he was going, and landed on top of the Warden's wife—a formidable lady called Mrs Fisher—who was asleep in a hammock, since it was a fine summer night. To her great credit, she didn't say 'I'm going to call the police.' John, who was a modest, quiet fellow, explained his predicament and she responded that if he went back the way he'd come, she'd say no more about it . . ."

Hoyland's first year at Oxford, where he was reading medicine at St Peter's Hall, ended. He went to teach for a few weeks at his old prep school, The Downs at Malvern, and during that time snatched climbing visits at weekends to Wales, the Lakes, gritstone, and the lime-stone pinnacles of Symond's Yat:

"John, armed with some fine rock-pitons which the local blacksmith had made to his directions, proceeded to explore Pear-tree Rock. He was some twenty to thirty minutes on the exposed 80ft face of this pinnacle, hammering in pitons and arranging all sorts of rope slings for himself. He at last reached the top to our united cheers, and we all swarmed up after him. The locals below were amazed to see seven young men standing on the top of the hitherto 'inaccessible' pinnacle."

Other memories are of him attempting, and just failing, to make a free ascent of Scafell's Central Buttress on his first visit to the Lakes; of the way "the mountains were always at the back of his mind"; of his exceptional genius for rock-climbing; of his "sixth sense, which brought us direct to the foot of a climb in thick Welsh mist without any trouble at all."

Nobody seems to know when he started climbing, nor how much he did before arriving at Oxford, except that his beginnings "were on Stanage Edge and Almscliff, with the aid of an old piece of box-cord." He left very few writings behind him, but those which do survive show a sense of humour and proportion allied to a precise descriptive style in conveying his emotional responses to a landscape. His handling of effects, too, is at times remarkably assured for (as he was at the time of the following piece of writing) an eighteen-year-old:

> I was inexpressibly lonely, not with the loneliness of a lonely man in a great city, nor yet with the loneliness of one alone under a wide horizon. It was a kind of companionable loneliness, wistful, kindly and sympathetic, expressive of a great yearning. I felt as if I would go on, and on, and on for ever, lulled to a walking sleep by the moving mist. Still there was nothing but snow, snow and a pair of boots mechanically moving forwards. Then something black appeared. I had consciously to focus my eyes upon it. It was some rocks and a cairn . . .

Frank Smythe's influence lies a little heavily on this, but he would, on the evidence of his last letters, quickly have outgrown those mannerisms.

The only new pieces of climbing he recorded were all in Wales: the top, and hardest, pitch of Pigott's; the top crack of what is now Hodgkin's Variation on Glyder Fach; and a long, rambling Diff on Ysgolion Duon called Hoyland's Route, climbed at the end of July 1934, on his last visit to Wales.

He went out to the Alps at the beginning of August, his first route being the Mer de Glace face of the Grépon, which was badly iced and up which he led a rope of four, including a complete novice. The Knübel Crack was in such poor condition that he elected to try it in socks, but fell off after ten feet and so donned his boots again and surged to the top. It was only the second British guideless ascent.

Bad weather came in. He and Wand retreated to Chamonix, then moved camp to near Montenvers. David Cox reminisces:

"I had an oldest brother who ran the old-fashioned reading parties that they used to have in those days, this privileged class at university. It was on a spur of Mont Blanc below the Goûter Hut. You were supposed to spend your time reading Cicero and people like that. It was absolute agony. But I got away on one day, hired a guide, and—it was my first excursion in the Alps—did the Pointe Albert and the Aiguille de l'M. Walking up to these, there was a tent visible at one point where John and Paul Wand had told me they intended to camp. I meant to go and call on them, but it looked rather a long way away. In fact, it must have been empty at that stage . . ."

On the 22nd of August, Hoyland and Wand arrived at the Gamba Hut from Courmayeur at 10 p.m. They were tired, and carrying extremely heavy loads. Next morning, the 23rd, at 9 a.m., they left the hut, informing the guardian that they would bivouac that night on the Col Eccles before climbing the Innominata Ridge. They appeared tired, and were last seen moving very slowly up the Brouillard Glacier. The following day the weather broke. Nothing more was heard from them. Their camp was not reoccupied.

Almost a month later Wand's guardian and Hoyland's father arrived in Courmayeur with Frank Smythe, who engaged two guides and went up to the Gamba Hut. After spending the night in the hut, Smythe and his guides set out next day up the Brouillard Glacier and reached the Col du Fresnay. Just above the col, its pick protruding from fresh snow, one of the guides discovered an ice-axe. Looking down from this point on to the Fresnay Glacier, the party could see "an object on [its] surface which did not possess the appearance of a stone". They descended, on their way down coming across "items of equipment . . . which included full-size table forks and spoons, heavy ski-ing gloves, heavy woollen sweaters, guide-book and underclothing, a condensed milk tin, a bivouac tent weighing at least six pounds . . . The bodies were lying some 50 yards beyond the bergschrund and it was obvious from the nature of their injuries that they had been killed instantly."

They were wearing crampons, which would have been positively dangerous in the soft snow conditions which had prevailed. Their bivouac equipment had not been used, and a watch on one of the bodies had stopped at 3.52, which suggested that they had taken nearly seven hours from the Gamba Hut to the Col du Fresnay. At that pace, in bad conditions, and with the weather due to break the following afternoon, Smythe concluded that "disaster *must* have overtaken them."

Their bodies were brought down and buried side by side in the graveyard at Courmayeur. Paul Wand was twenty-three, John Hoyland six months off his twentieth birthday. Fifty years on, Jack Longland sadly recalled that "he might have done much—but for that silly accident, deriving from inexperience, overloading and under-

John Hoyland and John Jenkins on top of Glyder Fach, July 1934 (photo: Rachel Gilliatt collection)

acclimatization." David Cox, too, reflects that "simply as a rock-climber and simply from the point of view of his absolute dedication to climbing, John was already terrific. To go on Cloggy in March with climbers who'd never done anything above V.Diff before was pretty ambitious. Similarly in the Alps, to go straight on to the Mer de Glace Face of the Grépon. The mystery to me is, how come he was as good as he was, and as ambitious . . . ?"

A few more fragments of recollection tumble out: he rowed; he was "just a very delightful man, very modest"; he was of average height, brown-eyed, broad-shouldered, strong-armed.

The span of his life was so very short, yet the memories endure with such clarity. The sage counsel is obvious—it was foolhardy, imprudent, fatal, to go where he went, to plan and dream as he did. No, you should not bolster up foolhardiness. But how can you not applaud courage? His sister states the case: "I find myself almost immobilized with ambivalence—of *course* I thought he was *wonderful*, but I would he had not died so young. Maybe the war would have got him if he'd lived—like it got Denys [his brother]. Better by far to have died as he did."

It is easy to look back judgementally or even wishfully—to imagine, for example, what might have been had he lived to team up with Robin

Hodgkin, who came up to Oxford in the autumn of 1934. That, surely, would have been a partnership to have matched any in climbing history. But those are the missing dates. Instead, we have to accept that his ambition overreached itself, colluded with adverse circumstance, and brought about his death. Yet all that rich promise he possessed is not a mere *ignis fatuus*—it is the ore, the essence, the inspirational element of our humanity, which only hard-won experience—which must sometimes entail loss—can refine or distil into achievement and perhaps beyond that wisdom:

> Somebody remarks
> Morello's outline there is wrongly traced,
> His hue mistaken; what of that? or else,
> Rightly traced and well ordered; what of that?
> Speak as they please, what does the mountain care?
> Ah, but a man's reach should exceed his grasp,
> Or what's a heaven for?

If there is a sport which is more fortunate in its front man, its chief communicator, than climbing, I have yet to encounter it. Chris Bonington endures much criticism, no doubt chiefly born of envy, from the climbing world. As an enthusiast to the core, he deserves it not at all, but rather our warmest admiration and support.

Chris Bonington at Fifty: Sketches from the Life
High 1985

TO THE NORTH of Skiddaw and Blencathra, the hills are smooth-browed, their flanks mine-ravaged and deeply incised. Carrock Fell and High Pike fall gently towards Caldbeck, the Solway Firth cutting a flat sheen into the green landscape beyond. From the old silver-workings on the northern slopes of High Pike I could pick out the house, and made my way down across plashy flats of reed and cropped grass to its unpretentious gate.

"Let's have a quick cup of tea," he suggested as he bustled me in through the door, "and then we'll shoot off for an hour's bouldering before it gets dark. There's an *absolutely super*"—his voice rises in pitch and the words are stressed almost to the breaking point where enthusiasm becomes comedy—"little limestone quarry a couple of miles away."

We gulp tea and rush out. At the crag he is already changed, and sets to work on its low-level traverse as I struggle with laces and lassitude. His commentary is vivid and sustained: "The first bit's tricky, you sort of . . . lunge . . . there . . . that's got it. Most I've ever done is three times across and back . . . terrific for getting you fit . . . this last section's *bloody* strenuous.'' He halts and looks back sympathetically. "It's much harder till you get to know where the holds are.'' I just smile ruefully and wonder at the contrast between this pleasant little 20ft wall of limestone—Park Head Quarry—with its strenuous, fingery moves above soft grass, and the summit of Everest, which he had reached just a month before.

"How d'you sustain the enthusiasm?'' He looks blank, as though the question had not only never occurred to him but was somehow invalid. And then, because it is of the nature of the excellent front-man he is required to be, offers up some bland assurance before getting on with the traversing. Arms throbbing, I drop off and watch. There is great efficiency in the way he moves. Certainly there are more aesthetic climbers, but his style blends effort and economy, weaves a fabric of bright motion across the loom of rock; feet shuttle along, arms reach and pull with crank-like predictability—it is, in its way, a very impressive performance.

A Charollais bull lumbers past, catches our movement and takes a baleful step towards us to end the session and usher us off the crag. We skirt hedges cautiously to reach the car, and stop off at the John Peel in Caldbeck on the way home. The regulars congratulate him on Everest. His handling of their queries—some of them elementary, others better informed—is again briskly efficient and at the same time brimming with pleasure, despite searching over the same material he has talked on for the last—Month? Year? Two decades?

Chris Bonington

The last light has drained from the Solway as we arrive at the house. Wendy, his wife, greets him. The lively youthfulness of the man spills out again in the fondness he displays towards her:

"We stopped off at the pub on the way back, love . . .''

He is almost sheepish, like a boy caught in some mild mischief who expects to be indulged.

"Yes, I thought you might,'' she smiles in response. In the car he has been confiding his respect and affection for her, talking of how difficult it has been for her at times, with him often away in hazardous places and her left with the upbringing of their two sons. The house reflects her presence perhaps more strongly than his—books everywhere, arrayed in a matter suggestive of use rather than decoration, musical instruments likewise, and in every otherwise vacant space the pottery she makes—*amphorae*, Celtic grave-goods, or flower-like sensualities of design. But upstairs, in his suite of offices, the purposeful, workmanlike aura of his climbing returns—lightness, functionalism, *three* word-processors!

We sit down to dinner and the rambling conversation of old acquaintance. He is as greedy as I am, devours the last potato with his eyes before dividing it between us. "Ah," I chide, "but if it had been on the South Col and I had not known, you'd have wolfed the lot." He laughs, and for the sake of argument denies the charge. His talk is easy and fluent. I had expected him to be more defensive, guarded in his responses, but he is not so. He treats each topic securely on its merits, and replies with frankness and candour. I mention to him that Red Rope had recently printed an extract from *I Chose to Climb* in their bulletin, describing his attempt to introduce Wendy to climbing, above the comment that it "illustrates the kind of traditional attitude to women that we can well do without." They are both convulsed with laughter, and Wendy promises to send Red Rope an account of how she introduced Chris to horse-riding. He looks pained at the memory.

There is a particular ghost hovering around our table-talk—that of Nick Estcourt, who died on K2 seven years ago—one of Chris's closest friends and one of mine also. We talk of climbs done together. I recall the three of us in the sea-mist on Gogarth one morning at six o'clock, fingers numb with the damp chill, seizing a route on which Chris's exuberance had insisted before a mid-day assignation in Manchester. And I remember another occasion, at his dinner-table seventeen or eighteen years ago—a silly woman present at whom I slashed a cutting phrase, causing her to depart in tears. In the awkward silence she left behind her, Chris's voice spoke softly but firmly: "That was unkind, Jim." Whenever lurid tales of self-interest and commercialism are told against him, or the old caricature of the "really good guy with two eyes on the main chance" is rehearsed, I hear in my conscience the moral authority of that quiet voice, and know which I consider to be the true version.

Talk for the activities on the morrow is of *Daedalus* on Eagle Crag—he had failed on it once when climbing with Estcourt, and Nick had had to complete the lead. I go to bed in pleasurable anticipation of the rare opportunity to touch some steep rock. The starlings in the eaves above where I sleep prolong my ensuing wakefulness. Next morning I scratch my stubbly chin and swap trivial remarks over a late breakfast with Ronnie Faux, the *Times* correspondent, who has brought round an interview for Chris to vet—but its subject has disappeared early on business to Carlisle, and trips in mid-morning to fulfil his obligations before we hit the crags. We are away before noon, but the first heavy raindrops from a darkening sky collide against the windscreen as we reach the Borrowdale roundabout out of Keswick. By Shepherd's Crag it has started in earnest. "Change of plan," he announces. "We'll go on that new crag of Colin Downer's." So we grab a couple of routes—a little groove at about VS and a very steep wall over to its right, lovely long reaches between sharp fingerholds—before the rock streams with wet. Again, the efficiency is paramount—in rope-handling and protection as well as movement. It is very difficult to believe, watching him, that he is fifty years old. The hair is long and thick, and only faintly flecked with grey, his body quick and youthful in its movements. But interestingly, it is not a body perfectly designed for rock-climbing. The torso is slender rather than muscular; he is not as tall as you might imagine—probably about 5′ 9″—but the legs and lower trunk bespeak great reserves of power and the rhythm of his movements promises stamina—it is a mountaineer's physique—less impressively so, perhaps, than Scott's or Boardman's—there is not the same strength and depth about the chest—but still near-perfect in its fulfilment of the demands a high-mountain environment would put upon it. The facial features are intriguing too—a broad, strong nose above full lips give the framework, but the eyes capture the attention. They are deeply recessed, deep-blue, and narrowed, skirted about with crow's feet as though concentrating in a continual process of weighing up chance and consequence. The dead metaphors of our language intrude on our reactions to such a face, and cause us to misinterpret. It is 35 years out there in the wind, squinting against the light from that snowfield, probing the icefalls, searching out a route on the shadowy faces above, that set the man's expression and perhaps carry the living metaphor of the climb, with its possibilities, difficult decisions and attendant risks, back into his life.

At Caldbeck again, we sit on a sofa, dogs supine between us, and watch the rain. He outlines his early career: the grandfather's house at Blackrock, near Dublin, solitary walks in the Wicklow Hills, seeing the Carneddau from the Holyhead train, climbing Moel Siabod in the winter of 1951, being avalanched from the Pig Track, and fleeing from Glyder Fach as the mist rolled in. Because the chronology of his subsequent achievements is so rich, it is very easy with Chris to accede to the "epics, dates and kings" view of history as a catalogue of tenuously linked events. To do that in a climbing magazine, where knowledge of the climbs is everyone's domain, would be a pointless exercise: Raven's Gully, Sunset Boulevard, Malbogies, Frêney Pillar, Eiger, Towers of Paine, Coronation Street . . . et al. The list *does* tell us something about the man, but there are other aspects which it leaves insufficiently characterized. Such as the fact that he was—it is a vague phrase but I use it here for convenience—a very good *natural* climber, who developed rapidly because he was thrust into a leading situation from the outset. I suppose in pure rock-climbing terms this ability is not all that obvious (I know of several modern climbers capable of leading at E5 and above who could certainly not claim it). But there are situations where it becomes very apparent. As it was on the occasion in the late sixties when Bonington and I went to do South Stack's Red Wall. I had already done a couple of routes on the wall, which had a fearsome reputation for being loose and serious at that time, and I was sitting above the normal abseil position on the opposite side of the zawn fiddling with boots and gear—Chris is always the first in a team to be ready to climb—when I noticed he had gone. I looked around and spotted him, rope round his shoulders, casually down-climbing the first of the abseils:

"Come on down—it's okay," he yelled up, so I set off and by the time I was 150 feet down at the foot of the first ridge he was halfway across a traverse of loose, wet, steep, vegetated slabs leading into the back of the zawn. Technically I suppose the ground was about Severe, but it was very frightening, on terrible material, and above an overhanging wall dropping on to boulders. He crossed it effortlessly, picked the easiest route down the bottom overhang, and obviously expected me to follow, which I did with great trepidation. By the time I caught up with him, he was tied on and belayed at the first stance and the loose ends of the rope were awaiting me. I suspect he knew the middle pitch was the most interesting, and had calculated it thus. When he came to lead that pitch—the route-finding on which, in those days before chalk and heavy traffic, was very complex—he did so with an unerring sense of its line. I have been very impressed with Bonington's all-round climbing ability ever since.

Two other aspects of that day stuck in my mind. The first was the banter in the South Stack cafe which Joe Brown and Mo Anthoine directed at Chris, and in which he appeared vulnerable—as who would not—at that time, when the foundations of his professional climbing career were newly laid. The second was his prodigious appetite for climbing—the way we ran over to Gogarth to snatch a route before the incoming rain, and the altercation that took place between us and two furies who descended on us as we took a short cut on our way there, and crossed what they claimed was their land—in which fracas he stood his ground and argued eyeball-to-eyeball for his right to travel responsibly where he pleased.

On this Caldbeck afternoon I reminded him of all this and he confessed to a pleasure and former competence in loose rock and movement on Alpine mixed ground, which led us on to a consideration of his involvement in mountaineering on a larger scale. He sketched out his initial contentment with British horizons until 1956, when he found himself, Sandhurst-trained, stationed in Germany. The first Alpine venture was unaccompanied, but the next year, in a state of total ignorance, he set out with MacInnes on to the North Wall of the Eiger: "I hadn't read much—Harrer's *White Spider* hadn't come out so I knew nothing at all about it. But the moment we got on to it I knew it was totally over the top, absolute lunacy."

The weather broke and they came down that night, to go over to Chamonix and do a new climb on the Aiguille de Tacul as his first Alpine route.

"Should all great climbers be totally ignorant of their predecessors?"

"I think most of them are anyway . . ."

In the course of the morning I had listened in fascination as Wendy had picked the word "commercial" up from Ronnie Faux's *Times* piece and volleyed it firmly back at him. Doing the equivalent of calling for new balls, I contested the same point:

"At what stage did the change in attitude from thinking of mountaineering as a very good thing to do for its own sake, to looking on it as a possible way of earning your living come about?"

"No such change did come about—at least not deliberately—it just happened. I left the army and went into Unilever as a management trainee, which turned out to be infinitely worse than the army. I was thinking of going to training college and becoming a teacher—purely for the holidays—and then that summer of 1962 we climbed the North Wall of the Eiger."

(I remembered the astonishing explosion of publicity that had caused, the lectures, the photographs—particularly that of Bonington at a bivouac eating his sardines with a channel-peg, which by itself had prolonged the fashion for artificial climbing far beyond its natural span.)

"We'd no concept of the fuss it was going to create. Because of the media-interest, Gollancz commissioned me to write a book, and I was able to lecture and so on. Really it was a case of grasping an opportunity because it happened to be there, with no clear picture of where it was going to lead. I slipped into it as the lesser of available evils and have been doing it ever since."

Had he encountered much resentment from the climbing world, and how did it affect him?

"Yes I did—and at the time I was hurt by it. Back in the early sixties you'd quite often encounter the accusation of cashing in on the climb or whatever. There's not the same kind of connotation nowadays, when so many are doing it, as there was when I started making a living around climbing."

What he had to say here caused me to ponder the analogy with the "gentlemen and players" debate which had been thrashed around cricketing circles earlier in the century. Should a man make of his sport his profession, and if he does so, then is his motivation called into question? Has he stepped over into playing for personal gain rather than for the ideals of the game? It *sounds* so antiquated these days, however valid are the moral questions raised. And the moral arguments anyway in my experience are devalued by the personal bitterness and resentment of those who most vehemently espouse them. (The psychopathology of those who adduce such moral arguments is an interesting study.)

I prompted Chris to continue:

"I think you'll always become a controversial figure by doing something successfully, but the important thing is to act from one's own ethical stance. I've always decided *what* I wanted to do, then capitalized on it as best I can, whether it's by doing a series of lectures, writing a book about it or what have you."

Nobody who knows Bonington would ever have any doubt that his primary desire is to do the climb, to be in the right mountain place, to *play the game* if you like, for its own sake. But there is another role he has adopted which bears upon this. He is *par excellence* in the public eye the front-man, the communicator, for the experience of climbing. Since he had introduced the concept of capital, I wondered if he considered this a due return on the investment made in him:

"No, not really. But I do feel a responsibility as a communicator to communicate as effectively and as truly as I can. I think the greatest impetus to that is creative satisfaction—you must want to produce something that is creatively good—as good as you can do, and often you're not happy with what you produce but at least you're trying for something which is as good and as true a picture as you can manage. You want it to hold water firstly with your friends, because you have a debt to them—whether it be your fellow team-members or those you've actually climbed with—and then, yes, you have a debt to the sport you're part of to produce something which is true to the sport. It's very important to me that the climbing world actually approves of what I've done. When you get a lousy review from that quarter, then it really hurts . . ."

The spectre of Robin Campbell—Banquo's ghost to the conscience of every climbing writer—reared its grim, Scottish head at this point —a review by him of *The Next Horizon* had obviously left its mark. I suggested that by Campbell standards the review in question was positively glowing.

"Yes, that's true," he winced, ironically, "but when you go through past reviews—and the same applies to any climbing author—you get a sense that the reviews are not about the book at all, but about what the reviewer thinks you stand for, and if he doesn't actually like what you stand for, you're taken to the cleaners on those grounds."

I wondered if that sort of occurrence might come about because of the quality of candour, ingenuousness almost, in his writing, which worked against the he-man image of the sport. "Was it," I asked, "just a literary device?"

"If you're going to write about climbing, the actual process of climbing is deadly dull—you're either establishing camp three some-where, or placing your right foot on a slightly rounded hold just below waist-height—what is interesting is people, your feelings for them, your interpretation of their feelings, and the interreactions of the two. To do that effectively you have to be honest. If you're going to be frank about other people, you've got to be frank about yourself. The only time you should ever hold back in your writing is when it's going to hurt someone. When that's the case, I won't write about a subject—I don't think it worth hurting anyone just for the delectation of the public, general or climbing . . ."

From writing we broached the subject of photo-journalism, and he explained how the apparent hiatus in his climbing career between the Towers of Paine in 1963 and Annapurna South Face in 1971 was due mainly to his acquiring the necessary skills for that profession: "I was using a fantastic amount of my own energies just learning how to write and take photographs."

"Satisfying?"

"From the point of view of acquiring the skills, yes, but I found the *voyeur* quality of being a journalist on other people's adventures increasingly frustrating."

"So what was the escape route?"

"Well at that time in the late sixties I was living in Bowdon, climbing a lot, chiefly with Martin Boysen and Nick Estcourt, and also doing a lot of winter climbing with Dougal Haston. We decided we'd have an expedition, and because the Himalayas were closed at that time we were going to go to Alaska. Then we heard the Himalayas were opening up, so we began looking for an objective. There was no great master-plan, we just stumbled on something. Dennis [Gray] showed us a picture which Jimmy Roberts had given him of the South Face of Annapurna, and our immediate reaction was, 'What a thing to go for!' So suddenly, instead of being just a bunch of the lads off climbing somewhere, we decided on that as the objective. And then we began to realize just how big a thing we'd taken on. I'd never thought of myself as capable of leading a large expedition—I remember Dougal and me trying to talk Mike Ward into leading an Everest South-West Face expedition in the mid-sixties which fell through—but no one out of that particular group was willing to take the job on, so I became leader by default. I made a fantastic number of mistakes on Annapurna . . ."

"Such as?"

"In the way I managed the expedition. I was very unsure of myself and spent too much time initially out in front, where you couldn't really control what was going on."

"Because you were enthusiastic about the route?"

"Yes—and I like being out in front if I can. Also, we were short of really experienced climbers—only Don [Whillans] and myself and to a lesser degree Ian [Clough] had experience of the Himalayas. But I learnt a lot from Annapurna South Face . . ."

Playing Devil's advocate again, I asked him about the accusation frequently reiterated over the last ten or twelve years—by myself among others—that he ran a kind of circus, in which a high degree of nepotism appeared to be the order of the day. His very straightforward rejoinder was that the expedition members were selected on a basis of friendship, tempered by pragmatism—it was important to know intimately the character and abilities of the individuals in the team, so inevitably the people chosen were friends—either personal or of other team members—and this is the only sensible way to select an expedition.

"So what happens," I quizzed, "when the necessity arises to discard some of those friends?"

"That's the nastiest and hardest thing of the lot. If you're organizing an expedition, then it's not just success, it's people's lives, and at times you've got to take decisions which cut across personal friendships."

"In consequence of which the friendships suffer?"

"Yes, and I think one's got to be prepared to accept that. I've certainly never done it lightly, and in some instances where the decision had to be taken, I've *bitterly* regretted the loss of the friendship."

If he felt so strongly about the loss of friends, what about their deaths?

"There's a terrific sense of loss—I've lost a very high proportion of my really close climbing friends. And I dread it happening again. You build up new friendships and then you think, my God, you know . . ."

His words tailed off and there was a look of desolate vacancy on his face, the features softened by it. It was after the bell, but I threw another punch. Did he feel a personal sense of responsibility for those who had died on his trips?

"No." The reply came back flat and hard. "If I'd taken a wrong decision which had directly caused someone to be killed, then yes I would, but I've never done that. The closest I've come was on K2, when I actually picked the route which went across the snow-slope where Nick was killed. It still edges me that I made a mistake then, but even there, though there's the regret, I don't feel a guilt, because my logic tells me that it's always down to the individual . . ."

"It's of the nature of the sport that an individual expedition climber never abrogates his responsibility to the leader?"

"Yes—even when you're leading an expedition, the people out in front have complete tactical command. There's no way that the people at the bottom of the mountain actually affect their route choice. In the same way, if anyone says 'that's too dangerous, I'm not going to go,' I would never dream of arguing with that individual. That's entirely their decision."

Sensing that there was only the stirring up of painful emotions to be gained from pursuing that line of inquiry, I switched the subject to the changing styles of Himalayan climbing and fastened on his Alpine-style ascent of the South-east Ridge of the West Summit of Shivling with Jim Fotheringham in 1983.

"That was without a shadow of doubt the most enjoyable route I've ever done. It was very committing, a beautiful line, would have been a

sod to get back down if either of us had been injured, and was really good climbing, mostly Severe or mild VS with the odd HVS pitch and a crux of about E1 thrown in. We even did an unclimbed route as the descent, because we hadn't the faintest idea where the ordinary way down lay. The whole climb took us four days and was absolutely wonderful. I much prefer small trips and after this last Everest one I hope I don't go on any more big expeditions. Four's a good number . . ."

"What about the Everest North-east Ridge in 1982—was four the right number for that climb?"

"No—it was too small, and we were constantly aware of the fact. In consequence it was the most exacting experience we'd ever had. But we'd wanted to go on it as a small team, and though we were stretched to the limit, until the final tragedy it was one of the happiest expeditions I've ever been on. There was a total unity of mind on how we should do it, despite the stress. Even the present expedition on that route is probably a bit on the small side . . ."

The point seemed inevitably to have been reached where I had to ask him for his own feelings about reaching the summit of Everest. Was it, at the age of fifty, the summation of his climbing career? Did the dismissive epithets applied to the route by Sherpas and echoed by people who'd never been near the mountain demean it at all in his eyes?

"Not a summation, but an immensely satisfying experience, and I was surprised at how good the route was. I'd never have got to the top without oxygen . . ."

"Did your age tell against you?"

"Of course it did! On the top bit I was definitely going slower than Bjorn and Odd—and as for the Sherpas, they just left all of us standing. But that didn't matter—I felt in control and I was going steadily and got to the top."

"The route . . . ?"

"Oh, it's very good—from the South Col it just goes on and on. It's probably only Alpine *Assez Difficile*, but it's a terrific climb. And the Lhotse Face is pretty easy-angled, but it's a huge expanse of bare ice."

"Where do you go from here? In mountaineering, what's left for you to do?"

"I think the seven summits, but by nice routes—things like the Cassin Spur on McKinley, the South Face of Aconcagua, Carstensz Pyramid and so on. Then there are lots of unclimbed peaks at about the 7000m level in unknown areas—like Menlungtse, which we're going for next year, if we get permission."

"How do you keep fit?"

"I run, but not fanatically, two or three times a week, and I rock-climb a lot."

Formal interviews between friends being generally rather odd and strained affairs, I thought to end this one with a politely-coded capping question quite aside from mountaineering. "Do you," I wanted to know, "feel a moral obligation to use the celebrity you have attained for the public interest and good works?"

"Yes—lending your name to things is easy enough, but Lepra, which is the charity I'm chiefly involved with, demands more than that. I'd helped them once or twice before, and when they approached me it was something which seemed worthwhile doing, and you are putting something back—it is a duty you have to fulfil."

I half-felt like speculating on whether he felt the same about the BMC, of which he had been newly appointed a vice-president, but desisted, knowing that he is certain to take a conscientious interest in its operations. So I switched off the tape-recorder, put note-pad and pen away, we had a last cup of tea, I drove off across the straight road over the open fells to Keswick, and turned south for home. It is a good thing to be able to talk and think favourably of your fellow human beings. Generally, fame is the spur to bitching, iconoclasm, and the unrecognized's despite. But in the case of Bonington, he is so enthusiastic, so basically honest and direct, that you come away from his company thinking well of him, feeling refreshed and invigorated by the character of the man. He is obviously and outstandingly the public face, the ambassador, for our sport. I doubt if there are many who could better fulfil the role, or remain such enjoyable company on the rocks or amongst the hills.

4: THE NATURE OF THE BEAST

In the cult television series of the sixties "The Prisoner", Patrick McGoohan finally exploded the computer which controlled the colony by asking it the question "Why?" So much, then, for a justification and a rationale to fit mountaineering. If you seek explanations, then your antennae must be attuned to the implicit, to aspects of the sport's attraction, to individual motivation. There is no whole story, no complete answer.

But I didn't always feel this way, as can be seen from the first thing I ever wrote about climbing.

A Note on Commitment
Climbers' Club Journal 1968

WALKING INTO THE Padarn Lake bar in Llanberis on a Saturday night, and looking around amongst the motley congregation, any preconceived pop notion of the type of "hard man" would surely go wildly amiss in picking out this sport's most polished performers: it appears that boots and beards cluster most thickly round certain shrines—a bandy-legged, close-cropped, short and sherpa-smiling man circulates in the central area, poking callous fun at all who come his way: and close at hand, his chief member of crew, scoring with a quick inward laughter at any crass comment thrown to him: on the other edges, before delving into the brash wilderness before the bar (land of brag, boast and bombast), a long and stooping man smiles with a slow acceptance, aloof as the respect for his ability allows. Everywhere between them the crew's petty officer wanders in wild abandonment, a fierce flurry of gesture, joke and endless enthusiasm signifying the nativity of each new half-commitment, each idea as yet or ever unresolved.

There seems a new attitude abroad for which all that is "classical" or "romantic" in mountaineering leaves us a little unprepared; an overt competition and mistrust of commitment in personal relationships which seems to stem directly from the nature of the sport's development; an attitude even or perhaps especially noticeable amongst its top performers. We sense a paradox: the more complete one's qualities of commitment on rock, the less is one's degree of commitment in life. Even to those who know him best, Brown remains an enigma; Boysen is a man whom few know closely; Crew's motives are completely his own, unquestionable through being unknown.

What qualities have the new hard routes these men are doing? Is there a new isolation, a new degree of utter commitment to certain sets of crucial moves which climbs (with a very few exceptions) had hitherto really lacked? Perhaps the best way of explaining what the attitude may be is to analyse my personal reactions to three routes which seem to me to be classics of the new era of climbing. I could have chosen other routes: the continuous coolness required by a route like South Stack's Red Wall, for example, or the short, sharp aggression of a hard gritstone climb, but the three I'd like to use here are Vector, Nexus and Troach, each of which could be claimed with some justification to be a classic of the last ten years.

With Vector, the crux moves begin at a large and very comforting runner (an aspect shared by Nexus)—a security which once left behind is unrecapturable. The first move off the pinnacle is one which I certainly couldn't reverse, a body lean and an awkward kick round into balance, followed by a layaway move up on to two small footholds; then the next moves up are the crux. To someone of my height (note the subjective factor) a delicate step up with a very rounded handhold gets you to a layaway hold, step up again, a breathless change of hand, bridge, layback and you're on the Ochre slab. (Vector on a hot day, hands sweating profusely and feet agonized in the confines of PAs has brought me nearer to my technical limit than any other route I'd care to mention.)

Having once left the pinnacle, you feel a commitment so complete that your only choice is to carry it through, a complete simplicity (within the framework of its particular technical complexity) of action, direction and situation.

Nexus is easier, but even more committing; the full-weight thread at your feet seems to possess a peculiarly rapid quality of diminution as you move away from it. Rounded layaway for the left hand, tiny fingerhold for the right, and for the feet nothing but friction flat against the wall. A few feet above is a layback round a roof; tentatively you try the first half-move, winding up the mind, then it's made, a sudden coolness and control of physical action, at the roof a pause, thoughts of reversal quickly put aside; laybacking with a restful detachment, talking about your situation to the people beneath with an almost complete objectivity, resting in the layback before making the next move up the thin groove. With a strange ease you have assumed an air of calm. Once committed, responsibility realized, there is an inevitability, no conscious effort, about carrying the action through.

On these last two routes, an act of commitment to a complex technical problem is faced in a comparatively safe situation. Troach offers a similar, but slightly easier, set of moves in a completely different situation. You may not, to borrow Eliot's phrase, feel:

> A fear like birth and death,
> When we see birth and death alone,
> In a void, apart.

But you will certainly be aware that your protection offers very little security in the event of a fall: you feel isolated, a small fly on a very large wall. To commit yourself to the crux moves is a very lonely and responsible action (the appeal of which Bentham perhaps defines to a certain extent in the following note: "Constantly actual end of action on the part of every individual at the moment of action; his greatest happiness according to his view of it at the moment").

In a situation like that below the crux of Troach, you are faced with this definition of happiness perhaps in the closest proximity to its ultimate form: the end of action is in view, its attainment demands for a few moments the total absorption in the problem of your mental and physical faculties—a totality of commitment.

In life the situation is a rare chance . . .

If the last piece hit the aspiring, confident note of youth and certitude, then the next is looking back in gratitude for an introduction to the outdoors which was as good as anyone could ever hope to have had, and it remains—so far as any of one's own work can hold such a position—one of my favourites.

Trains, Cafes, Conversations
High 1982

AN HOUR OR two ago I was sitting on the back step of a new house in Heaton Mersey, wondering if it would rain, whether I would get out to Pex Hill for some climbing tomorrow night, and what these streets would be like a century from now. Gazing vacantly across a neatly-mown and boundaried square of lawn at the disused and trackless railway embankment beyond, it occurred to me that this same embankment must have carried the railway from Manchester's Central Station along which the ramblers' specials to Chinley, Miller's Dale and Matlock rattled most Sundays in a period over twenty years ago when I first took to going out into the Peak District at weekends.

This train of thought once invoked, the most vivid memories came flooding back: of eager crowds waiting on gas-lit platforms in the dusk of a wet Sunday, and the comforting, warm, misty-windowed atmosphere of a carriage full of people come in from the rain, their flannels and cotton anoraks steaming, light patches spreading across the darkened fabric as the conversation, the incessant, friendly conversation flowed. And then the streaming out from Central or Victoria Stations into the city night and the buses for home.

I'm not basing this railway idyll on the celebration of such delights of a pre-Beeching era as might appeal to the Steam Buff—the blackened architecture, hissing and polished pistons, gusts of smoke swirling across platform ends, the dusty smell of third-class carriages, names of long-forgotten stations and the like. I feel no particular sadness at their passing, but what has gone, along with all these, and what had a special meaning for lovers of the outdoors, is the subtle sense of community which this mode of transport brought about.

It wasn't, of course, confined to railways or transport. I wonder how many readers remember Ma Thomas's Hathersage cafe in the days of her prime? When Ma Thomas died, a year or so ago, there were no notices or obituaries in the outdoor press, yet her influence on my generation of Peak District climbers was momentous. We all of us have scintillating memories of this ferocious little South-Walian woman. Her tongue was razor-fine, her politics sturdily Labour, her wit was fast yet kind, and her food . . . Well, I dare not say, perhaps less out of respect for her memory than from a sort of residual fear of ever daring to complain to her face. I remember Martin Boysen did so once, about an egg afloat in a sea of grease littered with the flotsam of white and sodden chips. The Prussian hauteur of Martin in his youth was speedily discomfited by Ma's summary rejoinder that if her food was not good enough for him, his custom was certainly not required by her.

I could write a great deal on the subject of Ma Thomas—the way, for example, she ejected Major Something-or-other, canvassing for the Conservative candidate, from her premises one weekday, when I was playing truant from school to go climbing on Stanage: "If my 'usband was alive you wouldn't 'ave dared set foot in this 'ouse, and you buggers needn't think I'm any different from 'im." All this as she chased him down the hall with a frying pan. And there was her partisanship for Richard McHardy, thrusting her daughter upon him, or him upon her daughter, I can't remember which, in preference to another suitor who, in her frequently-voiced opinion, "hadn't got the brains of a rat." The slapstick and the bias aside, there was something more about the place. Obviously you went to Ma's to eat and drink, but not just for that. She was a catalyst to good conversation, would listen in when she was not too harassed, and drop a cutting phrase across what, to her, was an inflated argument, or a commonsensical anecdote into a sympathetic theme. It was her personality which drew us there each Sunday to sit around the big tables after a day on Stanage or Burbage in a second-family atmosphere, the talk fizzing along, tea-leaves floating idly and an hour to go before the train.

Things that have gone! Sitting here now, I wonder if I actually do remember, or only dream I remember, being in Bala Station in about 1960 and seeing a train pull out on its way to Trawsfynydd? I certainly remember the stations at Bala, Corwen, Llanberis, and Bethesda, and they are now all long gone. And with them the facility to transport the walking population of a city *en masse* to some particular outdoor venue. You might think that this was not much used—probably these days it would not be—but you would be wrong. One such excursion comes back to me with great clarity. Again, it would be 1960 and I was thirteen at the time.

There was a ramblers' special to the Dee Valley from Manchester Exchange. I remember city streets deserted in the early Sunday morning except for groups of ramblers resolutely converging on the

Pex Hill balletics—choreography by Martin Boysen

station. The train was packed, twelve or more to a compartment. We went to Bala and the fare for me was, I think, less than five shillings. At that time I used to go out walking with a group of people from Oldham who called themselves the Kindred Spirits—there must have been hundreds of such walking clubs in the Northern cities. We went to Bala, raced up the Milltir Gerrig road at a steady four miles per hour before trailing along the Berwyn ridge in Len Chadwick's wake, to end up running along the last two miles of road between Cynwyd and Corwen to catch the train on its way back.

But most of all I remember the journey home, the carriage packed full and every other one likewise and all of them ringing with animated conversations, between people white-haired and ruddy, young and fresh-faced, friends and strangers, all clad in regulation garb of old flannels tucked into socks, cotton or gaberdine anoraks, heavy skirts for the women, Timpson's boots. Once the details of the day's activity had been recounted, discussed, and consigned to the vaults of memory, the talk started. There was a great, brown, jovial fellow, eccentrically clad in leather shorts, called Lees Shaw and he held forth in grisly detail about industrial accidents and the need for legislation on safety at work as the stations—Llangollen, Ruabon, Wrexham and Chester —clacked past. You could take that as the type of these conversations —a drift from the particular to the general—the telling of a tale and then its taking apart, its being held up to all sorts of differing viewpoints, from that of a jejune thirteen-year-old with no life-experience whatsoever to those of fifty or sixty-year-olds who had spent their lives working in cotton mills, taking WEA classes in the evenings, and walking at weekends and holidays. The tone was universally helpful, amiable, interested, courteous. In that train on that day there was a mood of light-heartedness, friendship, exultation, attentive consideration and community such as it is one of the greatest joys of humanity to achieve. And like the stations to which we were bound that day, it seems largely to have gone. We are no longer entrained together in humour, good fellowship, and joint purpose. Our television age and newspeak have undermined the capacity to talk. We no longer have the presiding spirit of a Ma Thomas in our cafes. Our clubs are not the same. The barrackers and the comics, the apprentices, the orators, the wise men and singers of songs have all been swept before the grey tide of personal, individual ambition at all cost, battered on the rocks of cynicism, or frozen out by the wintry sneer. We go out in our cars and strict couples, enjoined to secrecy, to tick the lists and climb the status ladders and the sense of community is gone.

Or has it? Have I grown older and gone beyond and forgotten, lost touch with all the good of it, or have my roots truly gone? I cannot see them, but perhaps I cannot see them for looking. There are still times, on the outcrops, say—perhaps on Pex Hill tomorrow if it stays fine—when an easy camaraderie will exist. But the times are rarer, surely, now? We are all intent on self-realization rather than the sharing and comparing and learning from the wider experience. Our new modes of education from the earliest age accent it thus. I cannot but think that in all this the last two decades have wrought another of those subtle and grievous losses in which our rich and progressive age abounds. And I cannot but wish I was wrong.

History is an odd concept, especially considered in relation to the mountains. What scale of time are we talking about—geological time? Human time? The last syllable of recorded time? The available perspectives bring out a wonderful sense of pretentiousness and futility alongside the undoubted skill and occasional nobility of man's activities in this sphere.

Ogwen Historical
Introduction to the Climbers' Club Guide to Ogwen 1982

It has always been the custom to let fall a little gentle scorn upon Ogwen, to suggest mildly that it is perhaps not much of a place to detain for long the ambitious expert, or satisfy a gourmet's appetite. The Ancients had a phrase which they thought apposite: "playing for knuckle-bones with Tryfan before tossing for crowns with Lliwedd." But history has the laugh on them, and the weary pilgrims who venture on to Lliwedd's dreary wastes are few these days, whilst Ogwen yearly revels in the pageantry of an ever-increasing popularity. Devotees throng, whilst the zeal of converts makes itself known on its infinite variety of cliffs. The range and contrast, accessibility, wealth, and sporadic excellence of its climbing seem by now to have put Ogwen beyond the grasp of mere fashion. So let us look back over its history, and see whether it ever has been that as which it has long been represented—a poor relation of Welsh climbing, to be visited of necessity rather than relished as an individual joy.

There is not much reliance to be placed on climbing history, especially early history. It is all dependent on report, and report must needs have its reasons, be they boasting or dismissing, probing, meticulously recording, or plucking from the flux of time. When we read, in Bingley's *Tour*, that at the end of the eighteenth century "a female of an adjoining parish" was renowned as having frequently made the jump from Adam to Eve, should we not wonder whether, similarly, many obvious mountain features were explored, ascended, and enjoyed by a curious native populace long years before bourgeois élitism seized upon the route description and its attendant pomp as yet another noisy means to self-glorification and the annexation of territory? The ascent, for example, of Lliwedd's Slanting Gully by miners in search of copper-lodes or Arthur's gold, 30 years before the

Abraham brothers' ascent, is the most wonderful demotic joke against all who take these seigneurial claims too seriously. So let us draw a veil over early history—say that early ascents of obvious features may have been made by shepherds, botanists, playful boys, Neolithic builders of cairns, inquisitive miners, reticent men, or even our forefather mountaineers—and proceed to cast our eye over the written record of climbing achievement.

How does it fit in with the rhetoric of an established view that the great leaps forward in Welsh climbing have taken place on Lliwedd, Clogwyn Du'r Arddu, or the Three Cliffs of Llanberis? The record darkly shapes itself through the 1890s in a succession of singular, dripping ascents of moss-grown and scree-filled clefts. The gully epoch it was later termed, in Geoffrey Young's *Mountain Craft*. On this succulent and strenuous diet was reared the first generation of specialist rock-men—Archer Thomson, Hughes, Reade, Puttrell, the Abraham brothers, Owen Glynne Jones. Look through the First Ascents List, and see the preponderance of gullies and chimneys climbed at this time—some of them severe struggles even for the present-day climber. It is hard to analyse in positive terms the attraction these unutterable places held for the early men, but it was strong, almost exclusive. The very few open routes on ribs and buttresses—Pinnacle Rib and Grey Rib by Archer Thomson, Rose's Ordinary Route on the Idwal Slabs —were in a tiny minority before Owen Glynne Jones's splendid series of climbs at Easter 1899. Hanging Garden Gully was done first, and perhaps its herbage held the cure. The Milestone Ordinary Route and Tryfan's North Buttress came next, breathing space before the "unjustifiable severity" of the Terrace Wall Variant shocked its ascensionists into silence and the decision that it should never be recorded. Of course, it was soon surpassed. Jones's seconds on the route, George and Ashley Abraham, made their own climb on Glyder Fach's Hawk's Nest Buttress, and followed it up with manful exertions on the Monolith Crack. The gully confines were left behind. Fresh teams of climbers took over from the earliest pioneers. Steeple and Barlow, Buckle and Doughty, made their generous contributions, as did the local man H. O. Jones. Ward and Gibson traced their great Direct Route up Glyder Fach's East Buttress. In its ascent was included a return to the foot of Gibson's eponymous chimney, to look at it on a rope. It turned out to be no chimney at all, but for all that it was led, to produce the hardest pitch of its day on Welsh rock. After this a fatal accident gained the cliff a wholly unwarranted reputation for unreliable rock, and it appears to have fallen from favour.

Ogwen, with its plethora of small and convenient cliffs such as the Milestone Buttress, the Gribin Facet and Bochlwyd Buttress, occupied a special niche in the designings of climbers in the years before the Great War, and perhaps even beyond that. Outcrop climbing enjoyed rising favour in the Peak, Northumberland, and Cheshire. The ideal

Paul Williams on the Holly Tree Wall
(photo: Steve Ashton)

transition from outcrops to the major mountain cliffs of Britain lay through these enlarged outcrops or scaled-down mountain crags. A new generation took note. Harold Porter, the arboreal exponent, added Cheek Climb to the Terrace Wall whilst casually soloing on Tryfan. John Laycock and Siegfried Herford explored the Gribin, attacked the Square Chimney of Glyder Fach, and went on to greater things.

And then the War came, and climbing passed into the hands of capable women, invalids, superannuated soldiers and academics. Mrs Daniells led Ivor Richards, the literary critic, up Hope, the best of the Slabs' climbs. David Pye completed Richards's education in the virtues by introducing him to Faith and Charity. All the time Richards's eye lay on the barrier above. A holly tree grew in its centre, offering the promise of safe anchorage, the insurance of retreat, if only it could be reached. In May, 1918, C. F. Holland, Dorothy Pilley, and Richards himself embarked on the attempt. They started "by means of a complicated and risky ladder, improvised with an ice-axe held aloft at arm's length by a second, whose position was so unsafe that he had to be secured with a rope." Late in the day the party admitted the holly tree to the circle of human acquaintance for the first time: "Here hope was very nearly abandoned, as neither of the two leaders could climb the crack above the tree, while the vertical and holdless walls on either side were impossible without the aid of methods of suction as yet undiscovered . . ."

Holland, however, descended a little, and then, in nailed boots, wandered out to an exposed ledge on the open wall: "Above this, progress seemed uncertain, but after many searchings of heart the doubtful step was taken. Wisdom was justified of her children in that excellent holds above led to a rocky bay, whence the top of the wall was reached by less intensive climbing."

The following day the same party climbed the Oblique Buttress of Glyder Fach. Neither climb marked a technical advance, but they were nonetheless substantial offerings; the Holly Tree Wall in particular, as it made possible what was rapidly recognized as one of the great Welsh itineraries—a route on the Slabs, the Wall, the Groove Above and one of the Glyder Fawr climbs.

The seven or eight years after the Great War saw little activity in the Ogwen region. Its pre-war adherents were for the most part crippled or dead in that carnage, and the attention of the few survivors was directed elsewhere. After the opening of the Climbers' Club Hut at Helyg in 1925, the pace quickened. A group of young climbers from Cambridge, inspired by Geoffrey Young, made it their base. Ivan Waller, with Stewart Palmer, climbed the elegant Belle Vue Bastion with a wind-up gramophone playing ragtime on the terrace above. Ted Hicks added Piton Route and Heather Wall. Then a quiet, awkward youth from Liverpool, Colin Kirkus, already esteemed a genius on his native outcrop of Helsby, appeared. In 1929, Hicks's Cambrige party took him with them up to Glyder Fach, where he espied a steep, right-angled groove capped by an overhanging crack. He begged a top-rope, then descended to make the lead of Lot's Groove. On the following day he and Hicks went to Tryfan's Terrace Wall, and he climbed the fearsome little Central Route, which no one could follow. Hicks, stimulated by these performances, added Ash Tree Wall on the East Wall of the Slabs, Wall Climb to Bochlwyd, and the exquisitely delicate Rowan Tree Slabs before returning to the autumn term in Cambridge. Welsh climbing was once more surging ahead.

The years 1927–1932 were unquestionably ones of considerable achievement in Wales. They were the years of the Clogwyn Du'r Arddu climbs, of Kirkus's two routes on the Nose of Dinas Mot and his admirable slab climbs in Cwm Silyn. There is, however, a remarkable aspect of this period to be considered in relation to the Ogwen district. The point is, that the climbs for which we remember this era, the classic VS's listed above, were not essentially any harder than the finest technical achievements of twenty years before—Gibson's Chimney, say, or Herford's Crack on the Gribin. In the Ogwen area, though, a process was going on which was more than consolidation, albeit in more impressive situations, of previous advances in technique. Climbs like Kirkus's Central Route, Hicks's Rowan Tree Slabs, and Edwards's Final Flake, marked a very distinct leap forward in standard, a realization of top outcrop standards in a mountain environment. Yet all of them were outdistanced by an extraordinary climb in 1930, one of those rare moments when a climber goes far beyond the technical limits of his time to mark out a point which will not be regained for years. At Easter 1930, Jack Longland led the Javelin Blade, a thin, steep, and committing groove which remains beyond doubt the hardest pre-war rock-climb on a British mountain cliff. It was not recognized as such for years. Longland himself seems not to have regarded it as particularly special:

"Quite frankly, I'd lost the way. I'd come to the famous thread belay at the end of the first pitch of the normal route, and I didn't know that the route ought to go right. I was a pole-vaulter, which I think gives you pretty strong fingers, and I remember the pull-out on to the actual blade of the Javelin was very strenuous, though not dangerous—I had a belay about 40 feet below me."

For all the unregarding modesty of the above, nothing climbed by Kirkus or Edwards was to approach the difficulty of this lead, and only after the next war was it to be outshone by a similarly startling and meteoric flight through the climbing firmament. So to the Edwards years. John Menlove Edwards had been introduced to Helyg and to climbing in 1930 by his elder brother Stephen, a Cambridge undergraduate. After matriculating at Liverpool University, he set about Helsby with gusto, and in the winter of 1930 opened up his Welsh campaign. Never have the damp and shrinking intimacies of cliffs been treated with such scant regard for their privacy as by this deeply-introverted, powerful, and ultimately tragic figure. He could, and did, create climbs of a clean and healthy character—the Sub-Cneifion Rib, the East Wall Girdle, Grey Slab, or Procrastination Cracks—but it is not for them so much that we remember him. It is not the place of a brief introduction to expound at length on character, but in Edwards's case the events of his life obviously turned him to the search for a correlative to his states of mind. The fissile, the dank, the rotten, and the vegetatious drew him when his life seemed thus. When touched by love and happiness, his climbs too became lighter, more delicate, more airy. Compare the 1933 routes with those of 1936. The former brought into climbing's purview the massive moulderings of Clogwyn y Geifr; the latter were notes and addenda to the staunch old text of Tryfan. Edwards's two guidebooks, to Cwm Idwal (1936) and to Tryfan (1937), were a service to climbing on which we still lean heavily today. They were works of commendable clarity, enormous charm, and minimal self-assertion, and they were in use for over twenty years. As much, perhaps, as any other single factor they established a popularity and an individual character for the Ogwen district.

Another war intervened. For six years the young men of the universities, the adventurers, the scarcely-reined-in freebooters, did not need to satisfy their craving for excitement through the medium of rock. The mountains were commandeered by the Army, and soldiers were trained on them to the pitch of fitness required for battle. This time, the techniques of modern warfare culled their victims from a wider spectrum of the population. More of the young men came back. Not surprisingly, it was a soldier, just after the cessation of hostilities, who made the next advance. About Chris Preston we know virtually nothing. Some say he was the archetypal wartime fighting man, peacetime misfit. Be that as it may, there is the fact of his two climbs in Cwm Idwal. One of them, Advocate's Wall on the right wall of the Devil's Kitchen, is a distinctly good VS, one of the standard courses of Welsh rock. The other, like Longland's route of fifteen years before, was in the order of a visionary leap forward. Suicide Wall Original Route is nowadays graded E2 5c, and it is not a soft touch at that grade. In 1945, without runners, climbed in gym-shoes, utterly serious and far harder than anything else in the country, it was an astonishing lead. It apparently had only two further ascents in the next fourteen years.

During the late forties and the fifties climbing in Ogwen reached the nadir of its reputation. Apart from John Lawton's Suicide Groove in 1948, probably as hard a lead as the later and much more celebrated Cenotaph Corner, nothing of note was added for years. It was dismissed as a place for beginners and wet days; the real thing lay

Opposite: Rusty Baillie on Suicide Wall Original Route (photo: John Cleare)

elsewhere. But some of the best routes remained to be found, as Ron James discovered in 1959, with Grey Arete and Devil's Nordwand. The leading climbers of the early sixties accorded it a certain amount of notice. Crew and Ingle climbed a second line on Suicide Wall, slightly easier than the original but equally good. Martin Boysen opened his account with the area in a typically esoteric and excellent climb on Gallt yr Ogof, Black Maria. Tom Herley climbed the superb Devil's Bastion, up the right arete of the Devil's Staircase, to point up the continuing value of these arcane cliffs; and Ray Evans proved that even the Gribin could provide worthwhile climbing, with his powerful and difficult Synapse. All these were admirably quixotic strokes by climbers whose main visions were to be realized elsewhere.

At the end of the sixties Boysen teamed up with Dave Alcock to add a series of routes which directed attention to major areas of unclimbed rock. They ascended The Crack and Hebenwi on Clogwyn Du, and Hades, next to Advocate's Wall. Two years later they were back, to add three routes to Suicide Wall. The style in which these were done was very much in the lackadaisical, straight-off-the-top-and-bolster-up-your-confidence-here-and-there-if-need-be style of the sixties, as opposed to a more stringent later ethos, but they were nonetheless difficult and pioneering efforts which really broke down a mental barrier for later generations, and put over the suggestion that Suicide Wall might well be climbable almost anywhere, given a sufficient degree of fitness and finesse. So it proved in the seventies, when this lovely wall, so understated in its features, became laced with an intricate pattern of routes.

In the last few years Ogwen has once more become recognized as an area marvellously rich in every style and grade of climbing. The stars of the moment no longer scorn its homeliness and familiarity, but search out its steeper facets to work out intricacies of their own. Livesey, Littlejohn, Fawcett, Redhead have all exercised their inventiveness here with pleasing results.

It is sad to end this chronicle of climbing achievements with a distasteful episode, but it is necessary to do so. In 1979 Martin Boysen discovered a couple of worthy little routes on the Central Block of the Milestone Buttress. One of them climbed the thin crack straight up the wall above a flourishing oak tree. It was a hard climb, and a good one, and he enthused about it to a few friends, including the guidebook author, but made no attempt to write up a description. Certain pundits have taken the view that this dilatoriness on Boysen's part was inexcusable, and a contributory factor to what follows, but this is sophistry.

At the beginning of April 1980 two young climbers spotted the line Boysen had climbed, and decided to "improve" it by cutting down the tree at its foot. They took a saw up to the crag and did so, thus adding a few feet to the climb. Then, laughably, they failed to get up it. They enlisted another leader, John Redhead (who had not known of their original action), who succeeded and saw fit to give it a crudely humorous name. It was soon discovered on the one hand that Boysen had previously climbed the route, and on the other that the tree had been cut down. On the one side, fury; on the other, a closing of ranks. The younger generation of active Welsh climbers, rather than disown a shabby action of the grossest stupidity, appeared to condone it and espouse its rationale by accepting, and still continuing to accept, the Redhead version and name as a significant discovery, and by protecting the identity of the lumberjacks. This guide makes the Climbers' Club view of the incident very obvious—it is one of appalled outrage at such irresponsibility. No one doubts the difficulty of the boulder-problem where the tree once stood, but the route and name in this guide are unequivocally Boysen's, and the action of the later vandals should be universally condemned and deplored. What would Archer Thomson, the Abrahams, Ivor Richards, Kirkus, Edwards, have thought on hearing of the fate of what, as a patient sapling, they must all once have known?

Perhaps the trees will grow again on these cliffs, though I cannot think when it will happen, as yearly the paths and routes grow the more bare. Yet a man's life is not so long as that of a tree. What will a later generation think of the deeds of this generation, as they stand, at some future date, by Ogwen or at the end of Llyn Idwal? As they stand there amongst a ghostly company; the men who climbed upon these rocks will have walked by that place minutes, days, weeks, or decades ago. A few individual actions stand out; certain trends can be discerned; the rest merge into silence and oblivion. Up on Glyder Fawr the last light lingers and fades. Shadows deepen on Clogwyn y Geifr. Lake water laps on the boulders, the Slabs gleam a little in the dusk; and stony streams chatter across the cwm as the grey rock gathers itself into night.

The Milestone Buttress

Lindsay Rogers, now of the League Against Cruel Sports, once teased me that I should use my monthly column in High *to a useful purpose for a change. I didn't need much urging on the subject he proposed—one which truly appals me, and the existence of which is inexcusable in a supposedly civilized country. As so often, Blake says it best:*

> *Each outcry of the hunted hare*
> *A fibre from the brain does tear.*

I have never yet heard a cogent argument in support of the so-called sport of hunting, and do not believe one exists. Now read on . . .

Country Matters
High 1984

THE FURIOUS YAPPING of dogs could be heard a mile away up the valley that afternoon. Curious, I set off to see what was going on. By the time I got there the badger had simply given up and the three sheepdogs were ripping and tearing away at it with unopposed manic savagery. The two men turned their heads and caught my eye, lips drawn back a little over their teeth and waiting for me to speak, not turning to face me. Then the taller one called off his dog: "I'll be seeing you, John," he said to the other, and nodded curtly to me as he got into his Land Rover and drove away.

John I knew quite well. At busy periods I'd given him a hand from time to time with work on his farm. He was a short, broad man of early middle-age, hospitable and I think slightly simple, his parents having been first cousins. He'd thrown his dogs into the back of the van by now and we began talking: "They're buggers, these badgers, you know. They bring TB into my herd, and they take eggs." The conversation continued uneasily for a few minutes before it was a case of, "Well, I must be getting on now," and he drove off in the direction of the farm.

I walked over to the fence. The old badger was still warm, his black-and-silver mask gouged and streaked with blood. He lay down the bank, slumped on to one shoulder. The wire snare in which he was trapped had virtually severed the tendon of his back leg. To my knowledge, from the moment I first became aware of the dogs, the baiting of him must have lasted an hour at least.

I hope that no reader of this magazine is in any doubt as to my abhorrence of what I saw in that isolated Welsh valley that afternoon. How relevant they think it, on the other hand, to raise this topic in a magazine devoted to outdoor recreation is a different matter. That two men could have taken pleasure in looking on at the savage death of a snared animal is an unpleasant fact to contemplate, but how does it affect this congregation of readers? Let me sketch out a case for its doing so. Badgers, otters, deer, foxes and hares have all given me a great deal of pleasure over many years through observing them in the natural environment. I would imagine that to very many people the sighting of them is a strong component part of the pleasure to be derived from going into the countryside, and that such sightings figure large amongst pleasurable memories of days out on the hills in this country. In fact, I would claim that seeing any of these animals can be as exciting an experience as, say, leading a hard rock-climb. There is the absolute concentration and alertness required, the bodily thrill of complete stillness, the aesthetic appreciation of watching a truly wild animal in its natural habitat.

The list above, as you will probably have noticed, is a fixed one, for each of the animals on it is regularly hunted by participants in blood

Stag-hunting in Devon—a country "sport" (photo: League Against Cruel Sports)

sports. Two of the species, badgers and otters, are now protected by law. Yet badger-baiting is widespread, particularly in the North of England, and badgers are also frequently killed, or have their setts blocked up, by terriermen who work with fox-hunts. Prosecutions, however, are seldom brought against these men because legislation is ineffectual, with laughably small penalties even in the unlikely event of convictions. In the case of otters, which are an endangered species, since the otter gained statutory protection the packs of former otter-hounds have turned to hunting mink. Unfortunately, the same rivers are hunted for mink as were formerly hunted for otters and this results in otters being killed at times by the hunts, the hounds not having learnt to differentiate, or respect the statutes. There is no record of actions having been brought in cases like these.

So much, then, for the advantages afforded to the badger and the otter by statutory protection. What of the other three species? The hunting of deer, fox and hare, using dogs, is at present quite legal in this country. It's not possible to distinguish between degrees of barbarism inherent in these pursuits, but the most overtly shocking seems to me to be stag-hunting. Over 400 stags a year are killed by the various West Country hunts. I quote from an account of a stag-hunt by *News of the World* journalist Maureen Lawless (6.3.83). After a six-hour chase, the stag has been brought to bay in a wood, "surrounded by about 40 hounds snapping at his heels." Ms Lawless continues thus: "He was exhausted, foaming at the mouth. There was nowhere else he could run. Bewildered, terrified, defenceless, he turned from side to side."

All this time, remember, the pack of hounds is frenziedly ripping at his legs, flanks, and belly: "He rolled his eyes at the followers who stood around as a huntsman loaded a shotgun. They were laughing and cheering as the huntsman shot him through the heart. He fell down into the pack."

It should be remembered that under the Wildlife and Countryside Act of 1981 it is an offence to kill a deer with a shotgun, except on land where crops are being damaged, and then it must only be done by authorized persons. So why are no charges brought against hunts in cases like this, which are commonplace? What connections exist between the hunt and the local Bench? And what is the rationale for the "sport"? The hunts, in their charity, claim they kill the old, injured, and poor animals. The stag in Maureen Lawless's account was a prime specimen. The joint master of Tiverton Staghounds, when asked his reasons for hunting, replied, "People should be allowed to do as they wish." Another man, who proffered his unsolicited opinion to me on the topic, stated with no trace of irony that whilst he didn't personally go hunting, "we should live and let live". Exactly!

Stag-hunting accounts for about 400 animals a year. Fox-hunting kills 30,000 and the minute you say a word against it up goes the cry from the shires that it must go on because the fox is a pest, and hunting is the most effective and humane form of control. The fox is probably one of those animals whose usefulness outweighs his occasional predations against lambs and poultry—and these are both, according to all authoritative research, *very* occasional. As to hunting being an effective form of pest control, I wonder that the fox-hunting fraternity hasn't passed on this argument to those gentlemen who find pleasure in shooting grouse and pheasant, for the two activities have one interesting thing in common—they both to some extent rear the creatures which they hunt. The joint master of the Beaufort Hunt, Major Gerald Gundry, reasons it out thus: "By building artificial earths on private land where the public cannot get at them, we do the foxes a favour. They can live at peace during the close season [and] it gives us the advantage of being able to keep the whole of our hunting country correctly stocked . . ."

Pest control? Apart from this unusually convoluted logic, the manner in which the hunts treat the animals is at times disturbingly sadistic. Two authenticated examples are as follows. I mentioned hunts' terriermen above. One practice which is quite widespread is for the terrierman to have a captive fox on which he sets his terriers from time to time to train the young ones and to keep the older ones "sharp". One such fox was called Tag, and was kept for eight years by a terrierman for the Derwent Hunt in Yorkshire. When the animal was finally freed by hunt saboteurs, it was skeletal, blind, and could only crawl on grotesquely twisted and broken legs. The man's comment was that "I keep four terriers and they've played with it, but the fox enjoyed it . . .". The other practice is of "bagged" foxes. This is usually undertaken for the benefit of visiting dignitaries, or to revive the interest of flagging subscribers who haven't witnessed a kill for some time. What happens is that a fox is captured in another area the night before a hunt, and kept in a bag. Next day it is taken out, stinking of its own excrement and therefore easier for the hounds to scent. Its paws are slit and it is set down in strange territory—foxes are confirmedly territorial by habit, so they are completely disoriented by this. One former hunt servant has it that "I've never seen a bagged fox survive longer than twenty minutes", and testifies that this happened on a day when Prince Charles rode with the Derwent Hunt some years ago—a fact of which Charles was, of course, unaware.

A couple more anecdotes should help to establish the character and influence of the hunt participants. At a meet of the Badsworth Hunt recently, four hunt saboteurs who were running along the road spraying the hedges with *Anti-mate* were arrested for obstructing the highway, an offence of which they were later convicted. Behind them, on the same road, blocking all traffic, 16 couple of hounds and 70 riders proceeded unmolested. One Pakistani member of the Huddersfield Hunt Saboteurs is, every time he goes out, subjected by hunt members to the most violent racial abuse and assaults: "You black bastard, fuck off back to Karachi . . ." and so on.

I've left hare-coursing to the last in this sad catalogue, not just because the hare is one of the most harmless and delightful of our wild animals, not just because it is a declining species, nor because one of the most entrancing things I have ever seen in the outdoors was a boxing match between a hare and a lamb, but because it is the one sport which cannot offer in its own defence even the most specious justification on the grounds of necessity. The hare is becoming more and more rare, yet each year up to a thousand are killed in *organized* coursing events. In November 1975 a bill to ban hare-coursing was introduced into the House of Commons and received a majority of 117. The House of Lords threw it out. In 1981 efforts were made to amend the Wildlife and Countryside Bill to provide for the abolition of hare-coursing. The Government firmly resisted them. In 1984, at the

Waterloo Cup, the premier British coursing event, one man was killed in a brawl between rival groups of supporters, and an anti-coursing demonstrator sustained serious brain damage after a blow from a shooting stick—an incident in connection with which the secretary of the Suffolk Coursing Club faces criminal charges. In the words of the Liverpool area secretary of the Hunt Saboteurs, "There has been an appalling escalation of violence against anti-blood-sports demonstrators over recent years."

According to the findings of an opinion poll conducted for the League Against Cruel Sports by Market Research Ltd, 65 per cent of the population disapprove of fox-hunting, 80 per cent disapprove of hare-coursing, and 81 per cent of stag-hunting. Yet the Government still allows hunting across, for example, Forestry Commission land, and the National Trust allows hunting across its land—a fact of which many of its membership are probably unaware and on which there has been no ballot.

On a subject like this it is very easy to get bogged down in data, statistics, conflicting opinions and reports, but two points seem to me to be central. Firstly, the conservation of our native fauna is every bit as important as any other area of conservation, yet it is probably the one which is most neglected and is certainly the least firmly fixed in the consciousness of the outdoor movement. Secondly, as a philosophical point, to kill for pleasure entails a diminution of humanity. That seems to me unarguable. To thrill at the death agony of a sentient creature involves the suspension of compassion, pity, mercy—all our finest human qualities.

On television recently, I have heard two astonishing statements. One was from a journalist being interviewed about blood sports, of which he was in favour: "Wild animals don't feel pain," he opined. The other was made by a well known footballer, in the course of a programme which showed a hare hunted down and killed by a beagle pack. To justify the death, he said that "hares don't die in their sleep, you know!" and then went on to add that the dogs "give hares the benefit of the exercise." They are comments which need no further comment from me.

On these so-called "sports" in general, for God's sake let us, in the outdoor movement, support all efforts to bring down the barriers of law against them. Masquerade under whatever guise they will, they are no more than the vicious indulgence of psychopathic tendency, and it is a very small step from this disregard for the sanctity of all life and the feelings of living creatures to that which could fashion lampshades from the skins of Jews.

(For assistance in researching this article, I am indebted to Lindsay Rogers of The Hunt Saboteurs, and also to The League Against Cruel Sports, 83 Union Street, London SE1 1SG. It pleases me as well to point out how responsible the attitude of the popular press, particularly the *Daily Mirror* and the *News of the World*, has been towards the subject over recent years.)

The mystical companionship-of-the-rope idealism with which climbing abounds sometimes gives me a slight feeling of unease. It's rather like the women's-magazine-type-syrup about babies, which serves to mask the fact that childbirth is a painful, messy and protracted business. Once, in a particularly sardonic mood, I decided to reveal some of the truth about climbing partnerships.

Pincushion and Silly Arete, Tremadog

Partners
High 1984

UNLESS YOU OPT for soloing, one of the fortunate or unfortunate —depending on the generosity or otherwise of your feelings about the human race—aspects of climbing is that it is an activity to be closely shared with another person. Because of the kind of experiences you undergo together, because of the responsibility for each other's safety which is involved, because of the intimacy and sometimes secrecy of the pact, these liaisons often seem to achieve a degree of intensity not exceeded by those of any other sport. Maybe I'm wrong. Maybe doubles players in tennis, for example, froth and inveigh against each other with equal savagery or interlock with similar success as do the combatants in climbing partnerships. But I doubt it.

I speak here as an observer from the sidelines of the great efforts of teamwork in climbing history, and as one who throughout his climbing career has enjoyed a thorough promiscuity in his choice of people with whom to climb. I wouldn't choose to elevate the latter to any higher ethical plane, but the point is worth making that the more people you climb with, the fewer your opportunities to cheat, because fresh acquaintance is usually more observant, interested and judgemental than those who are thoroughly inured to every strategic deceit and its later presentation in which the climber might indulge. To float a new theory of climbing history—albeit an extremely sardonic view—it is quite possible that the most rigorously ethical performers were those who were least likely to establish the cover of a regular partnership for their activities. *Folie à deux* needs a certain commitment to the twosome to get established. Without it, truth and reason stand a better chance of prevailing.

Flippancy aside, I've often wondered what it is that makes for a successful relationship between climbers. It's certainly not equal ability, I'm sure. Whenever that's been present, the team's usually performed well for a time and then split up under conditions of some acridity. At other times the obvious partnerships simply haven't come about. Why, for example, did Colin Kirkus and Menlove Edwards not climb together more often? They were both based in Liverpool, they got on very well together, were often staying at Helyg at the same time and on occasions without other partners. Yet they seemed to avoid each other when it came to climbing, and only joined forces in Wales on three widely separated occasions, two of them at the beginning of the thirties to climb Chimney Route on Cloggy and Neb's Crawl on Dinas y Gromlech, and once, poignantly, at Easter 1940, when at the very end of an era the two men who were its most profound innovators wandered together up Hope, the Holly Tree Wall, and the Cneifion Arete.

There's a very simple reason, of course, why equal ability doesn't often work as the basis for a climbing relationship. Climbers are very selfish people—they either want to hog the lead or rest as perpetual seconds. This can lead to workable arrangements along the lines of Jack Sprat and his wife. It can also lead to aggravation. If you, as a moderately ambitious climber, choose as partner a lead-hogger, the tensions will rise, particularly if you suspect that he might be a better climber than you are. This is a likely scenario: you set off to do, say, Winking Crack on Gogarth, and as you're gearing up on top of the descent gully, you toss a coin to decide who leads the top—which is the best—pitch. Heads, and it's you. So you rack your gear accordingly and down you go. He's away first, tight-lipped, and has uncoiled the ropes at the bottom before you arrive. Off he goes up the first pitch, storming up it in a bad temper, lashing himself to the belay in compressed fury, taking in the rope hard and jerkily so it continually twitches in your face, pulls you off balance, peremptorily orders movement and destroys rhythm. You arrive shaking on the small stance and, unaccommodatingly, he doesn't budge an inch but hisses at you to for Christ's sake breathe softly lest you, he, and the belay all fall down to the sea. He also produces a vast number of unfathomable heavy gadgets to further burden you, intimates but does not divulge prior knowledge of their usage on this pitch, pays out ten feet of slack and commands you to get on with it. Then he leans back to watch.

You stitch together a few frayed nerve-ends and set to. Half a move elicits five more feet of slack. You protest, and draw forth an abstracted apology as he takes six inches grudgingly back in. Since it's the first few feet of the pitch which matter, if they're at all difficult then you're obviously in for a hard time, and there's no way, in a situation like this, that you can opt for the total abrogation of responsibility entailed by falling off. So you just have to get down steadfastly to some work on it. Since you're not just unsupported, but are being actively willed into failure it is imperative to get away from his sphere of influence as quickly as possible. On a pitch like the top one of Winking Crack, this will probably extend to a point fifteen or twenty feet up, and above the difficult layback moves which start it, by which time a couple of runners will have intervened between you. But his influence will re-establish itself less strongly at intervals all the way to the top, only to be overruled by good holds, good runners, or the advent against all the odds of rhythm into your climbing. All this can be classified generically as the problem of the psychic crux, and the best safeguard against it is either to become, or choose as partner, a congenital second.

Most people, at some stage in their climbing life, have been congenital seconds and so can appreciate the peculiar difficulties presented to those who seek that role. Usually these can be moderated by an unbecoming degree of self-abasement—Ken Wilson is the great exponent of this technique—to ensure that the leader looks after you, but there are always occasions when you can be caught out, because there are routes in existence which are undoubtedly harder to second than to lead. Carnivore or the Atomic Finger Flake are good examples. The moment on Carnivore's first pitch when I unclipped from the peg 50 feet up at the top of the pillar, looked across at Martin Boysen a horizontal and runnerless 90 feet away from me, and knew that I had either to begin the descending crux traverse or risk the wrath of that inveterate lead-hogging god, is indelibly printed on my memory and belongs amongst my personal half-dozen times of greatest terror. This, mind you, was in the sixties, and I hadn't climbed enough with Ken Wilson at that time fully to appreciate the virtues and rewards of grovelling. What I should have done, and what my youthful modesty and idealism debarred me from, was to stand at the bottom assiduously managing the rope to cater for Martin's every need, and all the while keeping up an extravagant commentary, stopping just short of the suspicion of mockery, on how brilliantly he was climbing, interspersed with the inevitable trade-off of requests for runners here and there, long dangling slings, little detours to ensure additional safeguards, etc, etc. In other words, the technique is one of self-interested flattery raised to the province of an art-form.

If you could postulate the ideal workable climbing relationship, it would be along these lines. At the centre you have shared ambitions, but these are approached from different directions. The inveterate lead-hogger requires a belaying machine, whilst the congenital second's need is for a top-roping instrument capable also of placing many runners to safeguard his dignity, involve him in the task, and if necessary to supplement the natural quota of holds. So the symbiotic relationship evolves. You can throw in a few other qualities for good measure. The lead-hogger must be competent enough to get up the routes, for example, because congenital seconds are of all people the most intolerant of failure. And the congenital second must be possessed of a thorough efficiency in ropework and certain physical attributes. He is best designed at around six feet tall and weighing something over twelve stone, to act as suitable counterweight in the

"That inveterate, lead-hogging god"
Martin Boysen

event of flying activities. I know a few of these, but because of the stigma they would face in coming out, and for the obvious reason that they're bigger than me, I am very unwilling to name names. A final point on characteristics: if they come much heavier than twelve stone, then they must also be very competent at getting up the routes, lead-hogging whippets being generally incapable of winching up elephants.

Having read this far, you may well be sufficient of a misanthropist to conclude, along with me, that multi-pitch routes on mountain crags, which is where these relationships come into play most markedly, are just not worth the effort, and that the best form of climbing is to be found on gritstone, where you can be liberated from all the psychological compromises and wander along to solo, top-rope, or belay the occasional hero as you will. Or to go even further, perhaps it proves that Pex Hill, where ropes are distinctly out of order, is, as has long been thought, the best crag in the world. After all, the rope is as much a symbol of bondage as one of connection, so cast it off and be free.

There are moments of heightened perception accessible through climbing which have their counterparts in quite different areas of life. The same mood comes in so many different ways, in so many different places. But there is something more to it than that, as mystics, who lost themselves in God, have known.

(Apologies are due to Joe Brown for representing his language as more respectable than it actually is. The route we did is now called "Fools Rush In", and is unlikely to become popular.)

Venues
Climber's Club Journal 1981

1. The Hanging Stone
CIRCUMSTANCES ARE important. It is a perfect spring day. I am sitting in a small Derbyshire house, hard at work marking up a typescript. A knock at the door, a girl outside, and between us at that time the thrill of sexual curiosity: "Drive me to Swythamley Hall," she says and, glad to get out of the house, I willingly acquiesce. When we get there, she goes in to attend to her business, and I sit in the MG in the sun, hood down, my dog ranging the lawns, and get on with my work.

After an hour and a half of intense, mind-blanking concentration, the work is done. B, as I shall call her, reappears and we set off up the valley for a walk. Quite suddenly, beyond a wood, a striking gritstone buttress rears up. Reaching its foot, B and my dog scramble off up some steps leading round the side. I stand beneath looking up. Two plaques are set in the rock on either side of a nose. The buttress is 40 or 45 feet high, and on both sides at two-thirds height an easy traverse line leads back to the grassy slopes. Right at its top, on the prow of the buttress, a beautiful gritstone roof crack winks and leers. It looks about HVS.

Although I haven't come prepared for any rock, I take off my jacket, tighten my trainers, and set to on a technically difficult little wall past the right-hand plaque. It is all distinctly tenuous—feet slopping around in loose shoes and those in turn creeping slowly off the small holds. Obduracy and momentum see me through.

A little shaky from the lower wall, I move up to the roof. Putting in a jam, I bridge out and peer round the lip. A crack, awkwardly wide, continues for eight feet to the top. There is a flat hold. Leaning out, I explore its texture. Smooth rock, granular with lichen—using it without chalk from this angle doesn't appeal. I swing back to the ledge. It seems a long way up, the ground below falling steeply away into the valley. To the right I could almost walk off. B and my dog cast shadows on the hillside as they stand atop the buttress. I think about giving it up, but cannot. There is a wilful assertion in my mind that with rope, runners, EBs, chalk, it would all be so easy. I launch back out on to the roof and reach as high as I can from a squatting position, rocked right over on the good jam by the lip, but the best I can manage is an insecure fist-jam. A half-hearted pull before I think better of it and sag back down to cringe on the ledge. The red veil slowly draws down; I am getting very angry. Deep breathing to relax my tightened chest-muscles, and I plunge back into it. Back to the lip, rock over, fist in the poor jam, right hand on the flat hold, heave, stab left toe in the crack, a higher jam, and I'm on top, snarling with laughter.

My hands are tattered and sore. B and the dog have gone, so I trip off down, stumbling and unco-ordinated now, very shaky. By Dane-bridge, the sun is rolling down behind a light mist. I stop by a tree and watch, calming myself. The colours suddenly coruscate, explode. Shadows gape, weak rays of the sun flare violently, an oceanic feeling of great peace washes over my body, beatific, a well of infinite goodness. My steps float me away into a wood and, wandering amongst rhododendrons savagely bursting into bloom, I come across a dark glade with the remnants of a fire. Beyond it stands B, her eyes upon me, widening into black pools, inviting oblivion, above her a latticework of branches. I watch. Flesh drains, drips like melted plastic from her face. Cadaverous, she steps aside. Even thus, in my pride of strength, mortality haunts my trembling limbs. Love one another or not, we still must die. The black dog, Melancholy, stalks my heel and the sun goes out with a pop.

A seasick Joe Brown

2. Bryn Adda

Give me one bluebell from a springtime wood and I will show you an act of faith beyond compare, an iridescent marvel, sempiternal green flesh prayer-like in its sustenance. Once I looked across the glowing breasts of a woman, naked by my bed in the morning, to the bluebells which throbbed in the beauty of the sun. Such a moment as makes redeemable, whenever and whenever, our squalid and our paltry lives. Somewhere, to someone, this moment will come again. They will bathe in its numen, its light, hope thereafter forever renewable. And I? I cannot forget . . .

3. Brithdir

On the low ridge opposite my house, the sun sinks until it gazes right in, irradiant. Love is beyond the heart when the heart has ceased to beat. All quiet now, yet humming like a taut string. Brooding despatch of evil atomized in an instant. I have become the sun, and am extinguished thus. The planets swirl.

4. Mowing Word

"You're not abseiling off that," Brown said.

I didn't know whether it was a statement or a question, so I ignored him and threw the rope over. He watched. When I was ten feet down his face peered over the edge.

"Bollocks," I grinned up at him.

"Okay then," he agreed, "I'll tell Valerie to throw the rope down."

We crouched together at high-tide level. Grotesque gargoyles of draining rock crunched under our feet. The rope swayed down and hissed into the water. "Shit," he said flatly, and scurried away, leaving me to coil it.

"I'll get you for this, you little bugger," I yelled after him.

A glinting sherpa smile mocked around the corner. "Ha, ha, ha!" it said. I slung the rope over my shoulder, salt water dripping down my neck, and followed him.

He was waiting. A wave slithered along the cliff and his ledge was awash. We leapt out of reach.

"You're not going through that fucking cave," he yelled.

I carried on traversing, pausing on the corner to grin back down at him.

"Why not?" I asked.

His eyes narrowed, recognizing the game. We got to the cave, five feet wide, ten feet high, devil's-heart-black and the tide coming in.

"Pity about your legs," I jibed.

"They're telescopic," he replied.

A wave sluiced in before us, crashing and sucking, and another followed it. I moved before the qualms took over, bridging high up in the roof, stretching, going as fast as I could. Looking back, I could see him against the light, legs out at right angles, neatly plotting his way

Gogarth Bay (photo: Ken Wilson)

along. I was glad he couldn't see my scrabblings and lunges. Fifty yards of grazed shins and lurches in the dark and I was through, leaping across boulders to one well out of reach of the tide. He emerged, cat-cool and wreathed in smiles.

"Ha, ha, ha!" he cackled at me, hugely happy with himself. We raced across boulders to one which gleamed black and whale-like, ten feet from our line. He got there first and turned to laugh at me. Thirty yards out a big wave was bearing down on us. I leapt past him for a little, flat rock just awash, and thence to the marble-smooth base of the crack, thrusting a jam in, pulling hurriedly, swinging my body out horizontally as the wave careered by. Twenty feet higher I bridged across the groove, dried the soles of my boots, and asked if he wanted a rope.

"You fucker," he smiled.

"Better be quick, Joe," I parried, spying another wave on its way.

He waited. The little rock had remained obstinately submerged and the incoming wave splashed over the big one, dousing him. I roared with laughter.

"Get out of that, you little bastard," I cackled at him, and climbed another twenty feet up the crack. The next wave got him fair and square, soaking him to the waist. He jumped in before another one came, and waded across. Forty feet up the crack we had a wrestling match as I tried to stand on his head, then I sorted out the rope and belays as he fastidiously pulled wet cloth from cold flesh.

"You can lead," he said slyly.

I set off, trying to impress, but got it all wrong at a bulge and had to come down, attempting to look unconcerned. "Should've faced the other way," I told him, then climbed thirty feet without stopping. At which point the crack finished and things became loose. Forty feet away was a ledge, thirty feet down was my last runner. I put in half-a-dozen, tied them all together, and teetered onwards. "Bit loose up here, Joe," I shouted, prepared to call it quits.

"Ha, ha, ha," drifted out from the crack below. I kicked a block off in that direction to shut him up. An hour to climb forty feet, terror all the way. If I stand on it, will it move? If I press it this way, will it stay? What in God's name am I doing here? If you let me off this one, I swear I'll join the SDP, subscribe to *Newsweek*, and grow fat before the telly . . . Oh Lord . . .

The ledge, realm of broken promises and the return of arrogance, arrives. I put in eight nuts, tie myself intricately and variously on to them, hope that the block I'm sitting on will remain here longer than I intend to, and tell Joe to come up carefully. He does. Above us, a little curving diedre leads to the top.

"Up there," I tell him.

"Fuck that," he replies.

"Don't come on this ledge," I say to him, "or it'll collapse."

That pre-empts his move to take over my belay.

"How many nuts have you got in?" he asks, with more than passing interest.

"Eight, and that's the best of them," I answer, pointing to one jammed between a tuft of sea-pink and a fragile sliver of mud. I'm lying—a better one's behind me.

"Oh," he says. "Wouldn't you like to do this pitch?"

"No," I reply.

"Then we'll get someone to rescue us."

He puts two fingers in his mouth and lets out the most piercing whistle. Across the bay, Ben and Marion give no sign of a response.

"I don't think they can hear us," he says.

"Better do your pitch then," I prompt. "You're the experienced one . . ."

Joe Brown attempts to hold the cliff in place—Cilan Head

He grins, trapped.

"I'll just have a look at it." Twenty feet up he gets a huge runner on. "Watch me here," and swings across under the overhang.

"I've got you," I reassure him, but he's already gone and the rope runs out, slowly at first, then rapidly. I follow and find him sitting in a hollow amongst the bugloss and the thrift, his feet down two rabbit holes. He drags me down and punches me. We roll over wrestling till he gets me in a headlock.

"You're fucking mad," he says, grinning.

Ben and Marion arrive.

"What were you whistling about?"

We join forces to curse them roundly.

At the top of the path down to Broad Haven I stop, watch them head over the river and out across the sand. A woman and two small, greying figures ambling along the beach, the tide ebbing away, colours pale in the twilight, the beam of a lighthouse winking across the sea. Before the stumbling, sandy rise to the car park, I catch them up again. The engine fires, lights come on, we swing into the night.

5. A Prayer in Lud's Church

Malory's King Mark, with his "And but we avoid lightly, there is but death." Ha! It is all indissociable, all of this. It is all of a piece. I said to my soul, "Be calm." My soul spoke back: "Fight on, thrust through, the calmness comes. Where Gawain's neck was grazed my quest began. The places you shall reach all times are in your heart. Silk of the body fades and tears, sand rubs and blankets soft against the rock. Sea-battered, the cliffs break, but do not fall. Screech of an axe upon the stone, crash of a wave upon the shore. On the ebb-tide, we all go down."

It is astonishing how much assurance you possess at the age of twenty-five—to the extent, almost, that the rest of your life is spent trying to live it down. Still, it's right to dwell on the negative side of things from time to time: "If way to the Better there be, it exacts a full look at the Worst."

A Valediction
Climbers' Club Journal 1973

SCHOOL ENDS; THERE are more phases to a man's life than just one though each phase as it progresses brings a clearer realization of its own nature, or a firmer grasp on the security it seems to offer. I have been climbing intensively now for twelve years, and I have more or less had enough. I have come to see the nature of the sport; it is not a creative act and it has little left to give me. I expect to give offence or be criticized for what I have to say, and would thus like to define the conditions which lead me to say it. I am not referring to the mountain environment or to the quiet pleasures of days in the hills, not referring to the huge range of interest encompassed in this scene, not referring to the sheer bodily and sensual pleasure of movement on rock, although all these things impinge upon the central experience about which I write. The experience to which I am referring is the intense, neurotic urge to seek out the limits of subjective possibility on rock, the desire to push oneself to the extremes of endurance, adhesion, physical and mental control. I shall be making value judgements upon this experience; whether or not the reader feels intuitions of sympathy towards these is of little account. I have searched myself and found them valid to my situation.

I have heard people claim that climbing is an art form, a creative act, and read the same statement in essays such as Harold Drasdo's "Education and the Mountain Centres"; the people who make these statements have neither sufficiently considered the nature of a creative act, nor the nature of climbing. They are talking inflated nonsense; there is an element of the mystical about climbing, but the climbers are lost not in God but in themselves. This is valid enough at a certain stage in life, but it is a lesson which must not be allowed to harden into a habit. In a sense it represents a shaking off of the last egocentricities of childhood, and a coming-to-terms at last with the external world. The act revokes its own motivation. Commitment to a series of extreme moves on rock is a tenuous expression of belief in one's personal omnipotence; by its very nature it is an illusion, and one bolstered so often by the mean little tricks and dishonesties of the climbing world as to lose the integrity upon which its validity must rest. No one is omnipotent and on rock we all strive to be so. The ego and the will are the driving forces in climbing, the philosophy behind it is one of despair. Consider us and what we are: we are not well-balanced individuals, as long as we climb, because we have committed ourselves to a pure sphere of self-assertion and will. We turn from a world of which we cannot be the centre, to an experience so intense that we cannot but see ourselves at the centre of it. Every new trip up Sisyphus' Hill hardens the ego a little by proving to us that we can do it. Ego and will by no means lead to happiness; the times when I have been best at my climbing have been the least happy times of my life. Yes, there have been moments of desperate laughter and utter relief, even some warmth of companionship from time to time from an experience shared. But this continual focusing inwards of the climber's mind, this sifting and weighing of every fine weakness of response, this endless preparation for mental masturbation, these sudden explosions of the assertive will, are a path to restraint, and not freedom, of response. They are lessons to be learnt, not ones always to be lived by, and their repetition becomes not only absurd, for this element was present in its nature from the beginning, but also negative and destructive, and a denial of the potentialities of life. Obsessive climbing is a reprisal against nature for making self so small within it. The toying with death (any arguments that this is not so are utterly spurious) that represents so strong a part of the attraction of climbing adds yet another facet to the basic negativity of the sport. Each new death is a reiteration of the question, "Is it worth it", from the answering of which we always shy away. At Lawrie Holliwell's funeral every face was haunted by the realization of a death that could as easily have been theirs. Is it worth it? Yes, for those who are weak, aimless, discontent, strong and directionless, childless, unhappily married, unresolved or in despair. For all who fit these categories the activity is eminently worthwhile in that it brings them close to ridding themselves of an existence that could so easily become a burden to them, and by the proximity of that negation increases the attractiveness of life.

> I balanced all, brought all to mind,
> The years to come seemed waste of breath,
> A waste of breath the years behind;
> In balance with this life, this death.*

Well; all cannot be brought to mind; there is body and soul, there are feelings, intuitions of beauty and wholeness, softness, fullness,

* W. B. Yeats: "An Irish Airman Foresees His Death".

warmth. These things climbing alone cannot fulfil; the hard, cold world of intellect and will seeks to destroy the whole man.

I have learnt things from climbing: that the seemingly impossible can be achieved by precise, co-ordinated movement, by direction of energy and conservation and timed application of resources. That things are easier than they seem to be; that falling off is not the thing to do until every last possible scrap of resource has failed you; that a sufficiency of commitment will usually see you through; that a real and authentic desire is the only worthwhile spring to action. But these are lessons to be applied now to the creative act of living, in conjunction with the more warm, full and human values of love, feeling, knowledge, compassion. They are no longer ones to be squandered in the negative sphere of rock. We pass from one lesson to another armed with a new strength of knowledge, and should be glad that it is so.

This final article drew a curious response when it first appeared. One gentleman wrote in to express his outrage that I should have chosen to mention Al Harris in the same essay as Arnold Pines, and suggested that our brave RAF lads back from the glorious Falklands should strafe my house of that time in Bethesda. Fortunately this idea was not taken up, and I remain free to walk, climb and write upon the mountains for as many years as may remain to me. When the rocks and hills have been as important a part of life for as long as they have been of mine, then they're there for good, and I'm thankful for the gifts they bring.

For Arnold Pines
Climber and Rambler 1982

THE TITLE IS a deceit. I may never have met Arnold Pines, but even about this I am not quite sure. Certainly, I have met people who knew him, even knew him closely. And I may have met the man himself. But this is not the point. Arnold Pines is dead. I read as much in the obituary column of *Climber and Rambler*, and certain details set me wondering if I knew him. I shall come back to this later. On the same day as I read his obituary, I received a letter from my dear friend Kevin FitzGerald: "What with . . . a fresh fall of snow last night, and a general feeling developing that it can't be long now, and that I shall in consequence miss your novel, I am not in the best of moods . . ."

Well, I sit here today in my study, the Carneddau mist-shrouded beyond the window and rain dinning on the roof, washing away the last of the snow, and I am beset with thoughts of death. If this sounds morbid or melodramatic to you, let me confess straight away, in agreement with Montaigne, that "ever since I can remember, nothing has occupied my imagination more than death, yea, even in the most licentious season of my life." Indeed, I sometimes wonder how much mental activity I have accorded to subjects other than death and sex. There's a good Freudian opposition there, but I don't want to go over the life instinct *vs* death instinct argument here. It is not the purpose of this present essay.

It doesn't seem to me helpful to think about climbing without considering its element of risk and consequent death. This is a discursive essay on the acceptance of death as concomitant with the pleasures and rewards of mountaineering. You might not subscribe to Hazlitt's view, that "a life of action and danger moderates the dread of death. It not only gives us fortitude to bear pain, but teaches us at every step the precarious tenure on which we hold our present being." But you can scarcely disagree that the risk of death is indissociable from the thrill of climbing. The coward may die a thousand times before his death —likewise the climber upon his rock, weighing up the consequences and guarding against the contingencies of a fall; and as for vicarious deaths, those too, and by the hundred.

I am sometimes tempted to suggest to the BMC that, somewhere in their offices in that dingy, half-demolished area of Manchester, they should erect a roll of honour. Just such a one as you will find in schools, in village halls, on roadsides, in town centres, or chapel yards throughout the country, always inscribed with that lie about the men of these names having died for God, King and Country, which should more correctly be phrased because of Mammon, obligation, and politicians' stupidity. Only the mountaineering one would properly be inscribed to error, accident, and insouciance. The names come readily enough to the tongue. In the twenty or so years I've been climbing, the people I've met, known, been friendly with, who are now dead are many, and no single theory explains away all their deaths. What connection is there between the death of Lawrie Holliwell, whose abseil belay gave way on Craig yr Ysfa, and Nick Estcourt, killed by an avalanche on K2? Or between Dave Sales, who died after falling from Quietus on Stanage, and Arthur de Kusel, struck by lightning on the Grand Capucin? No explanations, no statistics, encompass or suffice, no theories would have prevented their deaths.

Consider, for example, the Cairngorm tragedy of November 1971. An enquiry quite stunning in its assemblage of a cast almost totally unwilling or unable to answer the questions put to them, failed to reach even the simple and unavoidable conclusion that if you place a party of young people on a high, bare mountain-summit in a blizzard then, no matter how well-equipped they are, in the course of a day or two most of them will die. It is in the nature of things. The mountains in winter are inimical to life. Even brute creation shuns a storm-swept mountain and cowers in its lair. Why then expect young, untrained human beings to survive? Why put them to the test? Which latter is really the crux of the matter. If they choose the test of their own volition, then fair enough. But to persuade, instruct, inveigle them into it—is that fair or wise? In a different context entirely, and one which fortunately did not end in a death, the major point of contention in the accident which befell Rob Taylor on the Breach Wall of Mount Kilimanjaro is not whether or not he and Henry Barber should have been there, for they had chosen to be, but whether or not Barber persuaded Taylor to lead a pitch against Taylor's better judgement, when the ice was in bad condition. In this aspect of the incident Taylor is as much at fault as Barber, in not resisting the latter's pressure. Responsibility cannot be abrogated by insisting that the other insisted. Nuremberg gave the lie to all that.

Men die in the mountains because the risks of mountaineering can usually be minimized or abated, but they can never be excluded. There will always be occasions when the human animal, with all his aspirations to dignity, power and control, is reduced to a limp bundle of crushed flesh and rags. How then should we react to it? Any death could as easily be our own. Lawrie Holliwell, as I mentioned previously, was killed when his tape belay for an abseil came off a rounded spike. Yet I can remember more than a few occasions when I have used unsuitable, unsafe belays for abseiling. Once on the West Wing of Dinas Mot when we retreated late in the day from the midway terrace rather than complete the scrappy upper pitches of a route. At the bottom, after a 150ft abseil, only the slightest flick was needed to bring down the rope. And there was John Taylor, killed soloing on Raven Crag a couple of years ago? How many of us have a terror story from soloing? My most frightening incident happened not on my drug-propped escapade on Coronation Street, but years ago, in the mid-60s, at the top of Covent Garden on Millstone Edge, 120 feet above the ground. With my hands on a detached dinner-plate of rock, both my footholds snapped off at the same moment. To this day, I have no idea why I didn't fall, or what quirk of fate saved me.

Then what of accidents on dangerous ground above and around cliffs? I well remember Hugh Gair falling from the steep ground between the top of Llithrig and the foot of Octo in 1968, landing terribly injured and dying on the path under the crag. A day or so before, I had done Red Wall on South Stack with Bonington. Instead of abseiling in we had blithely scrambled down the usual abseil ridge and climbed down into the back of the zawn, unroped and on appallingly loose, slimy rock. After Hugh's death, I had wondered then, as so many times before and since, why Hugh, why not me? I am no more careful. I had no more reason to want to stay alive. Why him? Why not me?

Of course the question is pointless, too compounded with our emotions, too simple, too wistful. We indulge ourselves in imagining

Yr Elen and Carnedd Llywelyn from Cwm Llafar (photo: John Cleare)

our own deaths: the things it would excuse us; the effect it might have on our friends; the judgemental finality of it all by which we might come to know where we stood, the crushing irony being that we would not know. I remember the curious sensation which Ken Wilson produced in me through a chance aside in a conversation about obituaries which he and I had some ten years ago: "Oh, I suppose I'd give you three or four column inches in *Mountain*." Francis Bacon wrote that: "Death hath this also, that it openeth the gate to good fame, and extinguisheth envy." I don't suppose many would be too envious of "three or four column inches in *Mountain*."

These are private considerations, secret imaginings. We cannot easily joke about death and yet it has a jokey aspect. I remember Tilman talking about it, coolly, sardonically, treating the whole thing as a huge jest, not much to be feared, rather even to be welcomed, in a conversation I had with him before he sailed in *En Avant* for the Antarctic on his last voyage. And at the time there were thoughts racing round my mind of what others who had sailed with him had said about what their reactions had been to his imperturbable manner in the face of peril. Tilman is the only man I have known who was undeniably prepared for his death. The source of his serenity, good eighteenth-century man that he was, lay in his Christian faith. What, then, of others who have not shared that faith? What of Jim Madsen's gloriously acerbic resignation as he slipped from his abseil rope at the top of El Capitan in '68. Falling past the team he was on his way to rescue, he calmly said to them, "Ah, what the fuck . . ."

Well, what does it matter? Of what account is our ceasing to be, our cutting apart the Gordian knots of life, our accepting future designs as by us forever unfulfilled, our transposition from the morass of experience to the flux of history? With all those questions goes the resounding affirmative response we can give to whether or not this activity of ours, which risks life and limb, is worth its occasional cost. Dr Johnson had it that "the known shortness of life, as it ought to moderate our passions, may likewise, with equal propriety, contract our designs." Why should it? Why make of life such a thing as an examination question, where due, balanced, and just consideration be given to certain elements before reaching a well-balanced and judicious conclusion? Is that a better way than to allow your mental and physical capacities a passionate engagement with the contingencies of life? Should we, in mountaineering terms, keep well within ourselves, opting in a balanced manner for what Harold Drasdo calls a "risk-free role", or should we explore our personal limits? Faced with that sort of choice, the obvious rejoinder is that it is based on the curious idea that we may avoid death. Yet accident, by its very nature, is adventitious. There is no such thing, in mountaineering or anything much besides, as a "risk-free role". Death, at some unknown point along the way, is inescapable.

To those who do not bear that in mind, what can you say?

"Beware, the Struldbrugs are coming . . . ?" In mountaineering terms, these are the mountain rescuers, who gravely pontificate on the dangers of the hills, and all the while they are unacquainted with them, only with their sometime consequences.

In great danger, there is great joy. Life is then very light; it weighs upon us hardly at all and could so easily be blown away: such a delicate, tenuous hold in this short span between laughter and oblivion. The rescuers, in their great beards and heavy boots, who stump along the roads with a dull emphaticalness, bearing stretcher and winch, bound down with heavy coils of rope and the weight of saving lives, will never know this joy of toying with death. All their pronouncements are virtuous and merciful rehearsals to place on a pedestal and praise that which we should treat with detachment, levity, disdain. Nothing so very dreadful about death, in the natural order of things. Sorrow in parting, yes. Unfulfilment, yes. A certain selfish grief at the loss of the company of friends. (How dearly I have loved, and would like still to be able to enjoy the company of, Biven, Tilman, Estcourt, Harris.) But nothing about it which is so very dreadful. A shocking moment, beyond recognition of accident, and then resignation. To attempt to

Opposite: Castell y Gwynt, Glyder Fawr (photo: Malcolm Griffith)

avoid the possibility of which is to follow the example of Aeschylus, of whom it was prophesied that he would be killed by the fall of a house, so he kept out of doors, only to be killed by a tortoise which escaped from the talons of an eagle flying above. Prudence, as the Greeks knew, is no guard against cosmic jokery.

And so to Arnold Pines. A month or two ago I went out one afternoon for a walk. Pen yr Oleu Wen first, that great escalator of scree above the Ogwen tea shack. I limped along the exquisite ridge above Ysgolion Duon in hissing squalls of hail and a blustery wind, stopped briefly on Carnedd Llywelyn to drink tea by the icy summit cairn and admire a coppery October sunset on Caernarfon Bay, then turned to run down over Craig yr Ysfa to Ffynnon Llugwy.

At the top of Craig yr Ysfa, a party of two had just finished Amphitheatre Buttress and another party was engaged on the final pitch—a couple of youngish men and one in his late fifties. There was a great deal of teasing and jocularity as the older man climbed. I sat and watched as they came up, then set off down slowly, as I had torn ligaments in an ankle and cartilage trouble in a knee. The younger members of the party overtook me on the zig-zags down to Llugwy, but not the older man. Darkness was falling over the lake and only a glimmer of light remained higher up. I sat down by the path and looked for the older man; I could see him well above me, faltering down the hillside, so I waited, and when he came up with me, I offered him some tea from my flask, foul though it was, thinking he might be tired. Then we set off down to the A5, well suited to each other's hobbling pace. On that walk down, I learnt several things about my companion, but not his name. I learnt, for example, that four years before he had been to Nanda Devi, that we knew some of the same people, that he was a doctor, lived in Hertfordshire, and some of the way he felt about being in the mountains, about the climbs he'd done, his family, and the times he would be back here. He accused me of being Jim Curran, which I vigorously denied. It was just a chance encounter, a half-hour's idling conversation as we walked down in the autumn darkness to the valley.

At the road we parted, he a few yards left to where his friends were waiting, and I to walk along to Idwal Cottage and my car. I don't know who he was, but a few weeks later a 58-year-old doctor from Hertfordshire, who had been to Nanda Devi, died in a climbing accident on Tryfan. His name was Arnold Pines, and he may or may not have been my companion of that evening. I don't know, and it doesn't matter. The point is simply that someone died in a climbing accident on Tryfan, that his death was unexpected, its time and place unforeseen to him or to either of us as we walked along that night. I end with another quotation from Montaigne, who would, surely, have appreciated the point: "Did you think never to arrive at a place you were incessantly making for? Yet there is no road but has an end. And if society is any comfort to you, is not the world going the selfsame way as you?"